I0884712

THEATER IN THE AMERICAS

A Series from Southern Illinois University Press

SCOTT MAGELSSEN
Series Editor

CHILDHOOD AND NINETEENTH-CENTURY AMERICAN THEATRE

THE WORK OF THE MARSH TROUPE OF JUVENILE ACTORS

SHAUNA VEY

Southern Illinois University Press
Carbondale

Portions of chapter 2 appeared as "An American Antebellum Child-Actor Contract: Alfred Stewart and the Shift from Craft Apprentice to Wage Laborer," in *Entertaining Children: The Participation of Youth in the Entertainment Industry*, edited by Gillian Arrighi and Victor Emeljanow. Published by Palgrave Macmillan, 2014.

Printed in the United States of America

18 17 16 15 4 3 2 1

Cover illustration: Little Mary Guerineau Marsh as Eva, Cincinnati, 1853–54. TCS 44, Harvard Theatre Collection, Houghton Library, Harvard University.

Library of Congress Cataloging-in-Publication Data
Vey, Shauna A.
Childhood and nineteenth-century American theatre : the work of the Marsh Troupe of juvenile actors / Shauna Vey.
pages cm — (Theater in the Americas)
Summary: "This study of the daily work lives of five members of the Marsh Troupe, a nineteenth-century professional acting company composed primarily of children, sheds light on the construction of idealized childhood inside and outside the American theatre"—Provided by publisher.
Includes bibliographical references and index.
ISBN 978-0-8093-3438-4 (paperback)
ISBN 0-8093-3438-0 (paperback)
ISBN 978-0-8093-3439-1 (e-book)
1. Marsh Troupe of Juvenile Comedians (Theater group : Philadelphia, Pa.) 2. Child actors—United States—History—19th century. 3. Theater—United States—History—19th century. I. Title.
PN2297.M285.V49 2015
792.09748'11—dc23 2015004645

Printed on recycled paper. ♻

The paper used in this publication meets the minimum requirements of American National Standard for Information Sciences—Permanence of Paper for Printed Library Materials, ANSI Z39.48-1992. ∞

To the memory of Joan Joyce Vey,
who loved childhood

CONTENTS

List of Illustrations ix

Preface xi

Acknowledgments xiii

Introduction 1

1. Beginnings and Success 14
2. First Losses, and a Battle Won 38
3. A Perfect Angel—Forever 62
4. Chasing Audiences and Aging Out 84
5. Tomboys Rule 99
6. Fathers and Sons 124

Afterword 142

Appendix: Actors Reported to Have Performed with the Marsh Troupe 153

Notes 157

Bibliography 195

Index 209

ILLUSTRATIONS

"The Marsh Children," circa 1857 27
Howard Athenaeum playbill, February 10, 1857 29
Georgie Marsh in eight characters 34
Howard Athenaeum playbill, 1857 45
Louis Aldrich, circa 1870 57
Little Mary Guerineau Marsh as Eva, 1853–54 67
Mary Marsh 69
Mary Marsh's tombstone 81
Engraved wreath on Mary Marsh's tombstone 82
Louise Arnot in ancient period costume 105
Louise Arnot in a queen's costume 111
Fifty-nine-year-old Louise Arnot, 1903 122
George Marsh as "Young Toodles" 130
Georgie Marsh, 1857 134
Georgie F. Guerineau's gravestone 139

PREFACE

In 2005, while reading the microfilmed pages of the antebellum *New York Clipper*, I ran across several notices of performances by the Marsh Troupe of Juvenile Comedians. As I continued my research on another topic, I began almost absentmindedly to look for additional items about the company, which had been organized by a father/impresario around his two children. My casual reading was stopped short by a notice that in early 1859, twelve-year-old Mary Marsh had moved too near the footlights, caught fire, and burned to death.

Fire was common in the nineteenth century; theatre history abounds with stories of theatres and performers that either survived it or did not. "Ballet girls" in their filmy skirts were particularly vulnerable. On one occasion, five sisters all perished in a backstage fire. Yet the story of Mary Marsh stuck with me. According to the *Clipper*, other performers were injured trying to help Mary, and her father had decided to quickly reopen the show. Three months after Mary's death, the *Clipper* published an account of a nasty contract dispute between the Marsh company and the angry mother of another of its child performers. I found myself fascinated by the conjunction of so many emotionally charged elements: parents, children, performance, business, law, life, death, celebrity, loyalty, and betrayal. It seemed like a mixture of *Little Women* and *Gypsy*. I wanted to know more, but the company suddenly seemed to disappear from history. By now I was hooked. As I searched through three years of weekly papers, however, I saw no more notices of Marsh Troupe appearances. After presenting a conference paper on the Marshes, I moved on.

In 2008 I received an e-mail from a graduate student at the University of Western Australia. While researching children's theatre in Australia she had come upon a mention of the Marsh Troupe. Finding the title of my conference paper online, she was hoping I could supply her with more information. Australia? The Marsh Troupe, I learned, had decamped for Australia and New Zealand, following a line of entertainers rushing to amuse the flush gold-rush audience.

The Marsh Troupe's travels encompassed at least four nations—plus rumors of appearances in Panama and Tahiti—and about a dozen U.S. states. Following their story has led me from theatre collections in New York City and Harvard to libraries in Cincinnati, Philadelphia, and Chicago. It has induced me to spend untold hours scrutinizing the (thankfully) digitalized newspapers of Australia and New Zealand, and to employ surrogates in Georgia and St. Louis. It has taken me to the top of the old Watervliet Methodist Church in upstate New York, where I brushed aside some mouse droppings and spent six hours crouched on a step, turning the two-foot-wide pages of a handwritten marriage register. And, ultimately, it brought me to Albany Rural Cemetery, where I knelt in sodden earth on a raw February day and—rubbing my mittens across the face of a fallen stone—I confirmed my hunch that there was more to the story than had been written so far.

ACKNOWLEDGMENTS

Long before this book was even an idea, I learned what a theatre historian was from Dr. Judy Milhous at the Graduate Center of the City University of New York, and I am still grateful. Since that time, numerous people and institutions have contributed to the realization of this project.

When I first brought a skimpy eight-page outline of an ill-formed idea to Bob Schanke, in his capacity as series editor for Southern Illinois University (SIU) Press, he saw a tiny sparkle within the dross and encouraged me to make it better. Without this early boost, the book would not have been written. Bob continued to mentor the project through several substantial reshapings before handing it over to his successor at SIU Press, Scott Magelssen. I am grateful to both Bob and Scott for their seamless support and to Scott for his own editorial insights and guidance. SIU Press's acquisitions editor Kristine Priddy has been a source of warm encouragement, information, and cheerful aid throughout the process. I am also grateful for the considerable and considerate efforts of SIU Press's editing and marketing personnel.

My thinking and writing were aided by the comments of many readers. I am particularly grateful to the SIU Press anonymous reader whose sensitive but keen criticism helped nudge the book toward all s/he thought it could be. Colleagues at the City University of New York who willingly put aside their own work to read and comment on mine include Victoria Lichterman, Philip Lambert, Helen Huff, James Wilson, Suzanne Epstein, and Alisa Roost, who deserves special mention for her multiple readings and super-rapid responses. Children's studies scholar Karen Sánchez-Eppler generously responded to a plea from a stranger with pages of useful critical analysis. The liveliest parts of the book owe a debt to the prodding of nonacademic writers Jeff Williamson, Christopher Brimer, and Paul Zakrewski. Jennifer Dobbins and Ann Redpath pushed me to write more clearly.

I owe a number of debts to my Australian colleagues, Gillian Arrighi and Victor Emeljanov. They graciously allowed me to use material on Alfred Stewart originally published in their edited volume *Entertaining Children: The Participation of Youth in the Entertainment Industry* (2014). My thanks go to Palgrave Macmillan as well. In addition, Gillian read my "Australian" section and offered several pointers. Victor organized the Entertaining Children Working Group at the American Society for Theatre Research conferences in 2011 and 2013 where chapters of this book debuted as papers. These sessions were enormously helpful and I thank all of the participants and questioners. Marah Gubar was especially generous in following up the conference with detailed suggestions and questions.

Other scholars willingly helped me clarify or identify items within their specialized knowledge. Aubrey Cannon explained gravestone classifications, Jane Eva Baxter shared sources from cemetery studies, John C. Frick supplied a reference on actor G. C. Germon, and David Rinear told me where to find W. E. Burton's cast lists. Rachael Hains-Wesson passed on leads to Australian sources.

Mrs. Cecelia Guerineau, widow of Georgie Marsh's grandson, was kind enough to speak with me and direct me to the family plot in Albany Rural Cemetery.

Diana Sera Cary is the generous expert-source-and-mentor extraordinaire. As a performer whose career as the vaudeville and film star "Baby Peggy" began just three years following the death of the last of the famous Marshes, Diana has tremendous insights into the material, psychological, and financial realities experienced by professional performing children. As the author of an autobiography and three well-researched historical works, she is a font of knowledge about all aspects of show business in the early twentieth century. As a woman who reinvented herself midlife and continues to be productive in her nineties, she is an inspirational role model; and as a friend, she is challenging and supportive in the best way. Her contributions to the book cannot be measured.

I am also grateful to Don Wilmeth for encouraging me at a number of crucial points in my career and for his championing of the *history* in theatre history.

This project owes a great deal to the continued maintenance of historical archives, and libraries, and their dedicated staffs including the Troy Room of the Troy Public Library; Harvard Theatre Collection; New York Public Library; Public Library of Hamilton County and Cincinnati; State Historical Society of Missouri; Rensaleer County Historical Society; Oneida County Historical Society; State Library of Victoria (Australia); Irene Wainwright, archivist of the Louisiana Division of the City Archives, New Orleans Public Library; Karin Suni, curator of the Theatre Collection at the Philadelphia Free Library; Siobhan Fitzpatrick, curator of the Museum of Early Trades and Crafts (Madison, New Jersey); Pete Shrake, archivist, Circus World Museum; Elizabeth Sherwood, Louisiana State Museum; and Lauren Leeman, State Historical Society of Missouri.

Some early research was performed during time made available by two PSC-CUNY Faculty Research Awards and by the CUNY Faculty Fellowship Publication Program. Much of the writing was accomplished during a one-year sabbatical. I am particularly grateful to my union, the Professional Staff Congress, for negotiating this leave and to New York City College of Technology for granting it.

My family supported the project in both material and nonmaterial ways. Helene and Tim Cline willingly fed and housed me while I searched the Philadelphia Free Library. Shelia and Michael Becker did the same during an extended trip to Cincinnati. Shelia Becker combed through Cincinnati's historic newspaper files to find a detail I'd missed. Sue Eggert was unfailingly supportive, as was Alex Wiesendanger. Lucas Wiesendanger endured hundreds of discussions, read and edited drafts, and formulated two score possible titles. Roger Kachinske and Stephanie Rogers roamed through acres of Rose Hill Cemetery to locate and clean Mary Marsh's gravestone and Stephanie and Cliff Kachinske drove to Macon to photograph it. I am grateful to them all.

The partner in my own graveyard research roamings is Jim Sherwood, now an expert in all things Marsh. Nothing in my life matches his no-holds-barred investment in this project, whether sitting on cramped steps in a church attic, re-editing a thirty-fifth draft, or excitedly debating casting for the imagined movie version. After nurturing this book for so many years, it is somehow fitting that it was put under contract shortly after our marriage. It emerges as the offspring of my hard work and his great faith.

CHILDHOOD AND NINETEENTH-CENTURY AMERICAN THEATRE

INTRODUCTION

It is possible, reading standard histories, to forget half the population of the country. —*Howard Zinn*

In Sydney, Australia, in 1863, a production of *Uncle Tom's Cabin* was presented by a group of professional child actors. The children were members of the Marsh Troupe of Juvenile Comedians, a touring company of about thirty children who performed adult material for general audiences. The Marsh Troupe was organized in the United States in 1855 and—after successes and tragedies—disbanded in 1863 shortly after their return from a Pacific tour. Writing about the Marsh Company almost a century and a half later, historian Benjamin McArthur dismissively "imagines" their Sydney performance to be "precious, rather than stirring."[1] The reaction of a contemporaneous spectator, however, was precisely the opposite. The nineteenth-century writer found the performance emotionally moving:

> Nothing, for instance, can be more beautiful in sentiment, or more poetic in composition than the solicitation of Eva (little Jenny Arnott), that her father (St. Claire) shall set his slaves at liberty—while the sweet ballad with which she concludes . . . cannot possibly be listened to without exciting admiration.

The enraptured critic extended his praise to the children's portrayals of adult roles:

> . . . we have in the haunted George Harris (Louise Arnott), a truthful picture . . . This character is sustained very effectively by Louise Arnott . . . and, indeed, the whole of the subsidiary characters are supported with an amount of evenness and ability that would tend greatly to the success of the piece. . . . The deaths of Eva, of St. Claire, and of Uncle Tom were severally portrayed in an affecting manner.[2]

Benjamin McArthur is a sensitive and knowledgeable historian whose comments about the Marsh Troupe actors are embedded in an otherwise excellent and entertaining study of Joseph Jefferson. Why would McArthur, a twenty-first-century writer, dismiss as "precious" a performance he had never seen, while a nineteenth-century spectator from the troupe's audience admired the "evenness and ability" of the children's acting? By telling the story of the Marsh Troupe of Juvenile Comedians, this book provides an answer that contradicts common generalizations about children and child actors and reveals the changing definition of childhood in the United States.

On stage, the star reigns, and theatre history tends to focus most of its attention on those who were most famous. But for each sensational Cushman or Jefferson or Forrest on the antebellum stage, there were hundreds of other working actors. The fabric of the nineteenth-century American theatre was woven of supernumeraries and walking gentlemen and traveling troupes and minor stars—and some of them were children. Child actors are both ubiquitous and invisible. Theatre historians have dutifully noted the individual careers of the brightest child stars of the nineteenth century—Cordelia Howard, the Bateman girls, and Lotta Crabtree—but these actors are generally seen as freaks or odd phenomena, rather than as competent professionals practicing their craft. We study stars because of their extraordinary-ness.

This book turns a microscope on the Marsh Children partly *because* they were never top-echelon stars. Rather, their experience exemplifies the lives of working juvenile professionals in the nineteenth-century theatre. This kind of microhistory not only recaptures the "experiences of hitherto obscure people," but it can also reveal larger patterns and new meanings. As Richard D. Brown observed, microhistory often begins with the premise that accepted generalizations may be based more on "slightly-informed assumptions than on empirical, archival evidence."[3] Many of our ideas about nineteenth-century child actors are generalized assumptions based on current constructions of childhood. This book focuses on only five members of the Marsh Troupe—one father/manager and four child performers—with the conviction that they are emblematic. Jill Lepore calls this belief a core assumption of microhistorians that "however singular a person's life may be, the value of examining it lies in how it serves as an allegory for the culture as a whole."[4] As members of a stock company led by an impresario, these children were involved on a daily basis with the antebellum theatre's bid for respectability, shifting business practices, and cross-dressed and mixed-bill performances. They encountered the deep influence of melodrama, the shift to a wage-based economy, and the need for workplace reform. Their particular experiences illuminate the lives of nineteenth-century players.

Because the Marshes were simultaneously working professionals *and* children, their story illuminates nineteenth-century culture and theatre practices, while also allowing insights into the broader dynamics of nineteenth-century childhood. Each career is examined in its totality because these profiles illustrate a variety of outcomes for the nineteenth-century stage child. The Marsh Troupe can serve as a prime case study because the story of each of these actors elucidates a different aspect of changing social arrangements regarding child performers. Their individual trajectories afford what Daniel Thomas Cook calls a "point of departure into theorizing" about childhood today.[5] Nineteenth-century conceptions of child performers differed significantly from contemporary opinions. Assessments of children's performance vary between the centuries, because the definition of childhood has shifted, and each writer sees children through the lens of his or her own era. The Marsh Troupe, operating at the moment when our society's notion of childhood began to shift, illustrates this change in the social construction of childhood at a moment when the identity of theatre was also in flux.

While children are living, breathing biological beings, *childhood* is an abstract concept whose meaning is fluid. Our visions and expectations of living children are filtered through our society's definition of childhood. In twenty-first-century America, children are seen as sacred and cute; it follows that their performance would be "precious." Neil Postman has defined 1850–1950 as the "high water mark of childhood."[6] Situated at the beginning of this era, and taking the fascination with mythologized childhood as its foundation, the Marsh Troupe is an ideal vehicle for an examination of how our construction of idealized childhood played out during a pivotal period in the development of American theatre, onstage and in the public arena.

In *Centuries of Childhood: A Social History of Family Life*, published in France in 1960 and in the United States in 1962, Philippe Ariès theorizes childhood as a social construct. Ariès argues that medieval Europeans did not conceive of childhood as a separate category, but that humans past infancy were simply merged into general society. For evidence, Ariès looks at painting, clothing, work, play, and language. In medieval and early Renaissance painting, children are denoted by small figures that resemble adults; there is nothing "childish" in the representation except for reduced stature. Likewise, Ariès finds no distinction between the style of clothing worn by adults and that worn by children; the children's clothing was simply smaller. At work and play, Ariès documents an intermingling of all members of a community, with none of the segregation by age that is common practice today. Children played the same games as adults, and labored alongside them in fields and workshops. With regard to language, Ariès observes that words now denoting age once denoted rank. The words "boy" or "*garçon*" meant "servant" or "menial." According to Ariès, "The idea of childhood was bound up with the idea of dependence."[7] It was economic, not biological.

Ariès notes that changes began to happen in the seventeenth century. In art, children became the frequent subjects of portraits that featured pink skin, chubby fists, and soft curls. Styles of clothing unique to children were adopted. A gulf opened between the categories of child and adult. Children were seen as needing protection. Adulthood, no longer automatic, needed to be achieved through training and initiation. Out of these changes emerged the notion of idealized or protected childhood, which would become the prevailing belief in the later nineteenth and twentieth centuries.

Along with other scholars, I am unconvinced by Ariès's assertion that "childhood" developed in a strictly linear fashion.[8] This idea does not square with the historical record of the nineteenth century—the apex of childhood according to Ariès—which saw protected children coexisting with child workers in mines, factories, and on city streets, as well as on theatre stages. To the contrary, idealized or protected childhood has existed in pockets of privilege throughout history. However, Ariès's foundational concept—that with the seventeenth century, Western society changed how it looks at children—has been widely embraced.[9] The changes are marked, not only in clothing, painting, work, and language, as noted by Ariès, but also in the mushrooming of schools, children's literature, pediatrics, and other child-centric practices that were previously nonexistent. As Steven Mintz observed in 2004, "Every aspect of childhood—including children's household responsibilities, play, schooling, relationships with parents and peers, and paths to adulthood—has been transformed over the last four centuries."[10]

The new idea of childhood that developed over these centuries has been variously referred to as protected, sentimental, idealized, or Romantic childhood—terms used interchangeably throughout this book. According to this notion, children are distinct from adults in almost every way. They are innocent, vulnerable, and pure, with ties to both the natural and the spiritual worlds. To preserve these sacred qualities, the new child needed to be protected from knowledge—including sexual knowledge—from work, and from adult society. The line between adult and child was no longer blurry, as children and adults were relegated to their separate spheres. Once the child had been excluded from the world of adults, this sacred creature needed a separate realm. Thus, literature, clothing, education, furniture, playthings, medical care, and recreation were particularized to suit children's (assumed) needs. For Ariès, the child had shifted from being an object of benign indifference to one of obsessive, claustrophobic love; from a life of freedom to one of confinement.

The personification of this idealized child is revealed in paintings such as Joshua Reynolds's *The Age of Innocence* (1788). Art historian Anne Higonnet has also noted the shift in images of children that began in the seventeenth century. In *Pictures of Innocence: The History and Crisis of Ideal Childhood* (1998), she demonstrates how the image of the "naturally innocent" child was created through the use of clothing, props, and settings as well as other elements of art.[11] As the eighteenth-century oils by Reynolds, Gainsborough, and others were followed by the nineteenth-century works of John Everett Millais, Kate Greenaway, and Mary Cassat, the image of the "Romantic child," as Higonnet labels it, wafted through Western consciousness via advertising. Although the idealized child existed in a realm apart from commercial affairs and labor, its image was quickly identified as marketable. Profitably linked with a wide variety of commodities and ideas, the image of the Romantic child in advertising parallels the use of children in theatre. In both instances, the buyer is responding to the sentimental appeal of the idealized child.

The value of children's sentimental appeal has been analyzed by economist Viviana A. Zelizer, whose insights have profoundly influenced my thinking. In *Pricing the Priceless Child* (1985), Zelizer traces the shift in society's definition of childhood by looking at changes in the economic value of children. She then juxtaposes economic and sentimental value. Twentieth-century children were much loved, but in contrast to the children of the prior century, they contributed little to household upkeep. With the twentieth century's "sacrelization" of childhood, the economically useful child was replaced by a creature that was economically useless but of immeasurable sentimental value to the family. Zelizer examines how this tension between economic and sentimental value informed struggles over the regulation of child actors, whose "work role . . . was ironically camouflaged by their fictional roles."[12]

While the idealization of childhood led to the ejection of most children from the workplace, it did not negate their impact in the economy. The increased focus on childhood in the twentieth century created a market for particularized, child-centered goods. Scholars have traced the connection between the creation of idealized childhood and the birth of new commercial industries in books such as Daniel Thomas Cook's *The Commodification of Childhood: The Children's Clothing Industry and the Rise of the Child Consumer* (2004), Miriam Formanek-Brunell's *Made to Play House: Dolls and the Commercialization of American Girlhood, 1830–1930* (1993), and Gary Cross's *Kids' Stuff: Toys and the Changing World of American Childhood* (1998).

Scholars of childhood acknowledge, of course, that the idealized child remained an abstract concept that never encased most children. Lived childhood experience is broadly diverse and includes an almost infinite number of social variations. Nonwhite children were excluded from the sentimental notion of childhood. The idealized child might have appeared to transcend class boundaries, but this child of nature was inevitably pictured and imagined as white and comfortably nourished. Idealized childhood never extended to the lower classes or the "lower races." Thus, thousands of poor and immigrant children could labor in streets and factories in the later nineteenth century, even as the cult of idealized childhood prevailed. The labor of African American children was accepted because they, too, were seen as existing outside of the realm of childhood. As Robin Bernstein has demonstrated, African American children were thought to be insensitive to pain, and thus capable of extraordinary labor.[13]

A bifurcated view of children continues to exist today in what Jared Diamond refers to as "WEIRD" nations (Western, educated, industrial, rich, democratic), where the comforts and protections extended to middle-class white children are still not deemed necessary for the poor.[14] Outside of WEIRD nations and in lower income brackets within them, there are myriad examples of children who capably work long hours both in and outside the home. Nayaka children in southern India "independently hunt small game." In New Guinea, a ten-year-boy may hire himself out as a porter and travel away from home for an indeterminate amount of time without consulting his parents, and three-year-old Sirionó girls in Bolivia spin and make baskets and pots.[15] By contrast, a typical, middle-class, nine-year-old girl in the United States adds nothing to the family purse, has meals prepared for her, and may never shop for the family on her own. These children exercise different degrees of agency.

The concept of agency has "served philosophy and social science since time immemorial" but is still unfamiliar to many people.[16] According to the *Palgrave Handbook of Childhood Studies*, agency refers to "conscious and deliberate human interventions" and is an attribute of people who are "active in construction of their own lives, the lives of those around them and of the societies in which they live."[17] Traditionally, children were seen as passive subjects, but since the 1970s scholars have begun to perceive of children as social actors. Allison James calls this shift in perception "One of the most important theoretical developments in the recent history of childhood studies."[18] The perception of children as social actors is key to this study of juvenile theatre workers.

In early America children often exercised agency, and their competence was a noncontested fact of life. Laboring children of the eighteenth century emerged as wholesome, industrious contributors both to their own families and to the growing nation. Well into the nineteenth century, parents recognized and respected their children's abilities. Robert Guerineau Marsh showed himself to be just such a parent when he founded the Marsh Troupe of Juvenile Comedians in 1855. He installed his two children, Mary and Georgie, as leading players in the company. The Marsh Troupe operated at the moment just before American childhood would be utterly transformed, when children's labor was still considered not only normal, but also essential to their preparation for adulthood and their own family's sustenance. Beginning in the decades after the Civil War and continuing into the twentieth century, laboring children appeared as exploited victims.

Where the solution sought by Progressives—eliminating paid labor from children's lives—has been successful, it has yielded a class of sheltered, often indolent, beings whose dependent phase can extend well past the age of twenty. After surveying the history of childhood in America, Steven Mintz urges us to "reverse the process of age segmentation," which has led to a "deepening contradiction between the child as dependent juvenile and the child as incipient adult."[19] What has been lost is common acknowledgment of the competence of children.

Today, the notion that all children need some period of protection from adulthood is universally accepted. "Childhood" is so established a fact that questioning its sanctity can be seen as immoral, disastrous, or both. Yet, in the rush to protect children from exploitation, the fact of children's competence has been glossed over. The iconic ten-year-old newsboy could successfully negotiate city streets and adult culture in order to buy and sell his papers. Children can—and do—function at a relatively high level of competence. This was common knowledge in Medieval Europe where, as Ariès noted, most children worked side by side with adults; it was still common knowledge in the early nineteenth century when children continued to work with their parents. In the middle and late nineteenth century, commerce and industrialization provided increased opportunities for children to work outside the home. As the circumstances of child labor became oppressive, however, well-meaning Progressives sought to separate children from work. When the ideology of protected childhood took hold, children were characterized not only as innocent, but as vulnerable and in need of protection. Vulnerability implied incompetence (for if children were competent, why would they need protection?). Thus, as Zelizer has pointed out, anything constructive that children did in the twentieth century began to be characterized as play or education: it could not be productive. Society could not reconcile a being who was both competent *and* in need of protection. As idealized notions of childhood took hold, the competence of children was denied. Today, children are frequently viewed not only as useless (in that they do not contribute), but also as helpless (in that they *cannot* contribute). To avoid the exploitation of industrialization, American society has robbed its children of competence. This view flies in the face of reality, both historical and contemporary.

Not surprisingly, discussion of child actors has tended to follow the same patterns. Film stars Baby Peggy, Shirley Temple, and Macaulay Culkin, for example, did draw laughs, emote on cue, and hit their marks on multiple takes, but discussions of their craft, labor, or competence are scarce. The performance of the Marsh Children is dismissed as "precious." Child actors are rarely taken as seriously as their adult contemporaries on stage. The success of antebellum child prodigies like Kate and Ellen Bateman is often attributed to clever promotion and/or fads for freaks. Some commentators assume that child performers have no craft at all. The kids are just playing, parroting, or simply parading cuteness, that is, their essential identity as children. Child stars, such as Cordelia Howard in the 1850s and Jackie Coogan in the 1920s, were credited with saintliness and innocence, but denied competence. They were admired in their identity as children. But as the study of the Marsh Children reveals, the truth is more complex, because acting is not like being a machine in a factory. It has nuance; it demands talent and thought. Child performers are neither parrots nor geniuses nor archetypes.

The professional child confounds the modern definition of childhood. Situated at the nexus of the freedom vs. protection knot, the professional child has features of both the "free," adult-like medieval child and the protected modern child. Like an adult, the juvenile performer earns income, exercises expressive agency, acts in the public sphere, and moves among adults. She is exposed rather than protected, free rather than confined. The professional child performer is a competent worker. However, like the modern child, she is legally dependent, financially dependent (for much of the history), and frequently ignorant. Child performers have always occupied a liminal space between child and adult. For child actors, a developmental linear timeline from naïve youth to savvy adulthood does not apply. At any moment, a child performer may embody both the innocent Romantic child and the more hard-boiled showbiz worker. Very few commentators (historical or contemporary) tend to look at the performance as a job the child is doing, and often doing well. While all actors substitute fictive, constructed characters for their biographical selves, this is doubly true in the case of child actors. Their public personae are often so well fashioned that the performers are both underrated as skilled practitioners of their craft and unacknowledged as laboring professionals. Neither artists nor workers, they are entirely camouflaged by the gauzy cloud of sentimentality supplied by the cult of childhood.

This book unmasks the professional identities of four antebellum child performers, bridging the fields of childhood studies and theatre history and drawing on scholarship from both. Performing children are an important subject for scholars of childhood because these actors, by muddling both historic and contemporary definitions, expose accepted norms. Stage workers need to be included in the history of child labor. Theatre history is better informed by situating these performers within this broader social change.

Nan Mullenneaux has pointed out the "wide variance of public personae" embodied by mid-nineteenth-century child performers, including the angelic innocent, the genius prodigy, and the audaciously independent child performer. While Mullenneaux theorizes that these paradigms evolved chronologically in a "rough periodization," the Marsh Troupe presented all of them simultaneously.[20] Mary Marsh embodied the Romantic ideal of sentimental childhood; Georgie Marsh, the genius clown; and Louise Arnot, the fearless tomboy. In the decades bracketing the beginning of the twentieth century, these actors remained well-known. Almost half a century after their heyday, critic Laurence Hutton would insist that every man of a certain age retained a fine memory of Mary Marsh, and that Georgie Marsh's comedic renditions of a famous character were preferred to those of many adult imitators since.[21] Thirty years after the troupe's dissolution, a *Los Angeles Herald* critic would still praise Louise Arnot's childhood performances.[22] Alumni of the troupe carried the epithet throughout their careers. Early twentieth-century memorials of former child actors who had retired at puberty inevitably mentioned their time with the "famous Marsh troupe." Yet, their fame did not survive beyond the lives of their audiences. A boy may have retained for life a childhood memory of those child actors, but when he passed away, so did word of the Marsh Troupe.

As childhood studies scholars often note, most of what we know about children from the past comes to us filtered through adults. Scholars like Karen Sánchez-Eppler and Jane C. Hunter have taken pains to ground their studies in the written words of children.[23] Such efforts admittedly tend to privilege the geographical areas and social classes in which children were most likely to be literate. Although most free girls who lived in the first third of the nineteenth century did learn to read, education was less widespread than it became in the decades after the Civil War.[24] For itinerant child actors, however, adequate schooling remained an issue well into the twentieth century. With regard to the actors of the Marsh Troupe who traveled steadily, there is no hard evidence that any of them were literate during their time with the company (save Louis Aldrich, who joined as a teenager after a year of college). We can presume that at least one of them, who became a printer, had managed to achieve literacy by adulthood. In any event, no diaries, memoirs, or letters by any of the Marsh Children are known to survive.[25] As a consequence, this book is based on records written solely by adults. Whatever personal feelings these child performers had about their work must be surmised or left mysterious. Fortunately, the degree of the children's agency can sometimes be deduced from a course of action—a decision to leave the troupe or to stay in opposition to a parent's wishes, for example.

This book offers both a record of the Marsh Troupe in aggregate and a chronicle of the individual case histories of its leading players—Alfred Stewart, Mary Marsh, Louise Arnot, and Georgie Marsh—as exemplars. The study of these histories explores complex questions surrounding the dynamic role of underage working actors on the world stage, and illuminates radical changes in the social construction of childhood, both in the Troupe's nineteenth-century context and today. Issues faced by the Marsh Children, such as parental control, education, financial agency, eroticization, and legal regulation, remain problematic in the twenty-first-century entertainment industry.

Chapter 1 tells the story of the troupe's founder, Robert Guerineau Marsh, and its first three successful seasons (1855–58). Marsh's history as an actor and as manager of an adult troupe informed the juvenile company's operations, repertoire, and advertising techniques. The record of positive critical comment and steady bookings, even during the financial panic of 1857, established the Marsh Juveniles as creditable theatre professionals. Less an exhibition of precocious phenomena than of fully staged spectacle, the Marsh Troupe made use of all of the grand promotional and production techniques that were available to antebellum impresarios. Unlike twentieth-century producers Hal Roach and Walt Disney, whose *Our Gang* and *Mickey Mouse Club* were populated by a renewable slate of juvenile hirelings, however, Robert Marsh invested in his own children, and a small cadre whose inevitable maturation did not allow him to expand or sustain his own Barnum-like ambitions.

Chapter 2 describes internal troubles the troupe faced: personnel problems in 1857 and 1858, and an unforgettable tragedy in 1859. Issues of the personal and legal agency of child professionals were exposed in the inevitable friction between Marsh and the parents of his young performers. The children's power is also revealed in their various salary agreements. Alfred Stewart's contract embodied an unstable arrangement that was partly a traditional apprenticeship, but partly reflective of the newer labor-for-cash mode. The conflict illuminates a paradigm shift in the training method of actors within the context of economic changes in theatre production. Throughout the dispute, Alfred Stewart seemed devoid of agency as his mother acted forcefully on his behalf. In analogous circumstances, Louise Arnot defied her mother, emphatically expressing her own employment preference, and displaying the character traits she would use to construct an independent professional and personal identity. In the midst of these legal squabbles, the company suffered its greatest loss with the death of little Mary Marsh in early 1859.

In chapter 3, Mary Marsh is situated at the zenith of the cult of the child. She is an embodiment of a sociological construct, the ideal child of innocence and purity. Her career is related to the popularity of melodrama, not only as a theatrical genre, but as a mode of interpreting daily life. This chapter also explores the eroticization of Mary and of the other girls in the troupe. Mary's accidental death was in some ways no different from those of the garment workers who perished fifty years later in the Triangle Shirtwaist factory fire, many of whom were around Mary's age. They were female workers who died on the job due to unsafe conditions. But while the factory fire spurred outrage, reform, and the organization of labor, reaction to Mary Marsh's death made scant mention of labor conditions, because Mary Marsh was not seen as a worker. Instead, her death was contextualized within the sentimental paradigms of nineteenth-century melodrama, in which angelic children met early ends before sailing blissfully to heaven. After death, Mary permanently assumed the angelic mantel of her fictional roles. Her gravestone and burial exemplify the sentimental values of the rural cemetery movement.

Chapter 4 tracks the company's reactions to a trio of crises: Mary's death, the approaching U.S. Civil War, and the unavoidable reality of children's aging. To revitalize his company, Marsh sought audiences among the gold-rush-swelled populations of California, Australia, and New Zealand. The thirty-seven-month Pacific tour engorged the company's coffers, but reveals the folly inherent in any enterprise reliant on the stability of childhood. In 1863, the troupe was undermined by the withdrawal of several major players, who married and moved on to adult careers.

Following chapter 4, the timeline splits. Louise Arnot's career is the subject of chapter 5, which analyzes her role as the troupe's original "leading man" and its impact on her sixty years on the stage. While devotees of the ideology of Romantic childhood lose interest when their subjects reach puberty, this text explores the entire span of Louise Arnot's career to demonstrate how childhood experience and training effectively prepared her to independently support herself as an adult actor. Louise's initial stage persona was a counterparadigm of fragile Victorian girlhood, but one readily found in the tomboys seen in novels and paintings of the era. While the transition to adulthood curtailed freedom for many girls, Arnot maintained a degree of personal and professional autonomy unusual for women of her time. Playing breeches roles both before and after Lydia Thompson transformed that convention, Arnot demonstrated the ability to adapt her style. She progressed from antebellum nautical melodrama through burlesque to twentieth-century vaudeville.

Chapter 6 returns to the fork in the timeline to examine Georgie Marsh's stage craft and trace the course of his later life, including his personal and professional relationship with his father-mentor. Like many nineteenth-century actors, Georgie Marsh played the same line of business for his entire career. Unlike most other professionals, however, during that career he changed from a cherubic six-year-old to a full-grown man. His ability to maintain a consistently praised characterization while making the necessary shifts in performance style over fifteen years demonstrates his highly developed expertise as an actor. This chapter also scrutinizes the relationship between parenting and management, which has been crucial in the lives of many professional child performers in every age. The father-son/master-apprentice dynamic between Georgie and Robert Guerineau Marsh reveals the complicated interplay between nineteenth-century ideas about the meaning of childhood and concepts of autonomy, loyalty, and talent.

These compelling histories offer documentary evidence that contradicts tropes concerning child actors. Exploring these stories in light of the larger histories of American childhood, American work, and American theatre can enhance our understanding of the changing position of underage workers in society as a whole.

CHAPTER 1

BEGINNINGS AND SUCCESS

The twentieth century was barely a year away when the sexton of Rose Hill Cemetery peered through the December dusk to see a fashionably dressed woman approaching the gate. He guessed her to be about thirty years old. Ignoring closing time, he waited for the stranger to draw near. The woman told him she was only in Macon, Georgia, for one night and must visit the grave of Mary Marsh.[1] The sexton recognized the name and, like most people in Macon, he knew the old, sad story. Before the Civil War, when Ralston Hall still stood on Cherry Street, and traveling entertainers played before blazing footlights, twelve-year-old Mary Marsh headlined a troupe of performing children. During a performance on January 27, 1859, her gauzy costume caught fire. Before the horrified but powerless mother, brother, father, castmates, or spectators could save her, the little girl was fatally burned. Later, a newsman would write, "Her tragic death caused gloom all over the city."[2]

Seeing the stranger's resolve, and reluctant to let a woman wander alone in the dark, the sexton admitted the visitor and offered to accompany her. When they reached the grave, she knelt down and wept bitterly. The astonished sexton stood silently aside until, at length, the stylish woman collected herself and rose. As they walked back to the gate through the quiet darkness, she told him that she'd been onstage with Mary Marsh the night of the accident. When the man couldn't believe this to be true of the youthful woman before him, she confided that she was an actress on tour. "You see, my looks are my stock in trade and not a member of the company has any idea that I am anything like as old as I am." The woman went on, "I don't mind telling you, however, that I am 55 years old. Mary Marsh would now be 52 if she were living, but I am three years older than she would be." The speaker was Louise Arnot (1844–1919), an actress whose six-decade stage career had indeed begun all those years ago under Mary Marsh's father.

In the fall of 1855, as the nineteenth-century vogue for childhood began to blossom, Robert Marsh founded a theatre company unique on the American stage, a professional acting company composed primarily of children drawn from many families. While a handful of child phenomena had drawn some attention and children were frequently featured in family-based singing, circus, or acting companies, an all-child acting troupe was a novel sight on the antebellum U.S. stage. Using the term "comedian" as a synonym for actor, Marsh gave the company a name that would draw attention to his status as founder, as well as to the youth of his players. The Marsh Troupe of Juvenile Comedians debuted at Philadelphia's Walnut Street Theatre on October 15, 1855. Louise was featured together with Mary Marsh as the pretty leading lady and her little brother Georgie as the clown. Alongside these starring players, Marsh gathered and trained more than two dozen other performing children for his troupe. An impresario as much as an artist, Marsh produced large spectacles involving up to fifty child performers, and he carried a company with musicians, machinists, scenic artists, nurses, and teachers. Playing primarily for adult audiences during eight years of incessant touring, they had success on two continents and created a legacy for a generation.

Family-based troupes were common in the antebellum period, but very few references exist to troupes composed, as the Marsh Juveniles were, of a large group of children from many families.[3] The *New York Times* called it an "unusual novelty."[4] And while most contemporaneous critics and commentators did not remark on this anomaly, an unidentified news clipping in the Harvard Theatre Collections stresses the innovation: "Juvenile companies of comedians have long been a principal attraction in the city of Paris; but *nothing of the kind*, on this extensive scale, was ever attempted in this country until the present troupe was organized by Mr. R. G. Marsh."[5] Troupes of children had been popular in England during the seventeenth century and *Pinafore* companies of children would tour the United States in the 1880s.[6] Later, in vaudeville, there would be all-children shows such as Gus Edwards's *Kid Kabaret*.[7] In early film, there would be the

Little Rascals, and in early television, the *Mickey Mouse Club*, but in the early and mid-nineteenth century, similarly constituted troupes were rare.

The phrase "children's troupe" has a diminutive, homey sound to it that may suggest a modest or amateurish enterprise. The Marsh Troupe was anything but. The size of the company, the extravagance of its productions, and the continuity of attention from the press reflect expertise. Additionally, the length and steadiness of their bookings in the face of economic downturns and pointed competition prove that the Marsh Troupe of Juvenile Comedians was big business. Nineteenth-century advertisements used grandiose claims that cannot be accepted as literal representations of what audiences saw. They do, however, indicate the troupe manager's sense of the public's interests and the company's strengths. Marsh emphasized scale and novelty.

Advertisements for the Marsh Troupe frequently highlighted the large number, as well as the youth, of the performers. A December 1855 ad promises "thirty four boys and girls . . . five to nine years of age."[8] By February 1856 they are "forty in number, under ten years of age."[9] An 1857 ad promises the appearance of, "43 beautiful children."[10] An 1858 production featured "thirty-six of the Marsh Juveniles and thirty-one highly trained little auxiliaries."[11] An 1857 puff piece promised "nearly FIFTY WONDERFUL CHILDREN."[12] Americans had already decided that bigger was better, and impresario Marsh aimed to satisfy them. Dances and specialty numbers were interpolated into plays—called for or not. In advertising them, Marsh also emphasized numbers of performers, as in these 1857 notices: "During the piece, the Serious Family Polka by 16."[13] "During the evening will be performed the beautiful FLOWER DANCE by 20 of our troupe as danced by the celebrated VIENNOISE CHILDREN entitled LES PAS DE FLEURS!"[14] An 1861 ad promised twenty-four members in a "Chinese" dance.[15] Like his contemporary P. T. Barnum, Marsh drew attention to his product using press puffery, animals on stage, and tie-ins to local events and enthusiasms. He was one of the earliest theatrical producers to seize on the newly developed photography techniques to produce and distribute portraits of his featured players.

The actors in the Marsh Troupe were professionals—accepted and judged as such by their audiences. They toured the same circuits and performed the same repertory as the adult companies with which they competed. As typical in nineteenth-century theatre troupes, each performer had his line of business. Little Mary Marsh was the versatile leading lady. A publicity piece enumerated Mary's roles: "now the pathetic heroine, now the pert and pretty chambermaid, now the lady of fashion, again the charming *soubrette*, and so on through all the paths and avenues of the tragic and the comic Muse."[16] Little brother George inevitably played the comic parts including a long list of amusing servants. "Miss Louise" played the powerful roles: swashbuckling brigands, nautical heroes, and the occasional stately queen. Alfred Stewart (1843–?) did Irish songs and sketches. Later, Louis Aldrich (1843–1901) would handle the tragic roles.

The historical record does not provide us with firsthand observations of rehearsals, and none of the performers left diaries or letters. Yet common theatrical practice in all venues would make it obvious that the Marsh children began their long day's work with arduous and demanding preparations. The company maintained a large repertoire. For example, during the 1857–58 season, twenty-seven different titles were rotated so the distinctive dialogue of each had to be readily recited. Almost all the plays included dancing and many involved swordplay. Some included military-style drills as well. Precise blocking and repeatedly going over scenes would be the daily agenda. Costume fittings would be frequent, necessitated by the variety of plays in the repertory, cast changes, and the children's growing bodies. With evening performances starting at 7:30 or 8 P.M., the children worked exceptionally hard and long hours.

Almost constant travel also burdened these competent troupers. "Draughty, unheated theatres, inferior hotels, and bad food in the lesser towns, devastating journeys by steamboat and unsanitary cars," were expected by nineteenth-century performers, but actor and diarist Harry Watkins bemoaned the other dangers: "All over the country there is great recklessness manifested on steamboats and railroads; scarcely a day passes without some dreadful accident which might have been avoided had there been the slightest caution on the part of those in command."[17] Those who survived illness might be maimed, but theatrical managers continued to tour.

While most of this book will focus on the child performers, the company's founder demands an introduction. Marsh was born Robert Guerineau (c. 1822–1907), and was a native of West Troy, in the present-day city of Watervliet near Albany in upstate New York.[18] Celebrated as home of the original "Uncle Sam" and a crucial supply site during the War of 1812, Watervliet was on the Erie Canal route.[19] Robert was probably born while it was under construction.[20] By the second quarter of the nineteenth century, the area's economy came to rely less on commercial activity and more on industry.[21] It was hardly a congenial locale for a hopeful actor with big ideas, and so Robert left town while still a young man. For his stage career, he relegated Guerineau to his middle name and adopted an old English appellation, billing himself as R. G. Marsh.

On May 5, 1846, Robert Guerineau married Jane C. Dutcher, also of West Troy.[22] For most of her life, Jane would play a supporting role in the marriage, going along with Robert's plans and helping out in a variety of ways.

Documentation of Marsh's early acting career is inconsistent.[23] Odell's *Annals of the New York Stage* identifies Marsh as "from the Troy Museum," but offers no supporting details, and none have been found.[24] Marsh spent his journeyman years in Philadelphia. Wilson's *History of the Philadelphia Theatre* lists Marsh as a regular company member at that city's National Theatre beginning in April 1845, and at the Arch Street Theatre beginning April 1846.[25] According to Col. T. Allston Brown—his contemporary—Marsh did not appear professionally until September 1846, when he performed at Philadelphia's Arch Street Theatre as Benserake in *The Gardener's Wife*.[26] From that point forward, the historians' accounts are supported by playbills and newspaper notices. Although many items list only the surname "Marsh," it is fairly certain that Robert Guerineau Marsh spent at least two seasons acting in Philadelphia, most of it under the management of the famous comedian William E. Burton (1804–60). Among the plays in which Marsh acted in Philadelphia was *The Naiad Queen*, later an important component of the Marsh Juvenile Comedians' repertory. In Burton's version of this fantasy, Marsh performed the role of Sir Rupert, while the celebrated comedian enacted the knight's page.[27] Marsh's later work reveals the close study he made of Burton's acting and managerial techniques during this period. Marsh would come back to Philadelphia to launch his Juvenile Troupe.

Both of Marsh's children were born during his Philadelphia period: Mary Eliza Guerineau (1847–1859) and George Washington Guerineau (c. 1850–1909).[28]

Marsh does not seem to have made much of an impact as an actor. In 1848, Burton took half his company to play at his New York theatre. These were "his most able and valuable actors."[29] R. G. Marsh was left in Philadelphia with the acting company that was, according to Burton biographer David Rinear, "simply not as strong."[30]

After a couple of seasons in Philadelphia, the young actor moved to New York, performing at the Brooklyn Museum, Castle Garden, the National Theatre, and the Chatham Theatre.[31] In August 1852, Marsh joined the cast of C. W. Taylor's (1785–1874) *Uncle Tom's Cabin*, the first adaptation of the novel performed on a New York stage. Marsh enacted the character of Sam Jenks, a Negro slave.[32] Blackface performance was common in this era and Marsh would make a specialty of it. In Stowe's novel, Sam is a sympathetic character who feigns incompetence to delay the slave trader tracking the runaways.[33] In the C. W. Taylor adaptation, the character was probably a low-comedy minstrel type, as it would also be in Conway's popular version. In that script Sam leads the opening number, inviting the chorus to "heel and toe it out."[34] Robert Marsh would later play other blackface roles including "Jumbo-Jum" in the "laughable Negro farce" of the same name and Uncle Tom.[35] On at least on one occasion, his Uncle Tom performance "won much applause."[36] One critic would later comment that Marsh's "negro [*sic*] characters [we]re his best efforts upon the stage."[37]

Marsh never entirely gave up acting. Later, while managing the Juvenile Troupe, he would occasionally appear with the company. In California, he took the role of Ali Baba in *The Forty Thieves*.[38] In many cities, he played "Amphibeo, the evil dwarf" in *The Naiad Queen*, a role that, according to one critic, he "carried out . . . with the facile agility which it require[d]."[39] In New Orleans he played "Mr. Lullaby" in *The Conjugal Lesson* for his benefit night.[40] Benefits were special performances negotiated as part of a performer's contract with the proceeds going to the performer.[41] As manager and actor, Marsh set up benefits for himself to take advantage of his local popularity in various cities on tour.

Uncle Tom's Cabin became a theatrical phenomenon and the most successful play of the nineteenth century. Between his appearance in the Taylor stage adaptation in 1852 and his founding of the juvenile troupe in 1855, Marsh seized upon *Uncle Tom's Cabin* as the vehicle for his first foray into theatrical management. Marsh toured *Uncle Tom* to Cincinnati, Chicago, and Williamsburg, Brooklyn. Partnering with John Ellsler (1822–1903) at the Utica Museum brought Marsh back to the familiar territory of upstate New York. The Utica and Syracuse Railroad had been running for over a decade in 1853 when it combined with other local routes to form the New York Central Railroad, facilitating travel across the state.[42] This new, efficient means of travel would have made it easier for Marsh and Ellsler to tour *Uncle Tom's Cabin* to Utica, Oswego, Auburn, Rochester, and Syracuse.[43] A good utility player, Marsh would over time act four roles in the play: the slave characters Sam Jenks and Uncle Tom, as well as two slave owners, the kind-hearted but weak St. Clair and the cruel, whip-wielding Simon Legree.

These tours laid the groundwork for Marsh's Juvenile Comedians in two ways: Marsh got his first experience as a manager, and his children got their first experience on stage. Perhaps the Howard family of actors had inspired Marsh. George C. Howard (1820–87) had staged a family-based *Uncle Tom's Cabin* at the Troy Museum using an adaptation by a cousin, George Aiken (1830–76). Howard played St. Clair; his wife, Caddie Fox Howard (1829–1908), portrayed Topsy; and their daughter Cordelia (1848–1941) acted Little Eva.[44] After great success in Troy, the show transferred to New York's National Theatre and made history, drawing record crowds from July 1853 to May 1854. Marsh may have known members of the Fox-Howard clan personally from his days at the Troy Museum, but he surely knew of their success. It is easy to imagine R. G. Marsh putting the pieces together. For an ambitious actor with a beautiful young daughter and direct experience with *Uncle Tom's Cabin* on stage, organizing a family-based production was almost inevitable.

Robert Marsh cast his daughter Mary as Little Eva and his son George in the smaller role of Little Harry. In some cities, Mrs. Marsh played the minor role of Aunt Ophelia.[45] Marsh acted Uncle Tom occasionally, but hired more prominent actors when he could find them. Greene C. Germon, famous from the Howard-Aiken version, played Uncle Tom for Marsh in Cincinnati where Marsh shifted to St. Clair.[46] In addition to his family and Germon, Marsh managed a well-staffed company of twelve men and six women.[47] Germon did not finish the season, however; he died in April 1854 and was replaced by Charles Whittle.[48] At the Utica Museum, Ellsler played Uncle Tom until the partners could bring in T. D. "Daddy" Rice (1806–60), the famous minstrel. Marsh portrayed Simon Legree while Mary and her brother continued their roles as Eva and Little Harry.[49] Through these tours Marsh learned how to fill theatres, while little Mary gained experience playing opposite many high-profile delineators of Uncle Tom.

The Cincinnati engagement played ten weeks, outlasting a competing production that opened and closed nearby during the Marshes' run.[50] According to a publicity piece published a few years later, six-year-old Mary "became at once the star attraction of the company." The "extreme youth, the fay-like grace, musical tones, natural readings and affecting pathos of Little Mary in her delineation of Little Eva, made her popularity boundless."[51] The claims for Mary's popularity are supported by announcements of her benefit performance for the last week in Cincinnati. Benefits gave audiences the opportunity to show their support of a favorite, and leading actors often had a benefit near the end of each run, but Greene C. Germon did not seem to take one. Neither the *Cincinnati Enquirer* nor the *Cincinnati Gazette* make any mention of a benefit for Germon or anyone in the company except Mary during the entire two-and-a-half-month run. And while the proceeds from a benefit normally accrue to the individual actor, in this case Robert Marsh probably pocketed the revenue from Mary's benefit.

Stage adaptations of *Uncle Tom's Cabin* varied widely in their attitudes toward slavery. Eric Lott declares, "To produce the play was by definition to engage in a divisive cultural struggle."[52] The Aiken-Howard version staked out a strongly abolitionist position, while others, such as Conway's, depicted minstrel-show-like scenes of happy life on a benign plantation. Marsh's own performance history and his managerial casting choices blur his position in this struggle. Greene C. Germon and T. D. Rice had appeared in simultaneous competing adaptations in New York City causing a theatrical war that spread to the newspapers and, occasionally, the streets, yet both performed under Marsh's management.[53] Evidence suggests that Marsh used an adaptation similar to the antislavery Aiken version. In his Cincinnati advertisements, Marsh published lists of characters and tableaux. These indicate a plot sequence that follows Aiken's script and Stowe's novel. Marsh utilized the character names that Aiken drew from the novel including Aunt Ophelia (rather than the Aunt Vermonty of Conway). Like Aiken, Marsh cut the character of Sam. An actor interviewed decades later by the *Chicago Tribune* claimed to have read the Marsh script and found it strikingly similar to the Aiken version.[54] There is, however, no evidence of a political slant in the troupe's business affairs. In common with almost all theaters of the era, the company performed before segregated audiences. Advertising notices frequently stated, "Colored people admitted only to the gallery."[55] Whatever abolitionist sympathies Marsh may have held, he did not exercise them in any way likely to rock the business boat. For most actor-managers, *Uncle Tom* was showbiz first, politics second.

At the time, there seemed to be unlimited audience demand for *Uncle Tom's Cabin*. Ellsler reported that he and Marsh did "phenomenal business" in upstate New York, and he expected the partnership to continue.[56] The public's fascination with *Uncle Tom* was not waning. Many family-based troupes took advantage of the play's enormous popularity which could support multiple touring companies simultaneously. Little Cordelia Howard would tour the role for nine years. Mary Marsh, about the same age as Cordelia, could have played Little Eva for many seasons. Georgie Marsh could have continued as Little Harry. Instead, R. G. Marsh, an iconoclast, chose a radically different course. He put aside the most popular play of the century, turning away from its road-tested format. He abandoned Ellsler, who became the first of several bitter ex-partners left in his wake. In October 1855, he launched the Marsh Troupe of Juvenile Comedians, an enterprise that would define his family's life, his own career, and their collective legacy.

Robert Marsh's decision to organize a children's troupe could not have been easily predicted. Children on the nineteenth-century stage generally performed within adult troupes or as individual phenomena. Marsh bet that the talent of children—his own and others—could sustain a company without the support of adult actors. Mary had proven herself on tour with her Little Eva, engrossing audiences in every town they played. The character Georgie played, however, is little more than a prop. In the play's most spectacular scene, his frantic mother carries Little Harry across the half-frozen Ohio River. The role gives no opportunity for the comic genius that Georgie Marsh would soon display. What proof of talent had Louise Arnot offered? Marsh had toured *Uncle Tom's Cabin* to her hometown of Rochester but there is no record of how he became acquainted with the eleven-year-old girl or why he chose her as a leading player in his new enterprise. According to an 1857 press piece, only three of the original troupe members "had ever seen the interior of a theatre or museum" before joining the company.[57] Yet, Marsh would stake his professional success on the talent and reliability of children.

Marsh had excellent timing. Interest in children was growing. Children appeared in more novels, plays, and paintings than ever before. These special creatures, who were beginning to be seen as so different from adults, increasingly fascinated the public. As Robin Bernstein writes, "By the mid-nineteenth century, sentimental culture had woven childhood and innocence together wholly. Childhood was then understood not as innocent but as innocence itself."[58] Marsh reflected this thinking when he explained his motive for founding the juvenile troupe. Its creation would "honor . . . and benefit" his chosen profession.[59] He felt that "something new and meritorious seemed needed in the world of dramatic amusements," which to Marsh, "exhibited a marked degree of degeneracy."[60] Children, by definition, were on a higher moral plain. For adults, contact with these special beings could be uplifting. Few in the antebellum world would question Marsh's hiring of children as workers, while many would enjoy the theatrical display of their innocence and youth.

After assembling his company, Marsh chose his repertory. In spite of the continued popularity of *Uncle Tom's Cabin* and his own success with it, Marsh excluded it. Eight long years elapsed before Marsh produced or acted in *Uncle Tom's Cabin* again. Instead, the Marsh Juveniles performed fantasies such as *The Naiad Queen* and *Beauty and the Beast*; romantic dramas such as *The Brigand* and *Ingomar, the Barbarian*; farces such as *Toodles* and *The Serious Family*; and melodramas such as *Black-Eyed Susan* and *Sea of Ice*; supplemented by ethnic songs and specialty dance numbers. Their large and varied repertoire was typical for the period and obviously chosen to please general audiences; many of the plays appear on David Grimsted's tables of the most popular plays of the first half of the century.[61] Significantly, Marsh made no attempt to choose repertoire particularly suited to child performers. If anything, the roles pointedly ignored their status as children. Virtually all of the characters were adults, and were often involved in the grown-up activities of courtship or battle. The play choices illustrate the Marsh Troupe's emergence at a pivotal moment in the social construction of childhood. While a current spectator, thoroughly indoctrinated in the modern ideas of sentimental childhood, might see a jarring dissonance, Robert Marsh saw professional actors performing the standard repertory of their peers. Only very occasionally did the newspapers of the day acknowledge that the roles or plot situations might not be appropriate for juvenile performers.

Unlike other nineteenth-century child performers who concentrated on (equally inappropriate) Shakespearean roles, the Marsh Troupe's emphasis on domestic farces, heroic drama, and fantastical situations made their repertoire roughly analogous to that of England's seventeenth-century all-boy companies. While the plays were well liked, most of the Marsh Troupe repertoire was backward-looking. It appears that R. G. Marsh chose plays that were first popular in his own youth.

From the outset, the Marsh Troupe enjoyed almost constant success. Following its debut at Philadelphia's Walnut Street Theatre in October 1855, the company boasted of achievements in Boston and Baltimore before arriving in New York City in December.[62] The *New York Times* review declared that the company was "destined to take the town by storm." Thirty children "toddling about the stage with all the elasticity of childhood in their limbs, and all the gravity of age in their faces."[63] The *Times*' prediction was correct: the New York engagement would last for a full year. Except for an August "vacation" when the children cooled off by performing in Buffalo and Quebec, the company performed continuously in New York City through November 1856.[64] They played at Mechanics Hall at 472 Broadway, which Marsh and his new partner Henry Wood had fitted up as a miniature theatre. They renamed the "new and beautiful temple of amusement" Broadway Varieties and advertised themselves H. Wood, Lessee and Business Manager, and R. G. Marsh, Stage Manager.[65]

Audiences were initially led to see Louise Arnot as part of the Marsh family. Reprints of the 1855 cast list show "Miss Louisa Marsh."[66] The 1855 *New York Times* review referred to Mary Marsh's "sister Louisa."[67] In a profile of the troupe published in 1862, Col. T. Allston Brown also identified the actress as Miss Louise Marsh, although he corrected this error in a later edition.[68] Other sources, however, consistently state that Robert Marsh had only two children.[69]

The company, now billed as the "Wood and Marsh Children," generally presented two pieces each evening. Their most frequent offerings during the early part of 1856 were *Black-Eyed Susan* and *The Wandering Minstrel. Black-Eyed Susan*, a nautical melodrama written in 1829 and advertised as "Jerrold's celebrated play," combined music, dance, humor, and spectacle, making it an ideal staple of the Marsh program.[70] The Theatre Royal, Bury St. Edmonds, England, offers this summary of the plot:

> Susan whose husband William is away at sea . . . falls on hard times. William returns a nautical hero and saves her from poverty, her crooked landlord and from the amorous advances of his drunken Captain. Despite his valour he is court-martialed for attacking a senior officer and is only saved from hanging in the nick of time by a sudden plot twist.[71]

The role of Susan was played by Little Mary, who epitomized the innocent heroines of the genre. Her leading man was not younger brother George, but Louise, three years older than Mary, and probably taller as well. Louise, playing the nautical hero William, garnered the greatest critical praise in this play. Master G. W. Marsh played "Gnatbrain," a gardener and waterman, and no doubt a comic character. Marsh believed in the dramatic ability of his actors to "put over" the show. The consistently strong audience response repaid his faith in them.

Although Grimsted lists *Black-Eyed Susan* as among the most popular plays between 1831 and 1851, Marvin Carlson writes, "[T]he nautical melodrama's great age was the 1820s and 1830s," after which it "was gradually replaced in the public's favor by other entertainments."[72] While the popularity of nautical melodrama may have declined generally, many prominent players such as the Bateman girls included *Black-Eyed Susan* in their repertory too.[73] Adah Isaacs Menken (1853–68), infamous for her risqué performance as Prince Mazeppa, would also use *Black-Eyed Susan* as a vehicle, posing provocatively as William and playing four roles simultaneously.[74] The novelty of Marsh's casting stands out when compared with Bateman's, which failed to entrust the two leading roles to children. H. L. Bateman bypassed his "phenomenal" daughters to play William himself opposite Mrs. H. F. Nichols as Susan. Unlike the Marsh Children, the Bateman girls played minor parts.[75]

Other plays in the Marsh repertory included *The Rough Diamond*, *My Neighbor's Wife*, *Beauty and the Beast*, *Faint Heart Never Won Fair Lady*, *Loan of a Lover*, and *Perfection*. On some nights, the company filled the bill with a single piece, *The Naiad Queen*. This fantasy spectacle served as a mainstay of the troupe for its entire existence. *The Serious Family*, *The Miser of Marseilles*, and *Nan, the Good for Nothing* were also added to their repertory during the 1856 fall season.[76]

At the Quebec Music Hall, the company introduced *Toodles*, a piece that became a trademark of the troupe as vehicle for Master G. W. Marsh, as little Georgie was frequently billed. The play, and Georgie's performance, were precise copies of William Burton's work as adapter and star. Burton had first appeared in Richard Raymond's play, *The Farmer's Daughter or Mr. and Mrs. Toodles*, in 1842. As David Rinear explains, Burton gradually developed and adapted Timothy Toodles into his signature role, and the piece became known simply as, *Toodles*.[77] Rinear offers this summary:

> The action revolves around Mr. and Mrs. Toodles' constant attempt at one-upping each other by purchasing ridiculous items at auction that they hope might be of future use. A door plate with the name of "Thompson with a P" finds its way into the house because Mrs. Toodles thinks that it might prove useful if she should ever give birth to a daughter who, upon growing up, married a man named Thompson. Mr. Toodles retaliates by purchasing a cheap coffin at an auction in the hopes that it might prove of future use in the event of his misguided wife's sudden demise.[78]

Initially Mary Marsh played Mrs. Toodles, but over the years various other little girls took the part of Georgie's foil. Audiences were delighted by the exactness of George's "marvelous mimicry" of Burton's *Toodles* persona.[79]

By December 1856, Marsh had ended his partnership with Henry Wood. The immediate cause is unknown but may have been connected to the fact that both the company and Marsh personally owed Wood money. Wood's name was dropped from the troupe's billing and the performers, now called the Marsh Children or the Marsh Juvenile Comedians, embarked on a year's tour beginning with an eight-week stay at the Howard Athenaeum in Boston.

After their year in New York City, the polished professionals who arrived in Boston were much appreciated. They stayed through the holiday season and well into the new year. The repertory remained stable but the company had grown. Notices in the *Boston Post* advertised "33 Little Misses from 4 to 12 Years Old," and the theatre's playbills frequently proclaimed, "40 beautiful Children will Perform!"[80] In addition to children and support staff, the large company also carried some young women performers. While programs typically list the first names of the child performers in the cast (for example, Miss Josephine, Miss Sallie, Miss Harriet, Master Waldo), Marsh Troupe cast lists also include about half a dozen female cast members listed by surname (for example, Miss Melville, Miss Secord, Miss Prowler).[81] These are probably young women in their teens that stand in the second row of the company pictured in figure 1.1. Significantly, none of the actresses who received "grown-up" billing ever played major roles.

Extant playbills and programs from this long and successful Boston engagement show sixteen different play titles with *Black-Eyed Susan* and *The Naiad Queen* recurring most frequently. There were also multiple performances of two showpieces for Georgie, *The Wandering Minstrel* and *Toodles*. A local critic called Georgie, "the most precocious child artist we have ever seen" who possessed "an innate drollery an older comedian might envy."[82] *My Husband's Mirror*, with Georgie and Mary as Mr. and Mrs. Delmaine, and *My Neighbor's Wife* both received multiple showings and praise.[83]

The children had two performances on Christmas Day, 1856, playing *The Invincibles* and *Nan, the Good-for-Nothing* in the afternoon and *Black-Eyed Susan* and *Toodles* in the evening. They had refreshment—if not rest—that day, possibly eating onstage between shows as the *Clipper* declared, "At the Howard Athenaeum ocular demonstration was given that the Marsh children had some dinner on Christmas day."[84] Steady business continued throughout January.

The popularity of the company may be suggested by the ticket prices. Ads listed a five-tiered scale for admission. Private boxes could be had for five dollars, the equivalent of $129 in 2013.[85] Dress boxes were seventy-five cents; dress circle and parquette, fifty cents; family circle and second tier, twenty-five cents; third tier, twelve and a half cents; and "Colored People admitted only to the Gallery." Children accompanied by parents were admitted to the parquette for twenty-five cents. The wide range of prices and accommodations indicates anticipation that the troupe would interest a broad spectrum of the populace. Most of the playbills include the announcement that, "There will be NO FREE LIST at this Theatre." As the end of the engagement neared, the theatre inaugurated a daily ticket auction. Playbills throughout the week of February 10, 1857, announced:

Figure 1.1. "The Marsh Children," circa 1857. The children are not identified in this early drawing, but it is tempting to assign names to the faces. The tiny boy in front row center must certainly be Georgie. To Georgie's left, one of the girls wears a round locket, similar to that worn by Mary in the 1853 poster for *Uncle Tom's Cabin*. None of the other girls wear jewelry, and the belt and collar of this girl's dress seem more elaborate than the others. She holds the hand of the girl half a head taller, perhaps Louise, whose hair is pulled back, without curls or adornment. Her face is long, not softened by full cheeks. It is easy to imagine her as Mary's leading man. Joseph Ireland's *Records of the New York Stage*; TCS 45, Harvard Theatre Collection, Houghton Library, Harvard University.

Auction Sale of Choice Seats

> At the solicitation of many patrons of the Troupe, and to afford all an opportunity of securing choice seats for the entertainments, the undersigned will offer the choice of seats at Auction, this morning at 10 o'clock, in the vestibule of the Howard. The sale will be continued every day, at the same hour, through the week. . . . SAMUEL HATCH, Auctioneer.[86]

In the hands of P. T. Barnum, the ticket auction was a "standard publicity device."[87] Its use here may be simply an example of the promotional imagination of R. G. Marsh, but coupled with the long engagement, it may also genuinely demonstrate the troupe's appeal.

Marsh fueled fascination with another publicity device that few artists were using at the time: the celebrity photo. Ten years before *cartes de visite* would come pouring out of Napoleon Sarony's New York studio, Georgie Marsh stood in the lobby of the Howard Athenaeum handing out small, silver-toned photos of himself.[88] A similar oval photo of Mary Marsh dressed as her *Loan of a Lover* character suggests that she did likewise.[89] Later, this device would become standard as Hollywood distributed millions of autographed 8 × 10 glossies to encourage the personal connection of adoring fans to stars, but in 1857 impresario Marsh was far ahead of the trend.

The three leading players took their benefits during their last week in Boston. Mary and Louise took a joint benefit in *Black-Eyed Susan*.[90] The bold, five-inch-high letters on the playbill for February 10, 1857, unmistakably blur Louise's identity by listing "Misses Louise & Mary Marsh."[91] Georgie performed *Toodles* for his benefit on the final night of the long engagement.[92] According to an unidentified clipping in the Harvard Theatre Collection, "There was a jammed house at the farewell of the Marsh Troupe on Friday, and, as during the week, tickets brought very excellent premiums."[93] R. G. Marsh thanked the people of Boston and promised the troupe would return—a promise fulfilled at the beginning of the fall season.[94]

Meanwhile, the Marsh Troupe moved south for the spring. Capitalizing on the increasing desire to see children on stage, they played at New Orleans' Pelican Theatre in March, before heading to Mobile, Alabama.[95] In June, they delighted audiences during two weeks at the St. Louis Theatre in Missouri. The children probably arrived by steamboat and may have mingled with the "drunken idlers . . . Indian beggars, travel-worn foreign immigrants . . . circuses, musicians, buskin-clad hunters and trappers,

HOWARD ATHENÆUM.

R. G. MARSH, ... LESSEE and MANAGER.
WM. J. NAGLE .... TREASURER
H. C. SPOHR .... MUSICAL DIRECTOR | E. PUTNAM & L. D. WHITE, MACHINISTS
J. V. CORNELL .... SCENIC ARTIST | A. CAMPBELL ...... PROPERTY MAKER

POSITIVELY THE LAST WEEK

A CARD TO THE PUBLIC.

Let it be understood that

THIS IS POSITIVELY THE LAST WEEK!

The Troupe can perform in Boston, an engagement of a most flattering and remunerative nature having been closed for New Orleans, to commence March 2d, 1857.

Remember, the Last Four Nights

The undersigned takes this method to express his grateful acknowledgments to the citizens of Boston for their very liberal patronage throughout the past seven weeks of almost incessant inclement weather. He will always bear in proud remembrance the flattering encomiums bestowed upon his Troupe of Little Comedians by the Press and Public of this City. He shall leave Boston with many regrets, and will ever recur to the season about to close as one of the most pleasureable and profitable, (the weather considered) that he has yet experienced in his theatrical career

AUCTION SALE OF CHOICE SEATS.

At the solicitation of many patrons of the Troupe, and to afford all an opportunity of securing choice seats for the entertainments, the undersigned will offer the choice of seats at Auction, this morning at 10 o'clock, in the vestibule of the Howard. The sale will be continued every day, at the same hour, through the week.

☞ Tickets not called for before 4 o'clock, will be sold at the Box Office, after that time.

SAMUEL HATCH, Auctioneer..

JOINT BENEFIT

OF MISSES

Louise & Mary Marsh

On (THIS) TUESDAY EVENING, February 10th, 1857,

Will be presented for POSITIVELY THE LAST TIME the Nautical Drama of

BLACK-EYED SUSAN!

WILLIAM .... Miss LOUISE
GNATBRAIN .... Master GEORGE W. MARSH
Admi·al .... Master Waldo
Captain Crosstree .... Miss Carrie
Doggrass .... Master Waldo
Jacob Twig .... Miss Sallie
Blue Peter, with song .... Miss Julia
Quid .... Miss Clara
Seaweed .... Miss Maline
Lieutenant Pike .... Miss Georgiana
Raker .... Miss Ada
Hatchet .... Miss Josephine
Plou:hsh·re .... Miss Harriet
BLACK-EYED SUSAN .... LITTLE MARY MARSH
Dolly Mayflower .... Hiss Helen

Sailors, Midshipmen, Marines, Officers, &c.

SONG, "To-day I'm Sixty-two," .... LITTLE JULIA

After which, LAST TIME, the Farce, by W. W. Clapp, Jr., entitled

MY HUSBAND'S MIRROR!

FRED DELMAINE .... Master GEORGE W. MARSH
Ricker .... Miss Carrie
Flouncer .... Miss Melville
Mrs DELMAINE .... LITTLE MARY MAR:H
Margaret .... Miss Helen
Children .... Miss Selma and Maline

Beautiful Dance, - - by - - Little Christine

To conclude with (LAST TIME) the Farce of

MY NEIGHBOR'S WIFE!

Mr Somerton .... Miss Carris
Timothy Brown .... Master Waldo
JONATHAN SMITH .... Mast. GEO. W. MARSH
Mrs SOMERTON .... Miss LOUISE
Mrs Brown .... Miss Harriet
Mrs SMITH .... LITTLE MARY MARSH

(TO-MORROW) WEDNESDAY EVENING,

Will be presented the Spectacle of the

FORTY THIEVES,

FIRST AND ONLY TIME!

☞ LOOK OUT FOR BALLOU'S PICTORIAL! ☜

Of THURSDAY NEXT, the 12th inst., as it will contain Engraved Portraits of the LITTLE COMEDIANS, executed by several of the best artists in the country. ☞ Get a copy.

PRICES OF ADMISSION.

Dress Circle and Parquette .... 50 cts | Third Tier .... 12½ cts
Family Circle, Second Tier .... 25 cts | Dress Boxes .... 75 cts
Private Boxes .... $5,00 | Colored People admitted only to the Gallery.
Children, with Parents or Guardians, to Parquette, ... 25 cts

☞ There will be NO FREE LIST at this Theatre. ☜

THE BOX OFFICE will be open from 9 A. M. till 3 P. M., when tickets can be had and seats secured for any Evening. Tickets for sale AT ALL THE HOTELS.

Times Job Press, 3 and 5 State Street, Boston.—J. H. & F. F. Farwell, and G. Forrest, Printers

Figure 1.2. Howard Athenaeum playbill, Boston, February 10, 1857. In spite of the misleading headline, the cast list includes no last name for "Miss Louise." TCS 66, Harvard Theatre Collection, Houghton Library, Harvard University.

farmers clutching their saddlebags, apple sellers with their baskets of fruit, [and] women of questionable character" who kept the levees crowded day and night. Charles Dickens, visiting in 1843, had found the St. Louisans to be "tobacco-spitting, slave-holding vulgar people," but they had responded well to Noah Ludlow's aim of presenting theatre that was "rational, moral, and entertaining." Professional theatre had been permanently established in the city since Ludlow opened the elegant St. Louis Theatre in 1837.[96]

The centerpiece of the Marsh Children's St. Louis engagement was four straight nights of *The Naiad Queen*, which had been much acclaimed in Boston. Missouri critics agreed, with the *St. Louis Leader* calling it "one of the most taking productions which the stage has produced for many years."[97] According to David Rinear, the story of the play came from a German melodrama called *Lurline, or The Spirit of the Rhine*.[98] The spectacle had been a reliable moneymaker for many managers. Sol Smith's 1839 New Orleans production cost $3000, played fifteen performances and was labeled "a really remarkable record for the period."[99] Various productions circulated during the antebellum period, including those by E. A. Marshall, Henry C. Jarrett, the Keller Troupe and Laura Keene's company, but the Marsh Troupe probably used William Burton's version.[100] This script tells the fantastic story of Sir Rupert who enters the realm beneath the sea.[101] Engaged to be married but short on funds, the knight determines to find the Queen of the Sea and charm her into giving him her fabled riches. He is accompanied on his quest by his squire, a comic fellow given to drink. A highlight of the play is the army of Amazon naiads and demon mermen the Queen later brings to attack the castle.

A great deal of stage time is taken up by the shenanigans of the squire, Schnapps.[102] This is the play's funniest role, the one played at the Arch Street Theatre by manager-star William Burton. "Schnapps" is first timorous of the adventure, then fortified by drink as well as his attraction to the naiad Idex. They banter, dance, and sing, often joined by the chorus of naiads. There are also songs for the rowdy knight-fellows of Sir Rupert, and two solos for the Queen.

Marsh cast his two children in major roles: Mary played Idex the Naiad, while Georgie enacted Schnapps, the squire, a role embellished with several German songs.[103] This meant that the siblings, aged eight and six at the troupe's founding, spent a great deal of the play flirting, jousting, and singing with one another. Louise performed the title role. According to one reviewer, the eleven-year-old "looked the Queen of the Naiads and performed as Queen of the Stage."[104] In a Gulliver-like reversal, the adult Marsh played the dwarf among the child actors.[105]

A dazzling set piece featured the large cast—one ad claimed "thirty-one highly trained little auxiliaries"—in armed procession.[106] As a local reviewer raved, "The military evolutions, marches, and counter marches are executed with a degree of precision and exactness truly wonderful."[107] These children anticipated the bands of girls doing Zouave drills that would sweep the nation in the early 1860s and the lines of tall girls in carefully staged drills, proffering their "Amazon marches" later in *The Black Crook* and George L. Fox's *Humpty Dumpty*.[108] Marsh may not have invented the idea of females in quasi-military formations, but he was savvy enough to be at the head of the trend. Another show in the repertory, "a comic military drama" called *The Invincibles*, also advertised "Military evolutions by the troupe."[109] R. G. Marsh would also utilize the device in his work after his eponymous troupe disbanded.[110]

Local critics heaped praise on everyone associated with the production, including the manager:

> Mr. Marsh deserves much credit for the manner in which he has placed *The Naiad Queen* upon the stage. Mr. Cornell's scenery reflects great credit upon his abilities; under the skillful conduct of Mr. Putnam, the machinery works to a charm; the dresses are in good taste, and a well-led orchestra is an important adjunct. The piece is certainly admirably mounted. . . . Every part is admirably played.[111]

The *St. Louis Missouri Republican* summarized the public's response: "The mounting of the drama elicits more admiration from the audiences that have attended the St. Louis this week than anything of the kind that has been presented in our city for many a day."[112] The engagement ended with a program of *My Neighbor's Wife*, *Faint Heart Never Won Fair Lady*, and *Forty Thieves* as a benefit for Miss Louise.[113]

From St. Louis, the Marsh children moved on to Cincinnati. Touring players could choose to travel between these two cities by river steamer or railroad. While the boats were slow and sometimes brought on seasickness, train rides could be torturous. Edwin Booth complained of the "gut-shaking" rattle of the cars and being forced to breathe "nothing but coal smoke."[114] Arriving in Cincinnati, actor Harry Watkins wrote in his diary, "Blessings on the man who will invent a plan to keep dust out of cars!

I could not have been much filthier had I been used as a broom to sweep the streets."[115] One can only imagine the condition in which the two dozen child performers arrived.

The Marsh Children were booked into Cincinnati's National Theatre for three weeks. As the centerpiece of the engagement, *The Naiad Queen* played every evening of the second week, while bills during the first and third weeks varied nightly. In Cincinnati, the most frequently played pieces were a "burlesque, localized fairy extravaganza" of *Beauty and the Beast*, along with *Toodles*, *Black-Eyed Susan*, and *Nan, the Good-for-Nothing*, which were each repeated three times, and *The Wandering Minstrel* which was played twice.[116] Audiences may have remembered Mary Marsh from her successful turn as Little Eva three years earlier. Mary and Georgie's benefit nights near the end of the run, on July 22 and 24 respectively, gave their fans a chance to show special appreciation.

On Monday, July 27, R. G. Marsh did some important business before leaving Cincinnati. He signed a contract with Mrs. Hannah Stewart, a widow, hiring her twelve-year-old son Alfred to perform with the troupe for two years. Three days later, an advance ad in the *New York Daily Tribune* boasted of successes in Boston, New Orleans, Mobile, St. Louis, Louisville, and Cincinnati, and announced, "Several valuable additions have been made to the Troupe."[117] Up to this point, only the names of Little Mary, Master G. W. Marsh, and Miss Louise had been regularly mentioned in the company's advertising, and these three were generally singled out by reviewers as well. During the southern tour of 1857, full cast lists were often published in the ads, which might include a bold-type notice of a "Fancy Dance by Little Jennie," but in general the focus remained on the original trio. With the hiring of Alfred, however, a fourth name became consistently prominent in the company's advertisements: "Master Stewart, Irish Comedian and Vocalist." Now, Robert Marsh had four strong players as his troupe's foundation.

A week after signing his contract in Cincinnati, Alfred Stewart performed at Laura Keene's New Theatre in New York.[118] The opening night drew "not a very large audience," but the company continued to play through the month at the grand white and gold building between Bleecker and Houston Streets.[119] Offerings included standards such as *The Naiad Queen* and *Beauty and the Beast*, as well as additions such as *The Serious Family* for Louise's mid-month benefit. Master Stewart was frequently featured in an afterpiece, such as *The Happy Man* or *Brian O'Linn*, or simply singing an Irish song.[120] In the months to come, he would often sing songs called "Whiskey in the Jug" and "Trust to Luck," playing characters named "Paddy Murphy" and "Ragged Pat" in compliance with a request from his mother, Mrs. Stewart, that Alfred perform "as much of Irish farces and his own pieces and songs" as possible.[121] Nevertheless, he would sometimes join the cast of the troupe's dramatic productions as he did for Mr. Marsh's benefit at Laura Keene's on August 25, 1857. The company presented *The Lady of Lyons* followed by Alfred's afterpiece.[122] Later, Alfred played the role of Rubaldo in *The Brigand* for the troupe.[123]

Now beginning its third year of operations, the company moved back to Boston for the fall of 1857. The *Clipper* announced on September 5 that the Marshes had taken a four-month lease on the Howard Athenaeum.[124] A month later, the Howard Athenaeum published a four-page "newspaper" whose masthead proclaimed, "Marsh's Juvenile Dramatic Era, Vol. 1, No. 7. *Devoted to the dramatic and literary interests of the rising generation; also the pecuniary interests of R. G. Marsh, manager of Marsh's Juveniles.*"[125] The newspaper claimed a circulation of two thousand copies, "distributed among the Large Audiences at the Howard Athenaeum every night; and also in the Howard Reading room." This promotional idea may have been learned in Philadelphia where free copies of the magazine *Wheatley's Gift* were available at the Arch Street Theatre box office under manager William Wheatley.[126] Clearly, R. G. Marsh anticipated another successful engagement in Boston. Among other items, the "Era" promised "nearly FIFTY WONDERFUL CHILDREN" indicating the addition of almost ten juvenile performers to the troupe since its last visit to Boston. The "Era" also featured sketches of Georgie in the characters of Schnapps, Sam, the Irish Broom-Maker, and Jeremy Twitcher. There is a plot synopsis of *The Golden Axe*, in which George took on the character of "Mose," and notices of other new pieces including *The Honeymoon!* and *Don Caesar de Bazan*.[127]

Much of the new repertoire was familiar to Boston audiences. According to Grimsted, *Honeymoon*, first produced in 1800, was one the "best comedies" of the first half of the century in terms of both popularity and critical acclaim.[128] Mary Marsh's role in this Tobin comedy had been performed at the Athenaeum by Mrs. W. H. Crisp in 1846, by Mrs. Warner in 1851, and by Mrs. Mowatt in 1851 and 1854.[129] In 1853, Mr. Wallack had toured *Don Caesar de Bazin*, the title role Miss Louise would play.[130] *Toodles* had been seen at the Athenaeum in 1855 portrayed by Mr. J. H. Robinson, and in 1854 by Mr. S. F. Chanfrau, who would repeat

Figure 1.3. Georgie Marsh in eight characters, and as himself. *Ballou's Pictorial Drawing Room Companion*. TCS 44, Harvard Theatre Collection, Houghton Library, Harvard University.

it there in 1858. Much of George's repertoire was doubled by Chanfrau who gained fame playing Mose. Mr. and Mrs. Barney Williams shared roles with both Masters Marsh and Stewart, playing both *Brian O' Linn* and the Irish Broom-Maker at the Athenaeum in 1853. Antebellum audiences were coming to see the performance; they were looking for the individual performer's mark on the familiar role. Just like modern moviegoers who flock to each successive *Batman* movie even after the title role is recast, nineteenth-century theatre spectators enjoyed comparing actors who played the same part. In this arena, the Marsh Children—especially Georgie and Louise—held their own.

In Boston Alfred Stewart was continually featured in Irish afterpieces, as promised to his mother. In *The Happy Man*, he played Paddy Murphy, supported by Miss Louise as Ram Rusti, the Resolute, and Mary Marsh as Ko-Ket, the Man Catcher.[131] In turn, Master Stewart joined the troupe in *The Naiad Queen*, leading the list of the "Demons of the Dark Blue Waters" in R. G. Marsh's former role as "Amphibeo, the Demon of the Rhine."[132] The full cast list for *The Naiad Queen* at the Howard Athenaeum in October 1857 lists the names of forty-five performers. Four receive large billing: Little Mary Marsh, Master George, Miss Louise, and Miss Carrie, who played Sir Rupert (the role Marsh had played for Burton). Large billing is also accorded to La Petit Angelina for her Dance preceding the afterpiece. The staff for the spectacle includes R. G. Marsh, listed as Lessee and Manager, as well as a Music Director, a Scenic Artist, a Property Maker, two Machinists, and the Ballet Directress Madame Angelina (which may explain the billing for the petit dancer). The little ones on stage were part of a large production that meant big business.

In January 1858, the Marsh Troupe paid a brief visit to Buffalo, playing a successful engagement at the Metropolitan Theatre.[133] By the end of February, they had traveled back south to New Orleans to begin a long engagement at Spaulding and Rogers's Museum and Amphitheatre, which would be their home base throughout the spring. "Doc" Gilbert Spaulding, the business manager of the partnership, was an experienced theatre manager and "a model of the new capitalist age."[134] He booked the company annually with great success.[135] The troupe's bills included the usual repertoire of farces, their sumptuous production of *The Naiad Queen*, Alfred Stewart's specialty Irish numbers, and *Cinderella* featuring a carriage "drawn by two beautiful Shetland Ponies."[136] Opening on February 27, the initial engagement lasted through the first week of April.[137] After a brief sojourn to Mobile, the troupe reopened at Spaulding and Rogers's on April 19 and played there until the last week of May.[138]

Meanwhile, the idea of the juvenile company had caught on. Companies with siblings performing together, both as children and adults, were common in theatre, music, and acrobatics. The Wren children, the Boone children, the Ravels, the Worrell sisters, the Hutchinson Family Singers, the Webb Sisters, and the Hanlon brothers were all sibling groups.[139] Marsh's distinctive assemblage of children from several families was an attractive model. In the spring of 1857, the Boone children were "vegetating," as the *Clipper* reported, and open to a new arrangement.[140] By August, the Boones, the Wrens, and other children were combined into a new troupe called Nagle's Juvenile Comedians.[141] The new group debuted at Philadelphia's Walnut Street Theatre, just as the Marsh Juvenile Comedians had two years earlier.[142] The venture looked promising, as "there [was] said to be considerable talent among these little people."[143] By November, the troupe, now billed as Nagle's American Juvenile Comedians, had leased "Christy and Wood's old place, 444 Broadway" in New York.[144] In less than a month, however, the venture had collapsed, as the *Clipper* reported:

> Mr. Nagle seems to meet with but ill success with his large family of little geniuses. Juvenile wonder won't go down any longer—the public has lost confidence in all such prodigies and won't pay the first red to see them; so Mr. Nagle has been unable to provide for such a numerous family as he has unfortunately gathered about him . . . and the consequence is that some of them have been thrown upon their own recourses, which, it seems, are two or three percent below par.[145]

The *Clipper* reiterated its negative view of the outlook for child performers in dismissive comments about little Anna Marie Quinn (1848–1920), a child phenomenon who also played New York in the fall of 1857.[146] "She's a nice girl, has talent, and all that sort of thing, but is altogether too little to fill such a big place as Burton's."[147] Quinn may have done better after moving on to Boston—where she reportedly gave "stiff competition" to the Marsh children—but it was a difficult time in the theatre business.[148]

Many theatres were suffering that fall from dreadful economic conditions in what became known as the Panic of 1857. Overspeculation in railroad construction led to the collapse of an investment house in New York in August, which led to the failure of the Bank of Pennsylvania a month later, ultimately affecting nearly every sector of the economy.[149] Years later, actor Louis Aldrich recalled the season "as dark financially for the profession" as anyone could remember. "Leading men's salaries came down to $10 a week and good men could be hired pretty cheap," he said.[150] Philadelphia's Arch Street Theatre reduced admission to twenty-five cents for all parts of the theatre. At the Boston Theatre, actors worked for half salary. When burglars broke in, "Funds were so scare there, however, that the burglars didn't even get the 'first red.'"[151] Summing up the season, the *Clipper* mourned:

> The theatrical season of 1857–58 . . . will long be remembered as one that tried managers' "souls," for business has only been kept going through the most energetic exertions on the part of those having the direction of our amusements, ably seconded by those in their employ. When the financial squall struck us, it was generally conceded that many a good ship would flounder in the torrent.[152]

Dreary economic conditions, the failure of Nagle's American Juvenile Comedians, and the pronouncements about the poor outlook for child performers all suggest something extraordinary about the Marsh Troupe. This company succeeded where many others failed. Enjoying multimonth residencies in Boston and New Orleans and continuous bookings throughout the so-called disastrous 1857–58 season, the Juvenile Troupe had made good on R. G. Marsh's gamble to do something "bold, hazardous and original."[153] Children with the talent and discipline of adult professionals had delighted thousands of spectators and proved their company to be economically viable.

Already, however, trouble was brewing, and the carefully assembled quartet of star performers was about to splinter.

CHAPTER 2

FIRST LOSSES, AND A BATTLE WON

While the Marsh Troupe had very successful bookings during the 1857–58 season, they experienced some personnel problems. In the summer of 1857, Louise Arnot's mother tried to remove her from the troupe. In the spring of 1858, Alfred Stewart's mother brought suit to free her son from his contract.[1] The two episodes had different outcomes but together illustrate the shifting status of child workers at mid-century. In early 1859, the company suffered its greatest trial and tragedy, the hideous on-stage death of Little Mary Marsh.

The autonomy of the individual child actors and the clashing authority of parents with manager Marsh were at the heart of the personnel conflicts. While the talent and professional competence of the Marsh Children were undeniable, their years of continuous success also owed much to the strong managerial control of Robert G. Marsh. Any power analysis of the Marsh Troupe places him firmly in the dominant position. As artistic director over actors, as manager over workers, as a male over a mostly female company, and as an adult over children, Marsh's position appears unassailable. In most stage companies, interdependency balanced power; all theatrical managers needed actors to create the entertainment product. That knowledge could lend individual actors some leverage but, given Marsh's authority over multiple facets, the troupe's arrangement appears less balanced than that of adult acting companies. Still, one wonders how often Robert Marsh's featured actors questioned his supremacy. There is no record of Mary Marsh exhibiting anything other than the smiling docility enshrined in nineteenth-century idealized girlhood, but each of the other leading performers—Louise, Alfred, and Georgie—would eventually break with the impresario.

In addition to matters of art, the manager of a nineteenth-century theatrical troupe contended daily with innumerable business arrangements and unpredictable transportation systems. Actors' memoirs are full of anecdotes about temperament, money squabbles, and the hardships of travel. The Marsh Troupe added an additional ingredient to this mix: parents. At the time, children often lived away from their parents, either with relatives or with an employer or master. This practice of children living away from their homes, however, was in flux—as were many issues involving children—during the antebellum era. Some children exercised tremendous independence, while others were kept safely by the hearth. The size of the Marsh troupe varied, but always comprised upwards of twenty children not related to Marsh. These children were away from their families for long stretches of time. How much personal or collective agency did these children exercise? What role did their parents play *vis à vis* manager Marsh? None of the Marsh children wrote about their experience, but the public record gives some glimpses of the balance of power among child performers, their parents, and R. G. Marsh. It certainly was not smooth sailing. "These Marsh children seem to have been a bone if not several bones of contention ever since their engagement was made known here," sniped a St. Louis writer in 1857.[2] Despite his company's success—or because of it—Marsh seemed to find himself frequently and publicly on the defensive.

The foundation for the conflict over Louise may have been laid in 1856 when R. G. Marsh partnered with Henry Wood to present the company at the Broadway Varieties in New York City. Although the engagement succeeded in terms of audience attendance and response, there were some budgetary problems. At the end of the engagement, the Marsh Troupe owed Mr. Wood three thousand dollars; Robert Marsh personally owed him another two thousand. Although it is impossible to know for sure what caused the dissolution of the partnership after only four months, this debt was a likely factor. The divorcing partners agreed that a Mr. J. Nagle would look after Wood's interests, traveling with the troupe and serving as treasurer on the spring 1857 tour.[3] Nagle held Wood's power of attorney. Fortunately, business in New Orleans that spring at Spaulding and Rogers's was excellent, prompting Mr. Nagle to demand full and immediate payment. According to the *Clipper*, Marsh "strained a point or two and paid off the judgment," discharged Mr. Nagle, and considered the matter closed.[4]

Mr. Nagle, however, had a new mission. He moved ahead to St. Louis, the next stop on the Marsh Children's tour. Upon his own arrival at St. Louis, Mr. Marsh was served a writ of *habeas corpus* demanding that Louise be handed over to Nagle, his former treasurer. Louise had been a mainstay of the troupe from its outset. She played title roles in *Ingomar the Barbarian*, *The Naiad Queen*, and *Beauty and the Beast* (as the Beast). She received frequent positive notices from the press and the public in the form of both applause and benefits. Twenty-four months had passed since the troupe's founding in June 1855, when Louise had been hired on a two-year contract.[5] It was time to renegotiate. Both Marsh and Nagle appeared in the St. Louis courtroom before Judge Hamilton. To the disappointment of Nagle, Louise was quickly remanded into Marsh's care.

There is no indication that the court considered Louise's desires at any point throughout the process. The outcome reflected a judicial climate that valorized property rights and the professional status of white men. Just a week before the Marsh Juveniles arrived in St. Louis, the Supreme Court had handed down its decision on the St. Louis–based Dred Scott case, which had become one of the most hotly debated court battles of the day. Scott, an enslaved man of African descent, claimed he had the right to sue for his freedom in the St. Louis Circuit Court in 1846. After a decade-long legal battle, the U.S. Supreme Court ruled in March 1857 that Dred Scott had no right to sue for his freedom because he was not, and could not be, a citizen.[6] The Court defended the slave-owner's position, asserting that no person of African descent had rights under the Constitution. The Dred Scott case ignited passions regarding slavery and states' rights, becoming one of the flash points of the American Civil War.[7] In the Dred Scott case, the court granted a white man ownership over a person considered to be of a lower order, just as Judge Hamilton would give Marsh control over a child.

Marsh had won the case but did not want to take any further chance losing this featured player, so he sent his attorney to Rochester, New York, to negotiate with the girl's parents. Louise's father accepted a payment of five hundred dollars to extend her contract an additional year. While an adult star of the era could easily earn three hundred dollars in a single night, Marsh paid Louise a higher wage than many bit players or supernumeraries as they were called. As Nora Titone writes, "In 1858, hardworking supes earned about $300 per season, about the same as unskilled laborers like farmworkers and hod carriers."[8] With Louise signed to a new contract, Marsh once again thought that the matter was settled.

Robert Marsh had not counted on competition. As the *St. Louis Leader* reported, "The parties in New York who are anxious to obtain Miss Louise for another, and rival troupe, persuaded the mother into making a contract with *them*"[9] (emphasis in original). Louise's mother and her lawyer, a Mr. Banix, traveled to St. Louis and demanded that Marsh surrender Louise to them. But Marsh, having recently paid five hundred dollars and been upheld by the court, was unwilling to surrender Louise.

The St. Louis newspapers covering the story identified Louise's mother as "Mrs. McLaughlin."[10] Although the young actress never used this surname, being generally billed simply as "Miss Louise" or very occasionally as Louisa Marsh, chroniclers have had no trouble tracing her identity. *Frank Leslie's Magazine* declared in an 1886 retrospective, "Louisa Marsh was properly Miss McLaughlin."[11] T. Allston Brown identified Louisa McLaughlin as Louise Arnot.[12] John S. Kendall, in *The Golden Age of New Orleans Theatre*, named Louise Arnot as part of the Marsh Troupe during its first appearance in New Orleans in 1856.[13] The Arnot (aka Arnott) surname first appears in the company billing about 1860. This text uses the Arnot designation throughout, because the actress was most widely known by this name, having performed as Louise Arnot for almost sixty years.[14]

When studying children of the past, a perennial difficulty is determining the degree to which they acted independently or influenced the actions of others. There is no indication that Judge Hamilton had consulted Louise before denying Nagle's *habeas corpus* demand. However, when Mrs. McLaughlin arrived at Marsh's door, Louise spoke up. We do not have her voice directly, but all three newspapers reporting the story agreed that Louise "declined in the strongest terms" to leave Marsh, with whom she had spent the previous two years. Louise also demonstrated her preferences in subsequent events.

After being rejected, the mother and lawyer departed, but returned after dinner, pleading for a chance to take Louise out so they could speak in private. Press accounts vividly characterized both Louise and her mother in the fracas that followed. Note the interesting attitude taken toward Marsh in the following account from the *St. Louis Leader*:

> Louise, suspecting something, was not willing to go, but partly by threats and partly by force was got into the street and . . . put into a carriage evidently previously provided for the purpose, and was about being driven off when the crowd attracted by her cries and the strangeness of the transaction stopped the horses. Mr. Marsh shortly appeared on the scene, explained the matter to the spectators, and then, with officer Pallis, got into the carriage and told the driver to go to the police station.[15]

In this account, Louise has a strong subject position. She is intuitive and wary. Once in the carriage she makes noise. She could be seen as performing a role akin to the strong characters she portrayed on stage. However, the structure and language of the story lends itself to another reading, that of melodrama. As Altman writes, genres are "ideological constructs, masquerading as neutral categories."[16] The popularity of melodrama as a dramatic genre influenced modes of thought related to off-stage life. The language of the news story is dark, utilizing terms such as *suspect*, *threat*, *force*, and *strangeness*. Details, like arranging to have a carriage waiting, appear sinister. This story casts Louise as a damsel being carried off. The townspeople hear her cries and gather round, mystified. They are called "spectators," the same word used for a theatre audience. The rescuer is R. G. Marsh, who masterfully takes command of the escape vehicle, quiets the crowd, and gives directions to the police officer. In the denouement, "All parties were introduced to Major Rawlings who remanded the child to the custody of Mr. Marsh and required $200 for the appearance of Mr. Banix [the lawyer] before the Recorder . . . to answer the change of abduction."[17] Good triumphs; vice is punished.

While generally consistent, the version of the story published the same day in the *St. Louis Missouri Republican* leads with the policeman: "Yesterday evening the attention of a policeman was called to a gentlemanly-looking man endeavoring to force one of the Marsh children into a carriage at the corner of Fourth and Olive Streets." Officer Pallis is the hero of this account, which omits mention of Louise's mother. The officer notices the struggle and gives chase, overtaking and arresting the culprit a block away at Third and Olive.[18] Casting a police officer in the role of rescuer is not surprising. Marsh, however, is a less likely hero to contemporary readers. He is a man who employs and manages child workers. This role would almost certainly make him the villain in a twenty-first-century tale of child exploitation. Here, however, the unlikely antagonist is the child's mother.

All the press accounts portray both the mother and her lawyer as villains. The duplicitous mother first acts against a newly made contract with Marsh, and then tries to hoodwink her own daughter. Louise suspects her mother; Louise resists her mother. Louise is overpowered by her mother and her mother's accomplice. Later in the century, a cult of motherhood would permeate public discourse, but the 1857 newspaper accounts seem far more inspired by a respect for property rights than a valorization of motherhood.[19]

The Louise news stories record actions taken by Mr. Wood, Mr. Nagle, Mr. Marsh, his lawyer (L. M. Shreve), Judge Hamilton, Louise's parents, their lawyer (H. C. Banix), and Officer Pallis. For all of them, except the police officer, Louise's economic utility is paramount. If the multiple newspaper reports are to be believed, the only reason to remove Louise from R. G. Marsh is her economic value. Her success with Marsh had demonstrated that she could please ticket buyers.[20] The news writers do not attempt to sentimentalize mother or child, as might be thought typical for the era. Economist Viviana Zelizer has written that children's sentimental value did not predominate until the twentieth century.[21] The presentation and outcome of the dispute over Miss Louise bears out Zelizer's claim that nineteenth-century children were valued primarily for their economic utility. The story also testifies to the success of the Marsh Troupe as an economic enterprise. Marsh presents as a respected businessman, and two courts uphold his position. Child performers were good business.

Louise functions as a professional actress in this tale in two different ways. First, defying her parents' wishes, she makes a professional career decision to continue with the Marsh Troupe. Second, drawing on her histrionic skills and experience with melodrama, she creates a convincing portrayal of a maiden in peril. Refusing to be bullied, she shouts loud enough to attract a crowd. Arnot's ability to act decisively will remain visible throughout the next six decades of her career.

With Louise reinstated and Alfred Stewart newly hired, the Marsh Troupe embarked on the successful 1857–58 season described at the end of chapter 1. Weathering the economic downturn with long residencies—fall in Boston, spring in New Orleans—R. G. Marsh might have felt comfortable. Audiences at Spaulding and Rogers's Museum and Amphitheatre in New Orleans responded well to the children, including Alfred Stewart, a featured performer.

Stewart had been born in Rochdale, Lancastershire, England, on October 4, 1843, and brought to America before his second birthday. As a young child, he acted at Cincinnati's National Theatre. Following his first appearance as Rolla's Child in *Pizarro*, he appeared in various small parts, including a cross-dressed turn as Little Eva in *Uncle Tom's Cabin.*[22] (In 1853, Mary Marsh had also played Little Eva in Cincinnati, at the Melodeon; a competing production at the National Theatre featured Viola Plunkett, not Alfred Stewart.[23]) We know little of Alfred's family except that his mother, Mrs. Hannah Stewart, had been widowed shortly before July 27, 1857, when she signed a contract with Robert G. Marsh. Children of deceased fathers were considered orphans, even if their mothers were alive. If Alfred had not begun working for R. G. Marsh, he might have been indentured by the state, as others were.[24]

At fourteen, Alfred was four years older than Little Mary and, from his first appearance with the troupe, given prominent billing as "Master Stewart, Irish Comedian and Vocalist." R. G. Marsh clearly thought a lot of the boy, casting him as "Amphibeo, the Demon of the Rhine," a role formerly played by Marsh himself in *The Naiad Queen.*[25] But the boy had been with the company only ten months when the connection was abruptly severed.

On March 26, 1858, the same date as Master Stewart's benefit, the Third District Court of New Orleans issued a writ of *habeas corpus* commanding R. G. Marsh to produce Alfred Stewart in court so the boy could be examined by a physician.[26] Unlike Louise's parents, who argued only commercial goals, Alfred's mother had sworn a statement that Alfred was "seriously afflicted in health by a dangerous disease." She feared for his life if he were not immediately treated. In a letter to the court, Mrs. Stewart claimed that she had ordered Marsh to restore Alfred to her custody, but the manager had refused.[27] Ten months after vindication in the Louise matter by the courts of Missouri, Marsh may have felt confident that his managerial rights would also be upheld in the southern state of Louisiana. He immediately filed a counter complaint against Mrs. Stewart asserting his right, under the contract, to retain Alfred within his care, custody, and control. The case of Alfred Stewart became one of the most protracted challenges to Robert Marsh's image. Alfred's story is both a parallel and a counternarrative to Louise's. While both had mothers who sought to redirect their children's careers, Alfred took no independent action. Economically and socially, Alfred existed on the cusp of the shifting concept of childhood, neither wholly dependent nor independent.

The seeds of the Stewart controversy were embedded in the original contract that balanced unsteadily on shifting ideas of childhood and children's

HOWARD ATHENÆUM.

ROB'T G. MARSH, - - - - - LESSEE AND MANAGER

L. C. SPOHR...... MUSICAL DIRECTOR	A. THAYER.....PROPERTY MAKER
MAD ANGELINA BALLET DIRECTRESS	E. PUTNAM & BRO.....MACHINISTS
J. V. CORNELL........SCENIC ARTIST	

MARSH'S

Juvenile Comedians.

THIS EVENING

Will be presented the Gorgeous Spectacle of the

NAIAD QUEEN

MORTALS.

Sir Rupert, the Fearnaught..................**Miss Carrie**
Schnapps, his Squire......................**Master George**
Rinaldo, the Honorable.........................Miss Georgiana
Carnell, the Doubtful..............................Miss Francis
Manfredi, the Ready...............................Miss Adelaide

Rodolph, the Wise..Master Ames	Alamo...............Miss Lelia
Ronaldo, the Disconsolate, Miss Amelia	Calot............Miss Josephine
	Baron of Lauchausen.Mast Waldo
Lady Una............Miss Sarrie	Bridget............Miss Helen

IMMORTALS.

The Naiad Queen.........................**Miss Louise**
Idex, with Songs.......................**Little Mary Marsh**

Fulvia..........Miss Melville	Spray, with Dances....Miss Anna
Sparkle, with Dances.Miss Jeannie	Coral Shell........Miss Matilda
Dew Drop " ..Miss Angeline	Sprinkle............Miss Proler
Brilliant " ....Miss Secord	Limpid..............Miss Rabauz

DEMONS OF THE DARK BLUE WATERS.

Amphibeo, the Demon of the Rhine..........**Master Stewart**

Finbach..........Master Charles	Carbuncle.... ...Master Welch
Goggle Eye........Master Henry	Scaly Skin.........Master Defitt
Phantom Face...Master Frederick	Sorreltop..........Master Wiley

NAIADS AND FEMALE WARRIORS.

Misses Ellis, Jones, Turner, Alderman, Anderson, Josephs, Andrews, Johnson, Fuller, Proler, Creuger, Crook, Morse, White, Secaux, Madden, &c.

Dance..............................**La Petite Angelina**

To conclude with the

HAPPY MAN!

Paddy Murphy, with a Song **Master Alfred Stewart**	Ski Hi, the Star Gazer......Miss Sibien
Ram Rusti, the Resolute·**Miss Louise**	Run Phast, the Active···Little Angeline
Foxi Fum, the Crafty···· ·Miss Carrie	**Ko-Ket,** the Man Catcher, **Mary Marsh**
	Sing Smahl, the Subdued····Miss Selma

Figure 2.1. Howard Athenaeum playbill, Boston, 1857. Twelve-year-old Alfred Stewart replaced Robert G. Marsh as "Amphibeo, the Demon of the Rhine" in *The Naiad Queen.* Harvard Theatre Collection, Houghton Library, Harvard University.

work. Robert Guerineau Marsh, Hannah Stewart, Alfred, and two witnesses signed the three-page, handwritten document; Marsh's florid signature is twice the size of the others. Extant employment contracts for nineteenth-century child actors are rare, so the Marsh-Stewart document is useful in positioning the Marsh Children with respect to other child workers. The contract gives the term of employment as two years, during which installment payments would be made to Mrs. Stewart at the end of every month. Alfred's wages would be $250 for the first year, and $500 for the second. The contract states that in addition to providing board, Marsh will bestow "care and attention usual for a father to furnish, taking care of [Alfred] in sickness and in health." All of Alfred's clothing, and any presents that the boy received, were designated as Marsh's property. In a short agreement subsequent to the original contract, Marsh consented to Mrs. Stewart's request that Alfred perform "as much of Irish farces and his own pieces and songs as can possibly be done by the Marsh Juvenile Comedians," and that Alfred would be taken out of any non-Irish pieces at his mother's discretion.[28]

The stipulations in the Marsh-Stewart contract match the facts revealed about Louise's employment during the "abduction" crisis. Recall that the crisis erupted precisely two years after the founding of the company, and that when Marsh extended Louise's contract for an additional year, he paid her father five hundred dollars, the same sum promised for Alfred's second year. These arrangements were probably standard for all Marsh company hires. In each case, parents at home received the earnings of juvenile actors on tour. The children in the company would have been completely dependent upon Mr. Marsh for all of their needs and wants. Marsh probably did not set aside any payment for George and Mary, his biological children, because at this time the wages of children legally belonged to the father.[29] Payments to Mrs. Stewart are not surprising because in the nineteenth century, children often supported widowed mothers. Even in two-parent families, the second breadwinner was more likely to be a son than a wife.

Little documentation on the salaries of other antebellum child performers exists, although in 1852, little Cordelia Howard and her mother had jointly been paid one hundred dollars a week.[30] While Marsh company salaries were much less than this, they still compared very favorably to those of children working in other fields during the 1850s. For example, machinist apprentice John Rogers earned fifty cents a day, and apprentices at Baldwin Locomotive Works were paid $2.25 to $3.25 a week, or just under $170 per year (not quite 70 percent of Alfred's first-year wages).[31] The equivalent purchasing power of a Marsh trouper's salary in 2013 dollars is $6,680 for year one, and $13,800 for year two.[32]

Alfred's contract may appear to be a simple economic exchange of labor for wages, but it includes several elements of the traditional craft apprenticeship agreements under which other boys worked at the time. The apprenticeship system that young America inherited from England served educational, social, and economic functions.[33] It fostered a transfer of knowledge from generation to generation that made advanced schooling unnecessary for most men. The system was essentially an exchange of labor for knowledge, rather than for wages. If a boy faithfully served his master through the completion of his apprenticeship, he would be equipped to perform adult work and gain economic independence.[34]Apprenticeship was a standard path to a career in many fields.[35] Apprentices were bound to masters for a specified period of time during which their duties could include almost anything the master ordered. The apprentice owed obedience and respect to the master.

This arrangement was not one sided, however—the master had responsibilities as well. The master educated the apprentice, teaching everything needed to practice a trade. The master cared for all the apprentice's needs, providing clothes, food, and shelter. Socially, the master functioned as a kind of father, both protecting and guiding his young charge. Apprentices usually lived within their master's homes. The master also served as a moral authority. Many extant letters include requests from parents, and/or reassurances from masters, that apprentices will be given guidance in all areas, including spiritual and financial.[36] The master and the father were in some respects alter egos. In the absence of the father, the master assumed a father's authority and responsibilities. Conversely, some fathers assumed the role of master, taking on their own children or relatives as apprentices.[37] The defining elements of the traditional craft apprenticeship were the combination of work and training for youth under a master's care.

Traditionally, many actors were trained in their youth through a kind of apprenticeship similar, but not identical, to those of their contemporaries in crafts. During the English Renaissance, boys performed in two types of professional troupes: adult companies and all-boy chorister companies. Renaissance scholar Edel Lamb notes that the adult acting companies imitated other legal structures of the time in the practice of apprenticing youths to masters.[38] The chorister companies initially used a different method, obtaining recruits through impressment, a practice in which the choirmasters utilized the Crown's authority to "press" boys into service. After 1606, however, a prominent chorister company also adopted a modified apprenticeship system.[39]

The tradition came to early America with the Hallams, who crossed the Atlantic in 1752. The Hallam company provided on-the-job training for their children, Lewis Jr., Helen, and Adam, and their niece Nancy, who joined them in 1759.[40] With this foundation, Helen, Nancy, and Lewis Jr. all appeared as adult actors. Nancy Hallam earned acclaim enough to be hailed as "our first 'star.'"[41] The early training received by Lewis Hallam Jr. sustained him over a fifty-year stage career, during which he served as boy actor, scene partner to his mother, leading man, and manager of the troupe. Hallam's theatrical path paralleled that of many sons of proprietors of other types of businesses, who often began as apprentices under their fathers and eventually assumed partnership of the firm.[42]

Nineteenth-century acting families continued the tradition by training their children in a similar fashion. When Cordelia Howard appeared as Little Eva in *Uncle Tom's Cabin*, she was coached by her mother Caddie Fox Howard, who had learned her own craft as a child actress.[43] Cordelia's parents were training her for an adult career, although she chose not to pursue one.[44] Kate and Ellen Bateman were also children trained by their parents, who were masters of the craft. Their father, Hezikiah L. Bateman, was a theatrical manager; their mother was Sydney Cowell Bateman, an actress, playwright, and the daughter of two actors.[45] For Kate, the early training formed the basis for an adult career as an actress and acting teacher.

These theatrical examples from the seventeenth, eighteenth, and nineteenth centuries illustrate an apprentice-like system in which children were trained in the craft of acting by their families or other professionals with the clear expectation that they would join, and later succeed, their parents as masters in the trade. The craft of acting was being transmitted via the same means as other crafts. However, the craft apprenticeship tradition, like childhood itself, was destabilized by shifts in ideology as well as economic trends.

Scholars of the traditional craft apprenticeship agree that by the mid-nineteenth century, the system had been eroded by a number of factors.[46] The emergence of factories undermined the need for individual skill.[47] The new system of manufacturing concentrated capital. Formerly, banknotes, gold, or silver were only used among the commercial classes engaged in overseas trade, land speculation or other large-scale business activities, while most people relied on the barter system.[48] As the economy shifted more and more toward cash-wage jobs, masters had to provide apprentices with wages and, in turn, apprentices increasingly had to pay for their own clothing and board. By the mid-1830s, many apprentices no longer lived within their masters' households.[49]

The substitution of cash for cohabitation broke down the paternalistic conditions on both sides. Masters frequently became less caring and lost their moral authority. For their part, boys became less respectful of masters. Apprentices had more autonomy than ever before, and felt entitled to make their own decisions or break their contracts. Apprenticeships became fragmented.[50] Apprentices increasingly asserted their right to decide matters for themselves or to walk out if they found conditions unsatisfactory.[51] Gains in independence and wages were offset by losses in education and security. Some factory owners undermined the term "apprentice" by using it simply as an excuse to pay low wages for work that included no training. Child workers lost the network of protection. As W. J. Rorabaugh writes, "In the end old-fashioned apprenticeship was swept away by a wave of change that engulfed traditional society and its artisan culture through the power of concentrated capital, the genius of mechanical innovation, and the ideology of individualism and self-help."[52]

The theatre was not immune to these larger economic trends, and the Marsh-Stewart accord reflects the shift in the nontheatrical trades. The contract contains elements of both the traditional craft apprenticeship agreement and the modern capitalist version of child labor for cash wages that would dominate the latter nineteenth century.

Although the term "apprentice" is not used in the Marsh-Stewart agreement, the document includes elements typical of apprenticeships: a specific time bond, housing, and the paternal care of a master. Virtually all apprentices were bound for a specific period of time; seven years was common but Ian Quimby, in his thorough and often-quoted study, notes bonds as short as two years and as long as twenty years.[53] The Marsh-Stewart contract stipulates a two-year period during which Alfred would be under the care, custody, and control of Marsh. The contract identifies Marsh as a resident of New York, and the widowed Mrs. Stewart as a resident of Ohio. Ohio law regarding the rights of widows would later emerge as a crucial legal strategy for Mrs. Stewart. In practice, the Marsh Troupe spent most of their time touring, but in any event, Alfred would not be able to commute from home. He would be utterly dependent upon Marsh for housing and board. The most traditional feature of the Marsh-Stewart contract is the language used to describe Marsh's responsibility. He would furnish "care and attention usual for a *father*" (emphasis added). This language, wholly absent from modern labor agreements, disrupts the contract's commercialist purpose. It harkens back to advice about the master's role published in 1821: "To them you stand in the parent's place; they are to receive the treatment of sons."[54] With his signature, Marsh accepted the paternal function of the master. The contract also uses a phase that today is more associated with marriage covenants than with labor deals: Marsh is to care for Alfred "in sickness and in health." Clearly, Marsh would be acting *in loco parentis*, just as apprentice masters had for centuries. In some sense, by joining the Marsh Troupe and acting alongside George and Mary, Alfred was joining the Marsh family.

In other respects, Alfred's situation diverged from a traditional apprenticeship. Historically, the small wages paid to apprentices covered their out-of-pocket expenses, but the Marsh-Stewart contract makes no provision for any pocket money at all for Alfred. Provisions for the end of Alfred's engagement also break with tradition. Most craft apprenticeships ended with the awarding of "freedom dues," a gratuity specified in the written indenture. The apprentice generally received some combination of clothes, tools, or money as freedom dues.[55] One traditional package included fifty dollars, a Bible, and two suits of clothing.[56] Since clothes were by far the most common form of freedom dues, as well as a nineteenth-century actor's most essential possessions, it is not surprising to find mention of them in the Marsh-Stewart contract—just not the kind of mention one would expect.

During the term of Alfred's contract, clothes were to be provided by Marsh, as was customary in virtually all apprenticeship agreements. At the end of the engagement, however, all of Alfred's clothing would revert to Marsh. This included not only his costumes, but "all wearing apparel, wardrobe, clothing or dresses of any kind whether used on the stage or not."[57] The contract also anticipates the possibility that Alfred will develop a gift-giving fan-base. It stipulates that any presents Alfred may receive over the course of the contract, "from the public or other parties," will also become Marsh's property; Marsh would then have the option of transferring them to Alfred. This stipulation stands in blatant contradiction to the custom of giving gifts to an apprentice at the termination of his labor and belies the paternal relations implicit in other aspects of the agreement.

The aspect of the Marsh-Stewart arrangement that resists easy categorization is training. Initiation into a craft or a trade was the *raison d'être* of the traditional apprenticeship, yet the Marsh-Stewart contract makes no mention at all of training. The term "apprentice" is not used; in the language of the contract, Alfred is "hire[d] to" Marsh. This language seems to indicate a simple business deal. Alfred is offered for hire as a finished product, rather than as raw material that must be molded by a master. It could be argued, therefore, that the apprentice label is inappropriately applied here.

While Alfred was not an apprentice *per se*, his contract represents a transitional moment in the history of professional child performers, as it contains both provisions applicable to a modern wage agreement and those of a traditional apprenticeship agreement. The training element, so germane to traditional apprenticeship, was *ipso facto* contained in the working arrangements between Alfred, an actor, and Marsh, his director. This is particularly evident when the age of the average Marsh trouper is considered; most of them could not have had much previous experience. Contemporaneous critics assumed that Marsh trained his performers.

The company's standard billing listed the troupe as "under the management of R. G. Marsh." While descriptive terms such as "coach" or "director" were not in common use, newspaper writers of the time frequently referred to the training that performers received. Here are representative comments from the *New York Times*, the *New Orleans Picayune*, and the *Argus* of Melbourne, Australia.

> Twenty-four Juvenile Comedians *under the direction of their tutor*, Mr. Marsh, have been engaged . . . for the Broadway Theatre.[58]

> . . . with splendid scenery, rich costumes, elegant paraphernalia, complete mechanical arrangements, abounding in startling effects, and . . . thirty-one *highly trained* little auxiliaries.[59]

> Here we have, then, a company of some 30 young people . . . who have been collected together for theatrical purposes, *instructed evidently with great care in the business of their profession*, several of them possessing considerable talent . . . [60]

These writers took for granted that Marsh actively trained the children who appeared in his troupe. The reference to him as the children's tutor signals an assumption that his role resembled that of the traditional master. Alfred Stewart joined the other children in many of the company's farces and, in at least one case, assumed a role previously performed by Marsh.[61] It seems reasonable to conclude that, in these productions, young Alfred was receiving performance training from R. G. Marsh.

Thus, the Marsh-Stewart contract comprises contradictory elements reflective of the shifting historical moment of its execution. Marsh is positioned as both an old-fashioned, paternalistic master and a modern profit-driven employer. Alfred is presented both as a boy who needs a father's care and a laborer in a wage economy. Mrs. Stewart has a dual identity as widowed mother and shrewd promoter looking after her property. Given these inherent contradictions, and the pervading climate in which boys felt emboldened to walk out if they didn't like working conditions, the arrangement's premature termination is not surprising.

In bringing her suit, Mrs. Stewart may be seen to be operating under assumptions associated with a traditional apprenticeship—for instance, that Marsh would act as a father. Therefore, by failing in his paternal responsibility to care adequately for Alfred's health, he had broken the contract. Marsh's businesslike response emphasized the legal obligation of the state of Louisiana to uphold a contract signed in Ohio. He petitioned that the writ of *habeas corpus* be dismissed and that Mrs. Stewart pay all of the court costs.

In response to Marsh's answer, Mrs. Stewart's counsel changed tactics and used a legal limitation to women's rights as a justification to challenge the legality of the original contract. Under the doctrine of *feme covert*, a married woman could not be the legal guardian of her own children.[62] More than half a century before women would win the right to vote, Mrs. Stewart used her impaired status to gain advantage, alleging, "At the time that the instrument was made, she had not been recognized by the state of Ohio as the legal guardian of said Alfred and therefore could not bind him." Mrs. Stewart was a widow and the court confirmed that, "By the laws of Ohio, a . . . guardian or tutor cannot bind the minor . . . unless he has taken the oath and has complied with the other formalities required by law." Mrs. Stewart had taken the guardian's oath on August 28, 1857, one month after she had signed the contract with Marsh.

On March 30, 1858, the court decided in Marsh's favor. An examining physician found Alfred "in every respect sound and healthy."[63] The *New Orleans Times Picayune* reported, "the case, after a full hearing, was dismissed."[64] Following events from afar, the *New York Clipper* announced Mrs. Stewarts's intention of appealing to a higher court.[65]

On the very next day, March 31, 1858, Mrs. Stewart filed an appeal.[66] The Louisiana Archive case file includes the three-page judge's opinion. Because the former court had already ruled on Mrs. Stewart's claim that Marsh had mistreated Alfred, the judge refused to revisit that charge. The opinion staked out the only remaining question: "whether the defendant detained the person of Alfred Stewart legally or illegally." The judge noted that Mrs. Stewart became Alfred's legal guardian one month after signing the contract with Marsh. At that point, she had the legal authority to terminate the contract. However, Mrs. Stewart continued to accept her monthly payments from Marsh; she even entered into a second agreement concerning Alfred's performance of Irish and non-Irish pieces. The final sentence of this short accord states: "This agreement does not conflict or make void any existing contract or agreement." The judge reasoned that the original agreement was validated by Mrs. Stewart's actions after she gained full legal guardianship, that is, her entry into the second arrangement and her continued receipt of profits:

> This last agreement is certainly in my opinion a ratification of the former one. Her incapacity at the time of entering into the first contract was relative not absolute and when she became capacitated by law; she had immediately the right to purge it of all illegality existing at the time. The [plaintiff] cannot be permitted now to claim the benefit resulting from an illegality when she has solemnly received those benefits by her own acts.[67]

The judge denied the application for a writ of *habeas corpus*; Marsh did not have to return Alfred to Mrs. Stewart. Thus, according to the court documents in the Louisiana Archive, Marsh prevailed in both the initial case and the appeal. The logical outcome of these decisions would have been Alfred's continued employment with the Marsh troupe, but that was not to be.

After April 1858, Alfred never performed with the juvenile troupe again. The *New York Clipper* proclaimed, "It has at length been settled by the New Orleans courts that little Alfred Stewart shall be delivered into the custody of his mother and will probably start out on a starring expedition."[68] Robert G. Marsh's featured quartet, so proudly assembled and advertised, had cracked. Alfred Stewart was the first of the four to go.

Alfred's voice is missing from the written record, and the degree of his personal agency is unknowable. Indeed, scholars of children's history have noted that we often know more from the "perspective of the adults who tried to educate, reform, or punish [children] than we do about their own strategies and aspirations."[69] Alfred's voice cannot be heard over the shouts of the adults struggling to control him. Following the court decision, Alfred Stewart started working as a solo performer.[70] By June 1858, Master Stewart was appearing in Richmond and the Marsh Troupe had moved on to St. Louis.

Robert Marsh may have considered the matter closed, but two months after it had been settled in court, the Marsh-Stewart controversy was resurrected in the press. The *Clipper*, a continual conduit for the dispute, published a letter from each side. The first letter came from Edward Warden, possibly the English actor of that name who produced the first U.S. version of *Ixion*, the burlesque later popularized by Lydia Thompson.[71] In his letter, Warden revived the original complaint, claiming that "Master Stewart was taken from the Marsh troupe on account of ill treatment."[72] Warden's accusation is contradicted by several court documents, including the letter from the examining physician and the judge's opinion. Moreover, both the *Clipper* and the *Picayune* had previously announced that Mrs. Stewart's case had failed. Was Warden unaware of this contradiction, or was he an ally of Mrs. Stewart determined to re-try the case in the court of public opinion? Warden's claims that Alfred was "the best Irish comedian now on the stage" and "destined for the highest honors" suggest his partisan position.

Warden's letter provoked a quick response from a Marsh supporter in New Orleans who wrote using the nom de plume "Justice":

> To set the minds of the public right on the subject, and to do justice to Mr. Marsh of the juvenile troupe, I would inform you and others that Mrs. Stewart signally failed in proving *any ill* treatment but gained possession of her son by breaking of the contact she had made with Mr. Marsh; because at the time it was made, she had not been *legally* appointed his guardian, which was done after the contract was made, she sought to annul it on these grounds and succeeded.[73]

The pen name and the italics in the original underline the writer's belief in Marsh's character, but his facts are shaky too. "Justice" seems unaware that the judge had refused to accept Mrs. Stewart's technicality as justification to set aside the contract. The means of Alfred's release were blurred—perhaps intentionally—by the principals and their surrogates. No other voices joined the fray and, again, the matter seemed settled.

That June, while the Marsh-Stewart surrogates were still sniping at each other in the pages of the *Clipper* and the children were performing in Missouri, Louis Aldrich joined the company, becoming Alfred's replacement in the Marsh Troupe. Aldrich and Stewart shared a home state (Ohio), a birth year (1843), and the fact of pre-Marsh stage experience. Their family situations, however—as well as talents, temperaments, and professional lives—differed significantly. While Stewart excelled at comic ethnic songs, Aldrich began his career in Shakespeare's tragedies. While Stewart's mother vowed to protect him with her life, Aldrich had been on his own since age ten. While Stewart's preferences are unknowable, Aldrich made strong choices in a long public life, later described in multiple interviews. While Stewart's success was brief, Aldrich enjoyed fame, wealth, and professional respect for many decades.[74]

In the summer of 1858, Louis Aldrich was already a veteran player. He'd gotten his theatrical start at age eleven at the Cleveland Academy of Music under John Ellsler, Marsh's former partner. Ellsler would become an important presence in Cleveland's theatre development as well as a first mentor to young Clara Morris, who was about the same age as Mary Marsh.[75] Ellsler billed eleven-year-old Louis Aldrich as "the Ohio Roscius," the first of many stage names applied to the young actor during the four years of his informal apprenticeship. Born Salma Lyon, Aldrich was repeatedly adopted via billing in keeping with the popular vogue for family troupes. He performed as Master Moses, Master McCarthy, and Master Kean on tours under Morris Moses, Minnie McCarthy, and Thomas Kean, respectively. Sociologist Daniel Thomas Cook has noted how children's "relative powerlessness" enables their identities "to be quite malleable."[76] The appropriation of the boy actor's identity by various masters also demonstrates how strongly patriarchy defined identity. Without familial connection, a child's identity had no substance. The list of shifting stage names also highlights the difficulty in tracking the careers of children. Taking control of his own billing, the performer chose the name Louis Aldrich for himself and legally adopted it shortly before joining the Marsh Troupe.

During his apprenticeship, Aldrich played Richard III, Macbeth, Shylock, Claude Menotte, Young Norval, and Jack Shepard. The *Clipper* would later refer to him as the Marsh Troupe's "tragedy manufacturer."[77] When his voice started cracking, young Aldrich dealt with the problem by using the money he had earned to enroll himself in White Water College in Indiana and wait out the change. Rejoining the profession, he found himself unsuccessfully competing with the popular Marsh Troupe, so he signed on with them. Deep-voiced, experienced, and just shy of fifteen, Aldrich could barely qualify as a child. Unlike most other company members, Aldrich undoubtedly negotiated his own contract and pocketed his own payment. Although the experience with Marsh would certainly be useful, Aldrich arrived in the troupe as a professional—a journeyman rather than an apprentice.[78] His career would not be the product of R. G. Marsh's coaching. While Aldrich's contribution certainly enhanced the troupe and he received periodic benefit performances, he was never prominently promoted as Alfred Stewart had been.[79] Aldrich may have assumed the mantle of senior boy in the troupe, but he did not truly fill the lost place.

The Marsh Troupe began its fourth year, 1858–59, by coincidentally spending most of September and October in Alfred Stewart's home town of Cincinnati. The performances were heavily advertised and, though Hannah Stewart must have been aware of the tour, she made no public comments during the fall. The robust Cincinnati engagement led off a season that would limp to its end after Mary Marsh's sudden tragedy.

The Marsh Children opened at Smith and Nixon's in Cincinnati on September 15, 1858. R. G. March had engaged a new Treasurer, W. M. McGill, who received billing along with the manager. For the opening production of *The Naiad Queen*, Marsh promised, "All the original music, magic, changes, transformations, processions, [and] tableaux."[80] The fantasy played for two nights, followed by *Sea of Ice* for two nights, and subsequently *Ingomar*, *The Brigand*, *Nan, the Good-for-Nothing*, and *Toodles*. After a week, the company moved on, while Smith and Nixon's continued to run ads until the troupe returned on October 11 for an additional fortnight. During this engagement Marsh showed his Barnum-esque flare for promotion by advertising "the beautiful Trick Donkey, Jenny," employed for *Forty Thieves*, and creating ties to local events.[81] For example, the Cincinnati Mechanics Institute Fair exhibited a "painting of *The Brigand* as performed by the MARSH CHILDREN" while the company played at Smith and Nixon's nearby.[82]

In Cincinnati, *Aladdin*, *Cinderella*, and other selections from the repertoire were grouped together and labeled "beautiful Fairy Stories," to

Figure 2.2. Louis Aldrich, circa 1870. *Notable Players of the Past and Present*; Billy Rose Theatre Division, the New York Public Library for the Performing Arts, Astor, Lenox and Tilden Foundations.

appeal especially to children. Although most performances took place in the evening, Marsh always made it clear that children were welcome. During its first season, the company had sometimes offered half-price tickets to the stalls for those under ten.[83] One notice proclaimed, "Families are respectfully notified that on each representation by the Juvenile Troupe the entire performance will close by 10 o'clock."[84] During some engagements, matinees were added "for the accommodation of children and families."[85] At Spaulding and Rogers's during the spring of 1858, for example, advertisements in the *Picayune* proclaimed in large bold type, "GRAND MIDDAY ENTERTAINMENT For the accommodation of Ladies and children."[86] These notices were the exception rather than the rule. In general, Marsh Troupe performances were not explicitly directed at children, although children undoubtedly attended. Indeed, Marah Gubar argues that young people were "omnipresent" as spectators to "virtually all forms of popular theatre from this era."[87]

Calling attention to the attendance of children at the theatre connected to the larger antebellum mission of elevating the stage. Marsh had expressed his feeling that the stage "exhibited a marked degree of degeneracy."[88] Like other nineteenth-century theatre managers, Marsh wanted to change that. He tried to attract the middle class, and frequently made claims regarding the honorable nature of his profession. Cincinnati advertisements asserted that the Marsh Children's names had become "household words among the first families of the Union."[89] Significantly, the ad praises the status of the audience. Those who aspire to high social class should imitate the "first families" and appreciate the Marsh Troupe. A notice from early in the Troupe's history proclaimed that the children had "performed to a succession of crowded and *fashionable audiences* in the cities of Boston, New Orleans, Mobile, St. Louis, Louisville, and Cincinnati."[90] The assertion of crowded houses and the number of cities listed emphasize the popularity of the troupe. The inclusion of the phrase, "fashionable audiences," is a clear appeal to middle- and upper-class spectators.

After Christmas, the troupe began a southern tour. Beginning on January 3, 1859, "the Marsh children played to crowded houses in Columbus and Macon, Georgia."[91] These towns were part of the "Georgia Circuit" that Sol Smith had established and William H. Crisp would keep intact until the outbreak of the Civil War.[92] Outside of the circuit, Georgians had to rely on "circuses, minstrels, menageries, and camp meetings" for commercial entertainment, but within the circuit theatres were bustling.[93] The Marshes were headed for a long stay at Spaulding and Rogers's in New Orleans. At about this time, Doc Spaulding's agent contacted Mrs. Stewart with an invitation for young Alfred to appear on the same bill with his former company. The choice of Stewart rather than another act to fill out the bill may have been a canny decision. The previous year, the press had called Stewart "the favorite among the company." His local popularity plus residual interest in the controversy might spark ticket sales.[94]

Receiving assurances that her son would have nothing to do with Marsh, Mrs. Stewart agreed, and the appearance was announced. But, as the *Clipper* reported a few months later, "For some reason not yet clearly explained, Stewart was not allowed to perform. . . . Another job for the lawyers perhaps."[95] Whether Robert Marsh had agreed to Alfred Stewart's appearance in advance or learned of the booking only after its announcement is unknown. Perhaps the bruises from the legal spat made the idea of a double bill just too painful, and he insisted it be cancelled. Apparently, Marsh once again owed money to a partner and used that for leverage. According to Mrs. Stewart:

> Mr. Spaulding . . . assured me that if Mr. Marsh had not been indebted to him for a considerable amount (and it was the only hope he had of recovering his money, and his motive for engaging Master Stewart was to make the business good enough to enable him to get his own) he would have insisted on the boy playing, or he (Mr. Marsh) should not have played in his theatre.[96]

In any event, Alfred did not play, but Mrs. Stewart only learned of the cancellation when she read the *Clipper's* taunt, published in early April. On April 29, she wrote a scathing letter—that Frank Queen obligingly published in the *Clipper*—declaring, "I sent the child to meet his engagement according to the contract, and the first intimation I had that he did not play it was through the newspapers." Mrs. Stewart is clearly not traveling with her son, whom she characterizes as a "little child." While he's in New Orleans, she writes from Cincinnati, over seven hundred miles away. In spite of the fact that Mrs. Stewart had succeeded in freeing Alfred from his commitment, she still wanted the public to think badly of Marsh. She took pains to paint a public picture of Marsh as someone from whom her son needed protection. In her view, Marsh caused the cancellation out of personal hatred of her.

> Which hatred arises from the fact that I took the child away by law because he outraged every condition by which he obtained him; he got the child by fraud and misrepresentations, which I was not willing to submit to, so I took him away from him and exposed him, and this is the whole secret.[97]

Throughout her long letter she emphasized Alfred's vulnerability by repeatedly referring to him as a child. There was, however, no indication of anyone acting in *loco parentis* for Alfred, who—at almost sixteen years old—was virtually an adult in that era.[98] Her letter concludes:

> I hope Mr. Marsh feels bigger since he has shown his littleness by venturing his spite on a little child whose only fault is being more talented than his own. Master Stewart has no father, but he has a mother who will defend him as long as she lives. By giving this explanation in your valuable paper, you will much oblige, Yours truly, HANNAH STEWART.[99]

By insulting Marsh's children, Hannah Stewart reveals the intensely familial nature of the conflict. The reference to Alfred's dead father recalls the role that she expected Marsh would play as a traditional master to his apprentice. Mrs. Stewart's angry rhetoric indicates a sense of personal betrayal by Marsh's failure to act as protector. The mother now has assumed the father's task and vows "to defend [her child] as long as she lives." The nobility of Mrs. Stewart's heroic defense, however, is called into question by her timing. Between mid-January, when Alfred's booking was cancelled, and April, when she wrote her letter, R. G. Marsh had suffered the greatest personal and professional tragedy of his life.

On January 28, the Marsh Troupe was still in the South, performing at Ralston Hall in Macon, Georgia, when Mary Marsh suffered her fatal accident. She'd performed the role of Idex hundreds of times, but on that night she made a terrible mistake. A member of the company described the horrific scene in quite plain language in a newspaper account:

> After the first act of *The Naiad Queen*, Mary, in her blithesome glee ran tripping across the stage so near a candle that the flare of it caught the bottom of her fairy dress, and in a moment she was a mass of flame. Her mother and Georgiana were instantly by her side, but she was literally a ball of fire, and in their efforts to smother the flame were themselves badly burned. Poor little Mary screamed terrifically and the house was in frightful commotion. It was soon all over with her. She died the next afternoon.[100]

Five weeks short of her twelfth birthday, Little Mary Marsh was dead.

Mrs. Stewart's attack on the talent of Marsh's children is dated three months to the day after Mary's hideous death. That Hannah Stewart was ignorant of the gruesome accident is barely conceivable; it had been reported nationally. The *Clipper*, which Mrs. Stewart read regularly and termed a "valuable paper," ran several items about Mary Marsh's accident and its aftermath.[101] The *Cincinnati Inquirer*, Stewart's hometown paper, had put the story of the fire on its front page and followed it with calls for improved stage safety.[102] Yet when Mrs. Stewart writes that her child has more talent than Marsh's, the wording and timing of her jeremiad make it unclear whether she is disparaging the talent of dead Mary, live Georgie, or both. In either case, clearly the perceived offense of Robert Marsh's behavior toward her own son outweighed her sensitivity to another parent's pain. One can only imagine the feelings of Marsh's silent spouse, Jane, reading these words just a few months after burying her daughter. No written response from Mr. or Mrs. Marsh was published.

Meanwhile, R. G. Marsh had responsibilities. He "resumed business as soon as possible after the death of Little Mary and the day of her funeral."[103] Heartbroken, though pragmatic, Marsh had forty children on his payroll and an investment in sumptuous sets. "Why should I leave here at once?" he wrote, "I have expended time and money to get ready. I engaged to play ten nights."[104] Marsh kept his contract. He recast the part and reopened the show—at double the ticket price. Advertisements throughout the triumphal 1858 season in New Orleans had listed admission at fifty cents, with children and servants half price. On February 26, 1859, the *Clipper* announced, "The Marsh Juveniles visited Columbus, Ga., after leaving Macon, and had full houses in Temperance Hall, at *a dollar a ticket*."[105]

The Marsh Troupe of Juvenile Comedians continued its tour of the "Georgia Circuit" moving to Montgomery, Alabama—with a benefit for Miss Louise on February 25—then on to Mobile on March 14.[106] In early April, the *Cincinnati Enquirer* noted, "The Marsh Troupe are at the Amphitheatre, New Orleans, playing to good houses. Their engagement continued several weeks longer."[107] On April 24, and again on May 22, the *Enquirer* confirmed, "The Marsh Troupe are still at Spaulding and Rogers's Amphitheatre, New Orleans."[108] The southern audiences remained charmed by the children and the troupe met its engagements for the entire spring season.

Alfred Stewart started appearing individually immediately after leaving the Marsh Troupe in 1858. His engagements can be documented through the beginning of 1860.[109] Colonel Brown writes that by 1870 Stewart was "connected with western theatres."[110] Corroborating information has not been found, however, and Stewart's name is not mentioned in any of the standard histories of nineteenth-century players. Master Stewart did not achieve fame as an adult. For all of the hubbub, Alfred Stewart left no mark.

CHAPTER 3

A PERFECT ANGEL—FOREVER

Mary Marsh's horrific death exposed one of the major dualities of her bifurcated existence. She embodied both the ephemeral, idealized persona of girlhood and a hard-working laborer with inadequate workplace protections. During her short life, she also exemplified the paradox of coexisting innocence and eroticism common to many child performers.

To members of her public, Mary Marsh possessed "an intellect far beyond her years" yet managed to retain "the sweet and fresh simplicity of childhood."[1] She was described as "a perfect little beauty,"[2] "an uncommonly attractive child, bright-eyed and graceful, fresh and fair."[3] This "perfect" child began her life on March 4, 1847, as Mary Eliza Guerineau. In her first appearances she was announced as "Mary Guerineau Marsh," but during the Cincinnati run of *Uncle Tom's Cabin*, her father experimented with billing. By the end of that run, notices for her benefit identified her as "Little Mary Marsh." Her legal surname had been dropped and would not be used again during her lifetime.[4] "Little" would become capitalized as part of Mary's name in billing for the juvenile troupe and, later, literally engraved in stone for posterity.

Performing professionally at six years old in 1853, Mary had made a hit in *Uncle Tom's Cabin*. Robert Marsh described Mary as the juvenile company's foundation, "the ground work upon which [the] troupe was founded.[5] Marsh claimed that his daughter was a "model for the whole troupe, both on and off the stage," yet we know little about Mary beyond the persona that he constructed for her.[6] Her idealized stage persona embodied both angelic purity and eroticism, while her dual identity as a child worker remained mostly obscured, until searingly revealed by her tragic death in the workplace accident.

Mary's "biography," published in *Marsh's Juvenile Dramatic Era* in 1857, consisted of platitudes about her goodness, and provided little real information.[7] Likewise, few of Mary's individual characteristics are discernible either in reviews or other advertising pieces. Her persona was simply *goodness*. James Kincaid has pointed out that the "good child" is often "so invitingly vacant that the goodness is utter blankness."[8] Audiences were invited to project their idealized image of girlhood onto Mary.

The Marsh troupe worked at the dawn of America's love affair with childhood, and Mary's constructed persona matched the nineteenth-century sentimental ideal.[9] "[I]n the average schoolboy's mind she was associated in some romantic way with all of the good and beautiful women of his history or his mythology."[10] The key words here are "romantic" and "mythology." Lawrence Hutton, clearly involved in the project of mythmaking, wrote these words a quarter of a century after seeing Mary Marsh perform. The myth was childhood. Childhood has never existed in the pure realm of romantic innocence evoked by Hutton's phrases, but most scholars agree that by Mary's debut the concept had been under construction for quite some time. As James Kincaid writes, "Few would question that the innocent child was manufactured by Rousseau, with refinements by Wordsworth and a thousand lesser writers, interior decorators, and producers of greeting cards."[11]

Anne Higonnet has argued for the additional contributions of "elite" eighteenth-century painters such as Joshua Reynolds and Thomas Gainsborough. Their visual imagery "introduced a new vision of the child" which was a "brilliant pictorial version of an invented definition."[12] The child thus imagined could be at once an object of the erotic gaze and the encapsulation of pure innocence. During the nineteenth century, the concept of Romantic childhood permeated Western society, and images of naturally innocent children were ubiquitous in novels, plays, poems, painting, advertising, and public discourse. "By the 1850s," writes Postman, "childhood was both a social principle and a social fact."[13] The stage career of Mary Marsh resulted from this fact. Her popularity, and that of all the Marsh Juveniles, depended on the public's newly awakened fascination with children.

The emergence of childhood coincided with the rise of the middle class, where the concept remained firmly embedded. Higonnet points out that elite paintings naturalized childhood: "The Romantic child makes a good show of having no class, no gender and no thoughts."[14] Idealized children, however, were inevitably of a particular type—pink and well fed. As Robin Bernstein has demonstrated, the nineteenth century understood childhood as "innocence itself" and "[t]his innocence was raced white."[15] Children of the working classes and children of color were outside the realm of "childhood." "Evacuated" of innocence and incapable of feeling pain, they did not require protection.[16] This bifurcation of the concept of childhood enabled late nineteenth-century industrialists to exploit and destroy millions of young bodies for capitalistic goals, while their middle- and upper-class contemporaries continued to venerate childhood.

Child actors represent a special case, as they have always dwelt within that blurry, liminal zone between child and adult. Their appeal derives from the precious, irretrievable ingenuousness of youth. As working professionals, however, their lives are circumscribed by the job. They are not segregated within the protected world of children. They spend their days amid adult coworkers at hours and locations that may put their health, safety, and education, as well as their innocence, at risk. Yet, their labor is often invisible, "ironically camouflaged by their fictional roles."[17]

Mary Marsh, and other juvenile actors of the period, created what Viviana Zelizer called a "curious paradox; they were child laborers paid to represent the new, sentimentalized view of children."[18] No one in antebellum America seemed struck by this paradox—the first legal protections for child actors were decades away.[19] In Mary Marsh's lifetime, almost all children worked, whether on the farm or in the shop. This was the legacy of the eighteenth century when the rural household functioned as the common productive unit, and families generally worked together.[20] Fathers owned their children's labor, and expected competence from them. In common with other child workers, Mary and her brother George were competent at their tasks and made significant contributions to the family's enterprise. Contemporaneous commentators accepted the Marsh children as professionals and evaluated them as such. Marah Gubar records that the same was true of child actors in Victorian England.[21]

Zelizer has argued that prior to the dominance of idealized childhood, most children were economically useful. In the twentieth century, as both middle-class culture and sentimental childhood became more widespread, children became economically useless. As they gained protection, children seemed to be endowed with less and less competence. Compare, for a moment, a modern middle-class child with her counterpart in a traditional society such as those Jared Diamond describes or in some parts of the Global South.[22] The child of the "advanced" nation appears helpless, while the "savage" or "third-world" child often earns a living and cares for siblings while managing a plethora of household tasks. From our vantage point in twenty-first-century Western society, we simply may not be able to fully conceive of the professional competence of antebellum child performers, or others since.

The idealization of childhood was immediately preceded by the idealization of women. The phenomena were similar in that both entailed separating the subject group from men and commerce by keeping them "safe" within the home. Barbara Welter's seminal essay on "The Cult of True Womanhood: 1830–1860" points out how this idealization held women hostage and kept them powerless. While venerated in name, a woman was to be "ever timid, doubtful, and clingingly dependent; [in] a perpetual childhood."[23] Many feminist scholars have noted how "protecting" women actually robbed them of rights. Whether married, single, or widowed, women lost the ability to act independently on their own behalf. Ann Douglas noted the change, for example, in opinions on widows, who in the eighteenth century were considered useful members of society, but by the nineteenth century were considered primarily as worthy objects for charity.[24] Similarly, the elevation of childhood and heroic "protection" of children may have actually been a smokescreen to hide the erasure of their agency.

During the nineteenth century, the home came to be defined as the exclusive sphere of women and children, while men moved in their own separate sphere of business and trade. Before the Civil War, fathers were more influential in the home, whereas in the latter nineteenth century mothers came to control the home.[25] Children were kept safe there from the world of commerce. The marketplace, polluted and dangerous, came to be depicted as the antithesis of the pure and safe home.[26] Boys would eventually enter the realm of men, but girls would remain forever pure within the protected ignorance of the home.[27] While this cultural wave would isolate many children from their fathers, Mary and Georgie Marsh spent their days intimately connected with their father, learning his trade. Thus, Mary Marsh was freed from what Jane Hunter termed the traditional "domestic apprenticeship" usual for girls at their mothers' sides, even as Mary embodied the Victorian ideal of girlhood in her public persona.[28] While all actors have double identities, not all are so completely at odds with the prevailing societal philosophy. By working with their father outside of the home, Mary Marsh and her brother transgressed the boundary between home and workplace at the very moment when it was being concretized in the middle-class Victorian mind. The Marsh family lived during a period of transition, but Robert Marsh's parenting style leaned toward the old-fashioned model of father as master and patriarch. Yet, ironically, the new ideas of childhood, which made children highly prized, contributed to the success of his endeavor.

That Mary Marsh began her career playing Little Eva, the eponymous angel-child, is not surprising. The role not only situates Mary within the context of a powerful cultural event that permeated both entertainment and American culture for the next half century, but it also brings into relief Mary's connection with Eva, a character whose tragic death only enhanced her purity. Before and after her own tragic death, Mary, too, would be an angel.

An image of Mary from Cincinnati's Melodeon Hall depicts "The Infant Wonder in her Great Character of Eva in Uncle Tom's Cabin."[29] The picture shows Mary seated on a tuft of grass, with her ankles crossed, a large book open on her lap over a wide skirt that fails to cover her lace-edged pantaloons. Mary's head is up, but she looks away from us, her gaze fixed in the distance. The image is clearly modeled on the iconic "arbor scene" illustration by Hammatt Billings that appeared in the *National Era* newspaper, the first and second editions of Stowe's 1852 novel, as well as in the facsimile edition published in 2011 by Oxford University Press.[30] This scene, found on handkerchiefs, ceramic figurines and countless other "tomitudes" has been described as "representing the highest 'moral moment'" of the novel.[31] In the Melodeon Theatre poster, Mary is pictured outside with sprigs of plants near her feet, but the image is cropped to create a rounded arch overhead. For those who may not remember the scene, a line of dialogue and a chapter reference are supplied: "'Uncle Tom, where do you suppose the New Jerusalem is,' *Uncle Tom's Cabin Chap. XXII.*" The image situates "Little Mary Guerineau Marsh" securely within the realm of sacred childhood. We know that the large book is a Bible. Mary's look is ethereal, already moving into the next world.

Visual and verbal references evoking religion (of mainstream Protestant variety) would often be applied to Mary Marsh. Sociologist Jane O'Connor, studying the child-star phenomenon of the twentieth century, speculated that public attraction to child performers relates to a need for

Figure 3.1. Little Mary Guerineau Marsh as Eva, Cincinnati, 1853–54. TCS 44, Harvard Theatre Collection, Houghton Library, Harvard University.

"a connection between the natural and the supernatural, or the moral and the divine."[32] The Cincinnati image invites us to see Mary/Eva as our link to a spiritual realm. Mary, as presented to the public, exemplified the good child described by James Kincaid as "more than just so-so good; it is angelic, holding out the promise of a happiness that is complete and divine."[33] The image differs significantly from the Billings illustration, which shows Little Eva in conversation with Uncle Tom. Mary's Eva is alone in the picture. Because she is not in conversation, she has no need to angle her body away from us as Little Eva does in Billings. Mary's shoulders are parallel to the picture frame; only her head is turned slightly to the side, as she gazes into the distance. Perhaps the angle of Mary's head suggests that the observer need not be distracted by thoughts of slavery or its abolition. Mary's solitary presence and her direct gaze draw all onlookers' eyes to her, "The Infant Wonder." Viewers are seemingly meant to focus on Mary's specialness, on her close-to-nature/close-to-God character, even as the advertisement works to entice ticket buyers to the theatre.

The emergence of melodrama as a dominant popular entertainment in the nineteenth century has been related to the emerging working- and middle-class audiences, but the correlation between its development and the creation of childhood has not been widely remarked. Melodrama's propensity to present, in John W. Frick's phrase, "life idealized," perfectly aligned with the emergence of sentimental childhood.[34] Child characters populated its stages, epitomizing the constructed image of a sacred child. They were close to the angels—and frequently sent to join them through an early death. The language used to describe the little girls who portrayed Eva overtly conflated her character with theirs. These actors "blur[red] any distinction between children and childhood."[35] Rose Bank has observed that melodrama functioned "as a form of imagination, of imaging (seeing) or conceiving."[36] Melodrama helped critics and audiences to naturalize sentimental childhood. Mary Marsh, and others of her ilk, embodied those fantasies for the public—"public" as Christopher Balme has defined it, as an entity distinct from the playgoers, whether individualized as spectators or collectivized as audience. The public is an "arbiter of taste and aesthetic judgment . . . a rhetorical entity of adjudication."[37] The public seemed to thirst for images of the pure and innocent child who possessed healing power and embodied all goodness.

The company's advertising promulgated Mary's "goodness." The description makes her sound like a fictional character rather than a real child.

Figure 3.2. Mary Marsh, undated photograph. Harvard Theatre Collection, Houghton Library, Harvard University.

She is an exemplar of the Christian virtues and feminine attributes taught in the era's conduct manuals:

> [S]he retains the sweet and fresh simplicity of childhood. Her genius, being genuine, excludes vanity from her disposition, laden with applause though she is. . . . She is beloved by all of her joyous professional comrades, for nature, no less than parental instruction, has taught her that the sweetest and highest honor in all this world, is to have a pleasant temper, a modest mind, and a frank good heart.[38]

The appeal of nineteenth-century child actresses was inherently tied to their angelic personae.[39] These characters were depicted as so closely linked to spiritual purity that when they died—which happened often—they could glide seamlessly into the afterlife. The actresses who played these children seemed to carry heaven within them all the time. Anne Varty describes the power of the child on the Victorian stage to "evoke the pageantry of immortality." Being in the presence of such a child could feel almost like being touched by God. The performance became a "metaphor for the afterlife. Heaven was displaced by theatre."[40] Within Stowe's novel, proximity to Little Eva could bestow virtue on Topsy or Tom. In the theatre audiences could believe that their own purity would be restored by their closeness to angelic children on stage. In Kincaid's words, the child's presence operated as "a purifying draught to take in and make part of one's own system."[41] As one of these angel children, Mary Marsh seemingly had the power to refresh human souls.

Coupled with innocence, child actresses were also seen to possess sexuality. Mary and her little brother George often played opposite each other as man and wife, or as a flirtatious pair, as in *The Naiad Queen*. Similarly, Kate and Ellen Bateman and Charlotte Cushman and her sister also played male/female pairs. Heather McMahon discusses how their youth and therefore assumed innate purity kept away any hint of incest, yet even the characters' names are sometimes suggestive. The "pert and pretty chambermaid" and "Ko-Ket, the Man Catcher" (in *The Happy Man*) were among the roles Mary played. When not playing opposite her brother, Mary's "leading man" was Miss Louise. The nineteenth-century practice of allowing only women to cross-dress made this acceptable, and perhaps amusing, to audiences. Few extant written reactions indicate the physicality of the performance or the degree to which the costumes might have been suggestive. A disapproving writer for *Putnam's Monthly* described the Marsh children as playing roles that they "happily cannot comprehend." He noted the tacit assumption that the young performers were unaware of the sexual overtones because "it would be shocking to believe [they] . . . understood." The humor, he believed, sprung from the contrast of the suggestive materials "with the innocence of [the] . . . young face and voice." Clearly under the suasion of the new thinking regarding children's innate purity and need for protection, he worried, "How long will a child, thus encouraged to say things of the meaning of which he is supposed to be ignorant, remain in ignorance of their meaning?"[42]

Many scholars have commented on the erotic appeal of the child performer during the Victorian period.[43] The image of Mary as Little Eva encapsulates both the innocence and this erotic appeal. While her countenance may be otherworldly, the ringlets framing it touch shoulders left bare by the broad lacy neckline. While Mary holds a Bible on her lap, below we can see her embroidered pantaloons. There is quite a bit of visual detail to draw the eye: The hem falls in deep scallops and a dotted decoration runs along it. Above the hem, the undergarment has further decoration in the form of sprigs of fern or flowers that grow up toward the knee. Between the scalloped edge of the pantaloons and the delicate high-button shoes, several inches of calf are exposed. Certainly tame by today's standards, the image is nonetheless different from the illustrations for Stowe's novel that inspired it.

In the Hammatt Billings illustration, Little Eva's long dress exposes only the tiniest bit of ankle, and although her neckline is lower, both shoulders are covered. Displaying the undergarments of seemingly innocent children would become commonplace in the century that followed Mary Marsh's career. Many commentators have noted Shirley Temple's very short skirts that revealed her underpants with every swish. James Kincaid mentions this as a recurrent practice in early twentieth-century newspaper comics, as well as later films and television. According to Kincaid, audiences enjoy

> shots of underwear, if they are made properly sneaky, provocative—Barthesian glimpses, flashes of forbidden wonder. The little Buster-Brown skirt-wearers in the long-running *Our Gang* films (1922–1944), the adorable Darla (Hood) most commonly, seemed always willing to pose in convenient positions for the display of underpants, and we see the same thing in any number of later "good-kid" Buster-figures, from Luke Halpin in the 1960s *Flipper* movies to Bobby Brady and Ricky Schroeder.[44]

Mary Marsh's Eva poster is a precursor to this trend.

Little girls have often inspired erotic thoughts. Mary Marsh started performing about the same age as Alice Liddell would be when she moved Charles Dodgson (Lewis Carroll) to snap her picture and entertain her with stories.[45] When the Marsh Juvenile Troupe launched, Mary was the same age as Nabokov's Lolita when first discovered by Humbert. Lawrence Hutton insisted of Mary, however, that "The passion the child inspired in the breast of her adorers was a pure one and . . . it did no harm."[46] Hutton's view illustrates the fascination with children that James Kincaid has called "child-loving." But Marah Gubar writes that the "ever-present threat of scandalous mistreatment and sexual precocity that hung over" child actresses was a "key part of their appeal."[47] The Marsh Troupe's advertising of its majority female contingent seemed to acknowledge this eroticization. While the phrase "beautiful girls" is common in the entertainment section of a newspaper today, we would find it unsettling if it were followed by the phrase "aged variously 6 to 12 years" as it was in ads for the troupe's 1857 appearances in Cincinnati.[48] It was lauded as "Composed variously of beautiful girls, aged variously from 6 to 12 years, and two boys, Master Waldo, 10 years of age, and Master George Washington Marsh, aged 7 years."[49] The attraction advertised not the talent or the script, but the beauty of young girls' bodies. Similarly, notices in the *Boston Post* advertising "33 Little Misses from 4 to 12 Years Old" called attention to femininity and age more than to talent or accomplishment.[50] Ads that cited accomplishments still highlighted the sex of the children: "Forty-three beautiful children will appear and execute grand marches of female warriors, military evolutions, combats and tableaux, living pictures."[51] The audience is clearly told of an opportunity to watch the display of beautiful female bodies. Earlier in the century, theatre manager Francis Wemyss had understood that the female warriors were the basis of the great success of *The Naiad Queen*: "Such a display of ladies' legs, no mortal man could resist the opportunity of seeing."[52] Was it so different when the warriors were girls rather than "ladies"?

Young female dancers and actresses were often dressed in filmy fabrics that may have inspired the dreams of spectators, but made the performers particularly vulnerable to the open flames of gas lights. Fire claimed the lives of many in the theatre, spectators and performers alike. Early in the century, the Richmond Theatre Fire resulted in seventy-two fatalities.[53] Every theatregoer in America had seen footlights burning; many had read about earlier accidents and could easily picture the speed with which a costume could be ignited. Reports vary as to what happened when Mary's naiad dress caught fire on the stage of Macon's Ralston Hall. Some place her mother onstage and rushing to help. Others tell of a gentleman spectator who bounded onstage and enveloped the girl in his coat. Another young cast member, Georgiana Mousely, suffered severe burns in her efforts to help. Mary Marsh was carried off stage and survived only a few hours after the accident. The story of Mary's accident was covered by papers in cities all over the country, including New York City, Troy, Cleveland, Cincinnati, New Orleans, and Chicago, as well as Macon, the site of the accident. "Never had the death of a child created such universal sadness in the community," a Macon historian would later write.[54]

Contemporaneous coverage supported Mary's image as an angel-child: "She died with the name of 'Mother' on her lips, and with the prayers of all her little companions in her behalf," reported the *Plain Dealer.*[55] As Alisa C. Roost observes, genres "influence how stories are structured, creating expectations, and conditioning responses."[56] Melodramatic tropes shaped the public response to Mary's death and provided R. G. Marsh with the imagery he needed to defend himself from complaints when he resumed business as soon as possible after the funeral. His long public letter was published in New York and Georgia:

> To the Intelligent Citizens of Macon:
>
> I address these few remarks to those who have extended their sympathies to us, Mary's bereaved father, mother, brother and little companions, not looking upon us as mountebanks, traveling with a company of oppressed and neglected children, but as a company who have now the respect of all with whom we have come in contact, as well as the love and admiration of thousands throughout the Union, who have witnessed their exertions in public. Our children's private conduct and public character stands pre-eminent. Most conspicuous among them all was Mary Elizabeth Guerineau, known to the world as Mary Marsh, daughter of Robert and Jane C. Guerineau (Marsh,) and sister of little George. She was a model for the whole troupe, both on and off the stage; she was the ground work upon which our troupe was founded—her modest deportment towards, and affection for her friends and enemies, won all hearts, and she was an idol—a comfort—to her mother—and advisor to her companions—a sister to her brother, and her father's guiding star. But we hope all is for the best, and rely on the inscrutable decrees of Providence. The living yet remains to be cared and provided for. We have a great care upon our hands—we have duties and engagements to fill—we are not prepared to relinquish our profession, which we dearly love, and have sought not to cut it down, as it will grow, but to dig around the roots and prune it, like the tree in the parable, that it may bear good fruit. It certainly will be hard upon our feeling to put

> one child here, another there, to fill her place, but after mature judgment and reflection, we find it must be done. I have been led to make this statement, from few unkind remarks, dropped within my hearing, (which, however, I cannot believe were intended to wound,) to the effect that it would be cruel for me to play here again—that I should break up all at once, &c. [*sic*]. If this is the general feeling, I shall know it after a night or two.
>
> Why should I leave here at once? I have expended time and money to get ready. I engaged to play ten nights. I am here among sympathisers [*sic*]; why go somewhere else and have the same expense in getting ready. The accident was one that could not have been foreseen, the victim having, full of extra glee and spirits, taken the trouble to go to a position she never occupied before. You, who are engaged in mercantile or any other business, who are at home, might delay your business for a few days, but oh! do not condemn me in your hearts, lest a misfortune should come upon yourselves. I do not want your pocket sympathies, as I give an equivalent for all I receive, but give my wife—my boy, whose little heart is almost broke, but who bears up manfully to console his mother and father—the sympathies of your hearts; we will deserve them. Here follows our announcement. Oh! world, oh! business, how can we embrace thee?
>
> R. G. Marsh
>
> *To the disinterested citizens of Savannah, from whom we have received letters of condolence; also to the kind friends in this city, who have come forward in kind words and acts, we would offer our thanks and love.* MARY'S PARENTS AND COMPANIONS.[57]

In this letter, Marsh continues to position his daughter as the epitome of ideal girlhood. While this is not surprising in words written just after her death, they closely resemble descriptions of Mary written two years earlier. In 1857 Mary's "pleasant temper, a modest mind, and a frank good heart" made her "beloved by all of her joyous professional comrades."[58] Following her death in 1859, Marsh writes, "her modest deportment towards, and affection for her friends and enemies, won all hearts." Mary continues to inhabit her line of business. Mary's role as the angelic-but-doomed heroine was written before her tragic accident. In common with the daughter characters of "Mary" in *Ten Nights in a Bar-room*, a popular reform melodrama of the era, and Eva in *Uncle Tom's Cabin*, Mary Marsh became the "martyred child."[59] In those scripted melodramas, the daughter-characters reproach their fathers and, with the child's death, the father-character comes to regret his past behavior. The fathers in these plays were guided by the daughters. While Mary Marsh's role was maintained, Robert Guerineau Marsh did not stick to the script. Even as Marsh referred to Mary as his "guiding star," he defended rather than renounced his actions that led inadvertently to his daughter's death. He justified these actions by utilizing themes of class conduct, professionalism, and patriarchy.

Marsh's first strategy was to separate himself from the lower classes whose behavior, almost by definition, was seen as morally suspect. His company was not made up of "mountebanks" or "oppressed and neglected children"; rather, he asserted, "Our children's private conduct and public character stands pre-eminent." Just as the company's advertising had frequently noted the quality of its audience, Marsh emphasized the status of the performers. In the Victorian mind, social class frequently correlated with moral status.[60] It must be remembered that in antebellum society, the Caucasian adult male occupied the highest moral position. Social and scientific theories including complementarity, social evolution, and recapitulation supported his superiority over women, children, and "the lesser races."[61] On the evolutionary scale, children (and women) were placed between men on the highest level and animals below. Marsh unapologetically claimed his position in this hierarchy when he addressed himself to his peers. Business was the province of males, and professionalization was another method by which one group could be distinguished from another. By addressing, "You, who are engaged in mercantile or any other business," R. G. Marsh aligned himself with this class. He stressed unwillingness "to relinquish [his] . . . profession." In an age that commended industry, Marsh accentuated his responsibilities and his willingness, as patriarch, to take them up, "We have a great care upon our hands—we have duties and engagements to fill." And although he stated that he would "rely on the inscrutable decrees of Providence," the concerns of this world could not be ignored. "The living yet remains to be cared and provided for." As for his own responsibility, Marsh glided by it easily, declaring that the accident "could not have been foreseen."

Mary's death highlighted her liminal position between what Viviana Zelizer identified as the useful and the useless child.[62] As a personification of idealized childhood, Mary exemplified the sacred child whose primary value is sentimental. Zelizer has pointed out that children's stage roles camouflage the reality of their work roles. This camouflage was mercilessly illuminated by the flames that seared through Mary's gossamer costume. Bereft of today's protection from the Occupational Safety and Health Administration, her identity as a worker became dominant. The public condemned Marsh's lack of sentimentality (reopening the show) more than for his responsibility for the accident (putting his daughter on stage, not masking the lamps, etc.). Media reaction to Mary's death was slightly mixed. Very few observers saw Mary's death as a call to action for changes in theatrical working conditions. In 1852, just seven years earlier, the city of Macon had experienced two catastrophic fires, one of which destroyed eighteen buildings downtown, extending "until the whole square was laid in ashes."[63] These events were so alarming that "the attention of [City] Council was engaged during the year in devising plans to procure water for the extinguishment of fires, and the organization of a Fire Department with a superior class of machines to those in use, which were found to be totally inefficacious."[64] Yet the local notices of Mary's death aligned with those of other cities, stressing only the tragedy of her loss and making no mention of the contributing conditions.

The *Cincinnati Enquirer*'s page-one plea imploring those in the profession to take action was unique among the surviving news stories:

> The shocking accident to little Mary Marsh . . . should be a warning to theatrical managers to cover the footlights with wire-screens. This necessary precaution, which should be a condition of licensing theatres, would save many lives. The only wonder is that more accidents of this same kind do not occur.[65]

In fact, similar accidents were not rare. During Mary Marsh's short career, burning costumes had caused the deaths of young performers at Wood's Theatre in St. Louis and in New York at Niblo's Garden and the Old Bowery Theatre, although none of these victims had been as young as Mary.[66] In light of these facts, Robert Marsh's assertion that Mary's accident "could not have been foreseen" appears foolish, if not glib. There's no indication, however, of public concern over safety conditions. It must be remembered that in 1859, a child's labor legally belonged to the father. Public opinion didn't take issue with a man's right to use his property as he saw fit.

Dead, Mary was available as a site for nostalgia. Ann Douglas has shown how nostalgia served as a useful tool in nineteenth-century culture. "Sentimentalism . . . asserts that the values a society's activities denies are precisely the ones it cherishes; it attempts to deal with the phenomenon of cultural bifurcation by the manipulation of nostalgia." Like the men Douglas describes, R. G. Marsh's values were economic, and his "regret was calculated not to interfere with [his] actions." His sentimental mourning for Mary literally did not stop the show, just as "Little Eva's beautiful death, which Stowe presents as part of a protest against slavery, in no way hinders the working of that system."[67]

The persona of Little Mary Marsh lived on after her death. Her beautiful innocence could not now be disfigured by maturation. Her burial illustrated Robin Bernstein's assertions that sentimentalism "constructed the death of a child not as dispossessive but as preservative, as a freezing that paradoxically prevents the essential child-quality from ever dying through maturation."[68] Many commentators have noted the sadness with which adults sometimes greet children's movement away from youth. In the first paragraph of J. M. Barrie's *Peter Pan*, Wendy's mother "put her hand to her heart and cried, 'Oh, why can't you remain like this forever!'" This is how Wendy learned she must grow up; Barrie's narrator calls it, "the beginning of the end."[69] James Kincaid phrases it even more brutally: "The child does not grow or even grow up; it becomes extinct. In part, these metaphors express the fact that the child becomes unattractive to the adult, becomes just another ordinary adult and no longer anything magical—disfigured by body hair and erupting skin and ungainly height."[70]

If Mary Marsh had survived into her early seventies, she might have seen the debut of "Baby Peggy," a silent screen star who performed from the age of nineteen months to seven years. "Baby Peggy" made hundreds of short comedies, gained international fame, and earned over a million dollars in the film business. She then toured vaudeville for an additional six years before puberty ended her career. The young actress experienced firsthand the unattractiveness Kincaid describes. Former "Baby Peggy" fans reacted to the teenager as if she had been somehow horribly disfigured. Years later, she still felt the sting of their appalled reaction, "You used to be so cute! . . . My, how you've changed."[71] One fan asserted that it was "positively wicked" of her favorite child stars to grow up.[72] By dying, Mary Marsh avoided the phenomenon "Baby Peggy" experienced and Kincaid describes when he notes that the loss of a child can come "either through growth or death."[73] By dying, and by dying dramatically, Mary could remain the figure about whom critic Lawrence Hutton could still dream rhapsodically thirty years later. Mary, although literally destroyed by flames, was less "disfigured" than she would have been by surviving into an unremarkable adulthood. A line from the verse inscribed upon her gravestone underlines this fact, "No Decay, / Nor Time, Nor Change, Can Steal Her Youth Away." She is safe.

The material culture surrounding her death helped freeze the memory of Little Mary Marsh. She was buried in Macon's Rose Hill Cemetery, far from her birthplace. Founded in 1840, Rose Hill exemplified the "rural cemeteries" that were taking the place of traditional church graveyards.[74] While clearly prompted by the geographic and hygienic necessity of an expanding population, the trend also reflected the Romantic and beautification movements of the nineteenth century. Rural cemeteries sought to deny or domesticate death while comforting and uplifting the living. Altering vocabulary was a first step in sentimentalizing death. The word "casket"—a chest for things—began to replace "coffin."[75] The word "cemetery," derived from the Latin *coemeterium*—meaning a place of rest or sleep—replaced "graveyard," a dark, creepy place associated with decay.[76] Ann Douglas has noted similarities between the language used to describe the rural cemeteries and that used to refer to the ideal middle-class home; both were meant to be an oasis.[77] The imagery in this description of Rose Hill Cemetery, written by its eponymous donor, locates the cemetery within the new Romantic ideas:

> [A]bove the city on the banks of the Ocmulgee river . . . through a lofty arched gate . . . a perfect picture of rural beauty . . . a rivulet murmurs over a steep and rocky bed on its way to the river. . . . The banks around it are high and steep, and thickly wooded. Above it tower giant poplars and the shady beech. . . . Two rustic bridges of rock and earth cross this valley. . . . Around it are several cypresses and weeping willows. . . . A variety of fine roses is also near it and in perpetual bloom.[78]

For the living, rural cemeteries became sites of leisure that attracted throngs of visitors.[79] The popularity of these sites prompted the adoption of common theatrical practices. Tickets were required to enter some rural cemeteries, while virtual visits could be obtained via stereopticon cards—"hundreds of different views mass-produced in thousands of copies each."[80]

These were analogous to the *cartes de visite* just coming into wide use by actors and others. Rural cemeteries then were sites of spectatorship. Mary's performance could continue there.

While audiences were drawn in by aesthetic attractions, the goal of the rural cemetery movement was "the improvement of the moral sentiments and general taste of all classes, and more especially the great masses of society."[81] According to Stanley French, Americans emphasized "the capacities of the garden cemetery for moral instruction."[82] The cemetery functioned, like melodrama, as part of a cultural formation. Rose Hill was particularly apt as a final "resting place" for Mary because it positioned her to continue to perform her Eva-esque role as, in the words of her father, a "guiding star." She became part of a landscape that performed instruction in gentility and morality.

In her study of children's graves, Heather McKillop found "burial practices specific to children and distinct from adults during the nineteenth century."[83] McKillop writes that the child-specific practices not only expressed the beautification of death, common throughout the era, "but also closely identif[ied] the child with the purity, innocence, and Christian values of the home, church, and heaven."[84] Mary's grave is consistent with this trend in several ways: its location in Rose Hill, the visual iconography, the inscription—including her name—and the inclusion of a personal relic.

It took almost a year to design and install Mary's gravestone. An 1860 newspaper item from Ohio's *Plain Dealer* carried this description:

> A handsome upright monument, ordered by Mr. Marsh, has just been completed at Charleston, S.C. It is an elegantly polished piece of Italian marble, with its edges chamfered, and enriched with an ivy vine with berries cut thereon, and surmounted by an urn enwreathed in immortelles. The stone springs from a marble base, which is set in a ground stone of brown freestone.[85]

According to Aubrey Cannon's classification system, this was a pedestal monument, one of the less common of the seven types used widely during the nineteenth century.[86] Today, the upright, rectangular marble stone remains, but the urn that topped the monument is no longer extant and no image of it exists. We do not need to see this part of the stone in order to comprehend its meaning. Immortelles flowers retain their shape and color when dried. In the typography of Victorian graves, the urn symbolized death and this plant's name meant everlasting life. Victorian culture defined death not as an end but as a passage to eternity.

Scholars in cemetery studies argue that memorials were chosen either to highlight membership in a group, such as a profession, or to "express personal relationships over group affiliations."[87] Mary Marsh's gravestone does both via engravings on two sides. In a way, the stone is a metaphor for her life, as well as for this book, which looks at the real, historic children behind the celebrated actors. One side of the stone represents Mary's material identity, and the other represents her theatrical persona. The first side of Mary's tombstone presents her simply as the daughter of Robert and Jane Guerineau. The engraving on the front of the stone is enclosed within a simple, scalloped frame. It gives her legal name and the bare facts: "MARY ELIZA ONLY DAUGHTER OF ROBERT AND JANE C. GUERINEAU, BORN MARCH 4TH 1847 AT TROY, NEW YORK. DIED JANUARY 27, 1859 AT MACON, GEORGIA." This inscription makes visible Mary's identity as a member of a family unit, a corporeal being with ancestral roots. The rural cemetery setting "ensured that personal relationships . . . were maintained after death."[88] Significantly, the language here bluntly acknowledges reality, shunning the popular euphemism of the era; the daughter is not asleep, but literally dead.

On the reverse side of the stone, leaves cascade from either side of a large bow, creating a wreath encircling the words: LITTLE MARY, "*MARSH*." Unlike any vine that exists in nature, the leaves of the wreath are of two different types. The oak leaves that curve along one edge of the circle are met by ivy that curves along the other. Ivy is eternally green and clings to a support. In the symbolism of Victorian gravestones, ivy could suggest friendship, love, constancy, immortality, or remembrance.[89] Oak leaves suggest faith, honor, and virtue, as well as strength and endurance. A wreath could mean victory, honor, or eternal love. Thus, the plant iconography works together to create associations complementing sentimental girlhood. The inclusion of her assumed stage name reasserts Mary's public persona, while the italics and quotation marks foreground its fictive theatricality. In contrast, the typographic presentation of the word LITTLE denotes this adjective as part her name, conferring eternal childhood status. Here again, Mary is an exemplar for her times. Lynn Rainville notes that "the sentimentalization of childhood is evident in endearments such as 'Little Nellie' or 'Little Guy'" found on children's graves of the period.[90] Mary's stage persona, with its diminution, is literally set in stone; even in death, she cannot escape the character constructed for her. The actress Mary, not the

Figure 3.3. Mary Marsh's tombstone, Rose Hill Cemetery, Macon, Georgia. This side presents her simply as the daughter of Robert and Jane Guerineau. Photo by Stephanie Kachinske.

daughter, is embraced within the symbols of eternal love and remembrance.

The two sides of the gravestone are linked by a verse, typical of the era's consolation literature which, as Karen Sánchez-Eppler has pointed out, was utterly conventionalized.[91] This enormously popular genre included "obituary poems and memoirs, mourners' manuals, prayer guidebooks, hymns, and books about heaven," which, according to Ann Douglas, "inflated the importance of dying and the dead by every possible means."[92] The verse on Mary Marsh's tombstone is addressed to the "Winds of Winter." It begins on the factual side of Mary's stone, and continues under the ivy-oak wreath on the reverse. Its message is that she is happy in heaven, and tears are only

Figure 3.4. Engraved wreath on Mary Marsh's tombstone, Rose Hill Cemetery, Macon, Georgia. Photo by Stephanie Kachinske.

for those who miss her. Typically, Mary is described in both romantic and religious images. She is "Perished Beauty" (like her character in *Beauty and the Beast*), and "This Pearl," as well as "The Lost," and "The Freed from Pain." There is little that is individualistic or distinctive about this verse.

One element of Mary's grave that was not at all conventional for child graves of the time was the inclusion of a relic.[93] In religious practice, a relic is often a fragment of the body of a revered, deceased person—a sliver of bone or a clip of hair. A piece that conjures a whole, *pars pro toto*, a relic was thought to hold the holy person's presence or *praesentia*.[94] Although most relics "begin their lives as integral parts of human bodies," Peter Brown writes that a bit of clothing, or something that touched the revered person, can also serve as a relic. This type of artifact, called a "contact relic," was held to be as full of the holy person's "*praesentia* as any physical remains."[95] All such objects "serve as the privileged interfaces between a celestial realm . . . and the faithful."[96] As part of her naiad costume, Mary wore a wreath of artificial flowers. The preservation of this wreath mimicked a traditional Catholic practice of encasing relics in elegantly designed, sometimes jewel-encrusted, containers called reliquaries. Mary's wreath was enclosed in a glass case—a reliquary—and mounted on her gravestone.[97] This spiritual practice melded with what Joseph Roach has described as "the refunctioning of religious conventions into secular public intimacy" with regard to celebrities.[98] He writes how—by seeing isolated accessories "tangibly available from abstracted and elusive wholes—ordinary people can experience a spurious but vivid intimacy with the public figures they represent."[99] Mary Marsh fuses both phenomena: the sanctity of her Eva-esque persona coupled with show biz celebrity.

Unlike the inscription, which is merely a remembrance of Mary, the flower wreath is a tangible object that touched her sacred head. Mourners and fans can touch the object that touched the girl (or at least its case) and thereby make contact with not only her saintly spirit, but the heavenly realm where she dwells. Thus is the power of the sacralization of childhood. The relic remained in place for at least two decades after Mary's death, before disappearing. Whether stolen by vandals or a passionate fan desiring even closer contact with the potent artifact is impossible to know. Mary Marsh's grave stands today as testament, not only to the bifurcation of her own life, but to the nineteenth century's treatment of children, who were venerated in the ideal, but whose bodies were too often destroyed while laboring for capitalistic goals.

CHAPTER 4

CHASING AUDIENCES AND AGING OUT

Marsh's featured quartet was decimated after losing both Mary Marsh and Alfred Stewart. The corrosive public squabble over Alfred Stewart and the nightmarish images of Mary's last moments must have undermined the children's spirits. The company met its engagements in the months immediately following the accident; however, as spring turned to summer and the 1858–59 season came to an end, the floundering troupe needed a new direction. Fixing on recent recruit Louis Aldrich, who had cut his teeth on Shakespeare, Marsh cast his juvenile comedians in *Macbeth* in Mobile, Alabama.[1] This ill-conceived experiment failed, and Marsh did not repeat it. Citing their weakened popularity, the *Clipper* observed, "The Marsh Children have about played out their juvenility." With the children growing up, the paper noted Robert Marsh's efforts "to reorganize with a new party of attractions in the South and West."[2] To rebuild his troupe, R. G. Marsh needed both new strategies and new talent. In August, the group returned to their headquarters in Knightstown, Indiana, with thirteen recruits who had joined in New York. The new members filled vacancies, but none of them became prominent players.[3]

In spite of the new recruits, things went badly as the company began its fifth year; 1859–60 would be its least successful season. The company started the fall in Indiana, but by October they were doing "a miserable business" in Philadelphia.[4] Most nights they took in scarcely enough to meet expenses, and "on one or two nights not money enough in the house to pay for the gas."[5] The news grew worse, with the troupe almost slipping to amateur status when they deserted Philadelphia's National Theatre for the Cheston Street Concert Hall to give "drawing room entertainments."[6] During the week that news of John Brown's October 16 raid on Harper's Ferry moved the nation closer to civil war, the Marsh Company had to stay focused on just getting by.

During the winter, memories of Mary's death were revived by a disheartening report on the condition of Georgiana Mousely, who, along with her sister Helen, had joined the troupe in 1855.[7] Georgiana had rushed to Mary's aid on the night of the accident. Unfortunately, like mythical Creon, who tried to save his daughter from Medea's vengeance, flames quickly engulfed the would-be rescuer. A year after Mary's death, Georgiana still had not recovered from her burns.[8] In February 1860, while the Republican Party gathered in Chicago to nominate Abraham Lincoln for president, the children headed south to Macon, Georgia, the site of Mary's accident. The long-delayed installation of Mary's gravestone during their visit may have brought the children some emotional closure.[9]

From its inception, the Marsh Troupe had toured both north and south, appearing in states that would take opposite sides in the approaching civil war. In the spring of 1860, with tensions rising and the war's first battle only fourteen months away, the Marshes continued to tour the future Confederacy where audiences still craved diversion. In New Orleans, with "operas, balls, hotels, clubs, cards and horse-racing, cocking mains [*sic*], and even bull-fights" to choose from, spectators cheered the children during three weeks of good houses at Spaulding and Rogers's Amphitheatre.[10] All too soon, however, New Orleans would "abandon . . . herself, heart and soul, to the cause of the Southern Confederacy."[11] Whether political rumbling triggered unease, or the location prompted unpleasant memories of the lawsuit over Alfred Stewart, or for some other, unknowable reason, once their engagement at Spaulding and Rogers's ended, the Marsh Troupe of Juvenile Comedians left the American South, never to return.

Instead, Marsh packed up his Juvenile Comedians—now numbering thirty-seven—and headed to California. Their journey was typical of many actors who made the trek west during these years. According to Louis Aldrich, the company traveled via Panama.[12] A steamer taking them from New Orleans would have first stopped at Cuba, before heading to the isthmus to catch the interoceanic railroad. Completed in 1855, about the same time as Marsh organized his troupe, the railroad across Panama had replaced the dangerous cholera- and criminal-infested route that, just a few years earlier, had robbed a young Ulysses Grant of one-third of his regiment and actor Junius Brutus Booth of every gold cent earned in California.[13] But safety and speed didn't come cheap. The forty-seven-mile train trip cost twenty-five dollars; fortunately for R. G. Marsh, children under twelve were half price.[14] Another steamer took them up the coast to San Francisco.

Every seat in the dress circle was taken when the Marsh Children opened at the Lyceum Theatre on April 4, 1860.[15] A number of infant prodigies had appeared in California—home-grown wonders like Lotta Crabtree, Sue Robinson, and Anna Marie Quinn, as well as touring sensations like the Bateman Sisters—but there were still plenty of spectators eager to see child performers. A decade after the rush of gold-seeking Forty-Niners, California's population continued to grow. The Marsh company enjoyed three successful weeks at the Lyceum, followed by overflow houses in a string of other California cities including Stockton, Placerville, Marysville, and Sacramento. R. G. Marsh himself took to the stage as Ali Baba in *The Forty Thieves*.[16] By this time, Mary's roles had been doled out among other young actresses with varying success. The lead in *The Naiad Queen* went to "Miss Ellen," although she didn't keep it long. Black-Eyed Susan was acted by "Miss Gironflo" who had played minor roles with the company in Boston five years before.[17] "Miss Harriet" received billing in a few pieces.[18] Good support for Master George Washington Marsh in his signature role as Toodles was vital, and ably supplied by "Little Jenny Arnot," six years junior to sister Louise. Alone among the replacements, Jenny would make the role her own.

Jenny was about ten years old when the troupe first played California, but it's not clear when she joined the company.[19] From early on, the company's bills had listed a "Miss Jenny" but this could easily have been a member of the Gourlay family alternately billed as "Jennie" and "Jenny." Starting in 1860, both Jenny and Louise adopted the Arnot surname. Members of theatrical families often change their names to differentiate themselves (for example, sisters June Havoc and Gypsy Rose Lee, or Olivia de Havilland and Joan Fontaine), but apparently, a visible family connection was considered desirable for the McLaughlin/Arnot sisters. The new shared surname, emphasizing family, may have been good for business, trumpeting the values R. G. Marsh strove to project. Yet, the sisters themselves demonstrated a desire, or at least a willingness, to remain connected. As adults, Jenny and Louise lived together in New York City for a time and sometimes performed together as well. Jenny's affect, however, contrasted with that of her swashbuckling sister. Lithe and light, Jenny emanated sweetness rather than strength, but she was no amateur. One critic described the young actress as "thoroughly *au fait* in her impersonations" which she played with "ease and finish." Within a year critics labeled her "one of the most accomplished, though the youngest, member of the great dramatic family."[20] At the start of the 1860–61 season, the troupe's sixth, the company seemed to have found its fresh start.

Audiences abounded in the West, but Robert G. Marsh chose another path. Years before, when he easily could have continued touring *Uncle Tom's Cabin* with all four members of his family playing roles, just as the Howard family did, Marsh the iconoclast had followed his impulse to create "something new."[21] Now, he once again eschewed the obvious path. On August 18, 1860, Robert G. Marsh herded his machinists, his conductor, and his thirty-seven juvenile comedians on board a ship and set sail for Australia, where they would avoid the U.S. Civil War and try to move beyond the loss of their little leading lady.[22]

For English speakers, Australia was a young land. The colonizing "First Fleet" had arrived only seventy-two years earlier with its initial load of convicts and their custodians. From San Francisco, the journey to Australia took two full months on a ship of average speed.[23] The travel experiences of the Marsh Children were probably quite similar to those of other U.S. entertainers who made the long voyage during the 1850s and 1860s, including actors Joseph Jefferson,[24] Laura Keene, Edwin Booth, Lola Montez,[25] Catherine Sinclair,[26] John Drew,[27] and Joey Guggenheim,[28] "Irish comedian" Billy O'Neill,[29] circus equestrian Mlle. Zoyara,[30] and minstrel performers "Wash" Norton,[31] and Charles Backus,[32] along with many performers from the United Kingdom. What drew the show people such a long way? They came for the money.

During the 1850s rich gold deposits were discovered in many parts of Australia. The gold rush of 1851 centered around Ballarat and Bendigo in the colony of Victoria (which also includes the city of Melbourne). Over the next decade, Australia "contributed more than one-third of the world's gold output."[33] Wealth—or the hope for it—transformed the British colony. Hundreds of thousands of prospectors streamed in, tripling the non-Aboriginal population in the decade between 1851 and 1861.[34] Almost half the colonists lived in the larger towns, with populations eager for entertainment.[35] Prosperous owners of sheep-shearing estates who spent much of the year at their townhouses also helped swell cities.[36] This urban population had tremendous amounts of discretionary money, as well as the time to spend it.[37] According to Australian historian Stuart Macintyre, during the second half of the nineteenth-century, "Australians earned more and spent more than the people of the United Kingdom, the United States or any other country."[38] Theatre flourished, along with sports and other commercial recreational activities, and the Marsh Troupe did well. A commentator would later remark that the Marshes "fairly coined money" on this trip.[39] The Marsh Children's tour ultimately took more than three years, and brought the troupe its last major successes.

The Marsh Juveniles who docked in Australia differed in significant ways from the "little chits toddling about the stage" heralded by the *New York Times* five years earlier.[40] The original Marsh Troupe cohort had both grown and shrunk—each remaining child was older and taller, but they comprised a decreasing percentage of the troupe as their numbers dwindled and younger, smaller members were added. The leading players, however, were teenagers—a fact clearly obvious to Melbourne commentators who "quarrel[ed] over the title of 'children,' insisting it was 'a misnomer.'"[41] The *Clipper* correctly claimed that the oldest troupe member to land in Australia was already nineteen, an age when most people were considered adults. In England, girls could marry at thirteen.[42] In the United States the age of consent varied from ten to twelve for girls, and fourteen to fifteen for boys.[43] In this context, Miss Louise Arnot and Master Louis Aldrich could hardly mask their maturity, and indeed, both of them would fall in love and choose a mate during this trip.[44] Since Mary's death, the troupe had recentered, and these young adults were now the company's featured performers, along with Georgie, the perpetual comic.

Nevertheless, the Marsh Troupe's reputation had preceded them, and the public highly anticipated their first appearance at Melbourne's Princess Theatre. A local writer confided, "Everyone has been on the tiptoe of expectation for some time past respecting these precocities."[45] As in the United States, a number of juvenile actors and actresses stoked increasing interest in children and child performers. Most prominent was Anna Marie Quinn, who toured Australia both before and after the Marsh Troupe. In between, she crossed paths with the Marsh children in New York and Boston.[46] As a solo phenomenon, Quinn presented snippets in the style of the Bateman Sisters and Master William Betty, a common comparison. After a humble start in the California gold fields, Quinn had established "an international reputation" and been hailed as a genius during her first

Australian tour (1854–57).[47] However, Quinn's act was very different from the Marshes'. Unlike the focus on individual precocity, the Marsh Troupe presented fully produced versions of popular plays. They emphasized polished, commercial spectacle. While audiences must certainly have noted the contrast between the ages of the Marsh Troupe actors and that of the characters they portrayed, this contrast would be starker in a mixed-age company where a child such as Quinn played one character and adult actors performed the rest of the parts. Like the Marshes, Quinn was an adept and accomplished professional. Nicole Anae suggests that Quinn may have been partly responsible for "the shift toward appreciating well-trained child performers as artists."[48]Analyzing the "sheer quantity of Quinn's press, her high media visibility, and the prominence of her popularity," Anae concludes that Quinn "raised the bar for the child players who followed."[49] The Marsh Troupe met the challenge.

Four days after Americans elected Lincoln president of the United States, the Marsh Juveniles played their first show "Down Under." The company opened On November 10, 1860, with Planché's *The Brigand*, a staple of their repertoire. Sixteen-year-old Louise had the starring role. The *Clipper*'s Melbourne correspondent confirmed that the "high praises" for the troupe had "been justified." The writer particularly appreciated Louise's singing, the costumes and the incidental music. The *Melbourne Herald* found "their groupings . . . picturesque" and their stage business "wonderfully accurate."[50] The *Argus* (Melbourne) wrote of their "extraordinary success" reporting that the Princess Theatre had "not been so crowded since the days of Mr. John Drew, and the furor created by the young people bids fair to throw even that gentleman's first successes into the shade."[51]

After several months of "crowded audiences" in the colony of Victoria, the company moved north to New South Wales.[52] By July 1861, the troupe had happily settled in Sydney, described by Joseph Jefferson as a beautiful city with "tall, white stone buildings and church spires" where "parrots in the gaudiest coats of plumage fly in flocks chattering and screaming through the air."[53] At Sydney's Royal Victoria Theatre the "novelty and variety" of the juvenile troupe attracted "very respectable audiences."[54] *The Brigand* earned "enthusiastic applause."[55] Critical response confirms the fact that the troupe maintained impressive production values on tour. Reviews admired the "effect and gorgeousness" of both *Sea of Ice* and *The Naiad Queen*, although the local reviewer found *The Forty Thieves* to be "utterly destitute of either plot, incident, or humor."[56] The order of benefits bore out one writer's observation that the "great popularities" were "Miss Louise and Master Marsh."[57] Befitting their relative status, Louise received the first benefit (July 19) and Georgie Marsh the second (July 30), followed by Jenny Arnot (August 2), who also received featured billing as "Mrs. Toodles."[58]

Constant travel dominated the life of every nineteenth-century trouper, and the Marsh Children were certainly used to it, but some conditions impressed even local commentators. On one typical morning, about six months into their tour, the Marsh Troupe boarded an early train in Melbourne headed south to Geelong, about fifty miles along the Australian coast. This journey would have been taken by most entertainers hoping to capitalize on the gold rush audience. Disembarking a little before ten o'clock, the twenty-six girls and four boys, along with their "physicians, nurses, teachers, and musicians," boarded two overland coaches to complete their journey to Ballarat, about fifty-five miles inland, beyond the reach of the rail line. Before very long however, the "bottomless condition of the road" made further passage impossible and the whole troupe had to get out and "walk a considerable distance, to their intense discomfort." About midday they came up to a mail coach stuck fast in the mud, and the Americans pitched in to help. As the *Argus* reported, "The adult members of the company, opportunely, were able to lend a hand, and get the coach out of the difficulty."[59] Whether the travelers had sincerely adopted the Australian pioneering sensibility or were motivated to create good public relations, we can never be sure, but by this point, the Marsh children had undoubtedly seen a lot of mud. Then, as now, Australia was subject to El Niño/La Niña's Southern Oscillation and its cycles of heavy rainfall and drought that obliterate roads. Conditions could be primitive. Outside of the coastal areas, arid wilderness dominated most of Australia. While it was home to the Aboriginal people, the European immigrants who made up theatre audiences lived only in cities or in outposts scattered sparsely. Even the major cities "lacked sewerage" and "the primitive sanitation was noisome during the long hot summers."[60]

In August, 1861, the troupe returned to Melbourne—this time at the Theatre Royal—before heading inland again.[61] During September and October, the *Star* (Ballarat) published reports of a "very successful tour" as the Marsh Troupe wound its way through the surrounding districts, including Sandhurst and Castlemaine, before taking up residence at Ballarat's Theatre Royal in December.[62] Robert Marsh's talents as impresario and business partner are well illustrated by this stretch of the tour. As he had in the United States, Marsh linked his troupe with local events, for example, awarding the "Marsh Troupe Silver Jug" to the winner of the Champagne Stakes horse race in December 1861. Marsh had the silver vessel engraved with the names of all the Marsh players and topped by the figure of Georgie Marsh in character as Toodles.[63] Apparently Robert Marsh pleased the Australians, for the Sandhurst community presented him with a gold watch. The affection was mutual. In January, with much fanfare, the Marsh company gave "a grand complimentary benefit" to the Theatre Royal's manager, Mr. D. Symons.[64] By March, however, Mr. Symons joined the long list of Marsh's bitter ex-partners. Symons and Marsh sued each other over board and production expenses.[65] The impresario's display of dramatic flair created what one reporter called "a great field day in the County Court." Symons demanded £170, but ultimately had to pay £24 to Marsh, who had a way with judges. In every known legal battle—against Mrs. McLaughlin in St. Louis, Mrs. Stewart in New Orleans, or Mr. Symons in Ballarat—R. G. Marsh won the decision.

Back in Melbourne, Marsh set himself up as the "Sole Lessee and Manager" of "Marsh's Royal Lyceum."[66] The troupe had been successful enough to finance, and justify the creation of, a semi-permanent home on the site of the "Late Prince of Wales Theatre" on "Lonsdale, opposite the Hospital."[67] Here, Marsh flaunted his talents as skilled manager and promoter of spectacle. He augmented his company's dazzling showcase, *The Naiad Queen*, with "Pyrotechnic Displays."[68] Their dance interludes grew more outlandish, including the "highly amusing Oriental Ballet de Grotesque, or Grand Chinese Dance," performed "in real Celestial costume."[69] The troupe infused songs like "The Garibaldi Hat" with "humorous local allusions," and awarded silver goblets to champion cricket players in onstage ceremonies.[70] In October 1862 Marsh celebrated the success of the All England Eleven, an Australian cricket team, by giving the victors a complimentary benefit of *The Naiad Queen*, followed by the presentation of a "prize bat" to the two highest scorers. Marsh advertised that young Miss Louise would address the team, "in the name of the company, and on behalf of the colony of Victoria."[71] Though only a visitor, Robert Marsh was not shy in claiming to speak for the entire colony.

Marsh refreshed the company's repertory by adding recent hits from the New York stage, including *Our American Cousin*, *The Drunkard*, and *Uncle Tom's Cabin*. Tom Taylor's *Our American Cousin* had enjoyed enormous popularity since Laura Keene's 1859 production in New York, which ran for 140 consecutive performances and featured Joseph Jefferson (1829–1905) as the comic Yankee character Asa Trenchard.[72] The role became a standard vehicle for Jefferson, who played it in Melbourne at the same time as the Marsh Children. With Georgie Marsh doing a "capital miniature representation" of Jefferson's performance, the juveniles once again stood up well to adult competition, giving the veteran comedian's production "a decent run for its money."[73]

In contrast to the light comedy of *Our American Cousin*, William H. Smith's *The Drunkard* was a didactic melodrama powered by the passionate temperance movement.[74] Although marketed in Melbourne as "a new moral Temperance Drama," the play had made a sensation at its 1844 debut in Boston.[75] P. T. Barnum's 1850 production in New York garnered even greater acclaim. Marsh's production coincided with the burgeoning Australian temperance movement, which had begun two decades earlier but grew under the influence of the United States. Morality was not the play's only appeal, however. Like most popular nineteenth-century plays, *The Drunkard*'s allure was theatrical as well. Audiences were both repulsed and fascinated by the portrayal of its title character suffering from the *delirium tremens*. As Amy Hughes has demonstrated, the *delirium tremens* scene was "powerful and popular" and relied "exclusively on the actor's expertise" for its success.[76] Once again banking on Louise Arnot's talent and power, Marsh cast her in the title role of Edward Middleton and she carried the play.

Despite the worldwide popularity of *Uncle Tom's Cabin* and Mary's early success as Little Eva, the Marsh Juvenile Troupe had never performed the play. After Marsh terminated his partnership with John Ellsler in 1855, he moved onto other repertoire. Now, for the first time since the founding of the children's company, R. G. Marsh returned to the most popular play of the century, advertising a script "adapted expressly for the Marsh Troupe." While he may not have been a "moral entrepreneur," Marsh clearly aimed to cultivate the genteel audience with these plays and the announcement of matinees "for the accommodation of Schools and Families," assuring these viewers that the house would be lighted "as at night."[77] Marsh also altered the mode of production by eliminating afterpieces, and presenting these plays as full-evening entertainments in long runs. *Uncle Tom's Cabin* repeated for twenty-four nights.[78] While Marsh's original repertory may have seemed old-fashioned, these changes marked him as *au courant* with the changing economics of theatre production.

A decade earlier in Cincinnati, four members of the Marsh family had appeared with other adult actors in *Uncle Tom's Cabin*. In the Marsh Juveniles' production, only R. G. Marsh reprised his role, playing Uncle Tom "in a truthful, quiet manner."[79] Mrs. Marsh is not credited with any stage appearances on the Australian tour, or at any time after Mary's death. With Mary gone, Jenny Arnot performed a sweetly affecting rendition of Little Eva. Georgie Marsh had played Little Harry at only three or four years old. Now, twelve or thirteen and an acclaimed comic, he cross-dressed to play Topsy, the show's funniest role. Nineteen-year-old Louis Aldrich portrayed the evil slave driver, Simon Legree. True to her usual line of business, Louise cross-dressed, but in an uncommon move, she also donned blackface to enact "the haunted George Harris" as well as Legree's slave mistress, the proud and powerful Cassy.[80]

The casting of Georgie, a Caucasian boy, as Topsy, an African American girl, demonstrates how the line of business superseded gender. The local critic thought Georgie's "make up was admirable," but did not otherwise comment on the cross-dressing, finding Georgie to be "as quaint and comical a Topsy as it was possible to see."[81] Robin Bernstein has demonstrated how stage versions of *Uncle Tom's Cabin* had altered Topsy from the character in Stowe's novel. While living children are fragile, the stage plays "configured Topsy as invulnerable to pain and invited audiences to laugh at the sight of Topsy's tears."[82] Society constructed childhood as innocent, vulnerable, feminine, and, of course, white. The caricatured Topsy, a cartoon, fit none of these descriptors; race excluded her from the protected sphere. As Bernstein explains, depicting Topsy as insensate placed her outside the borders of childhood. If Topsy is neither a child nor a female, but simply a comic figure, the role slips fluidly into Georgie's line of business. Critics in Australia and New Zealand praised his hilarious performance.

In February 1863 the Marsh Troupe increased attendance by pairing their production of *Our American Cousin* with a performance by the "famous trapezian" Bartine. Of all the promotional techniques R. G. Marsh had tried over the years, this choice had the greatest permanent effect on the troupe. Bartine was a "remarkably well-formed young man, apparently of great strength, with a fine open countenance, a dark bright eye, and a bodily development that betokens immense muscular power."[83] By April, he had charmed more than the audiences and, in the words of the *Brisbane Courier*, the man on the flying trapeze had "managed to fly into the affections" of Louise, who declared her intention to marry him. Now a woman, Louise demanded dominion over her own life.

R. G. Marsh did not fight to retain her as he had in St. Louis six years earlier. As she was now "of full age and out of her time with Marsh," he had no argument, and the young couple married. Louise moved out, severing her long professional connection with R. G. Marsh, who lost the third member of his featured quartet.

A few days after Louise's exit, ten-year-old Jenny Arnot gained permission to visit her sister, but did not return. Marsh did not try to separate the sisters, but he refused permission when yet another troupe member asked to visit them. Sent to her room, this troupe member reportedly tied her bed sheets together and lowered herself out the window. Alerted by a watchman, "Mrs. Marsh ran out, and reached the street just in time to see the errant damsel received into the arms of Bartine, placed in a cab, and hurried off."[84] Thus, the Marsh Troupe lost three members, including one of its leading players. There is no record of comments from R. G. Marsh, but a news account reports that he "quietly packed up" and moved the troupe to New Zealand.

Two years earlier, prospectors had found gold in Central Otago and forty thousand hopeful colonists had poured into the South Island of New Zealand.[85] Accordingly, the Marsh Juveniles headed to Dunedin, the port of entry for gold-seekers and New Zealand's most populous region. The *Otago Daily Times* reported an "eminently successful" engagement at the Princess Theatre there with "crowded audiences" nightly, as there had been in Victoria and, earlier, in California.[86]

The troupe's enthusiastic reception in New Zealand derived from both the quality of the entertainment and the remoteness of the performance venues. For example, European settlers had arrived in Invercargill only ten years earlier, and its mainly Scottish immigrants may have found life somewhat bleak. One local writer hoped that the winter evenings might be "rendered a little less drear" by a visit from the Marsh Children, but worried because the company's advance agent had "reported somewhat unfavorably on the mud."[87] Some residents recognized their inadequate facilities. The *Otago Daily Times* wrote of the need to construct a large room for performances since Mr. Marsh was "(naturally enough) not pleased with the Masonic Hall."[88] Communities willingly accommodated the troupe's needs because, as the *Mercury* in Hobart, Tasmania, reported eagerly, the performances of the Marsh children had "excited a furor in the neighboring colonies."[89]

In spite of the glowing reports, the size of the crowds at the Princess Theatre in Dunedin surprised at least one reporter:

> [W]e did not expect such a state of things as we found at ten minutes after eight o'clock. We fought our way through a dense crowd that surrounded the entrance to the stalls . . . [and] seemed most indignant that Mr. Wolfe would not allow their money to be taken . . . although he assured them that they could not possibly get inside the house. We got to the top of the stairs leading to the dress circle; and we remained there in a crowd for nearly an hour. By dint of standing on our toes and craning our neck almost out of joint, we several times caught a momentary glimpse of the stage—but we could not manage more. We know that the audience were laughing and applauding vociferously. . . . But we cannot at present attempt any description of *The Naiad Queen*.[90]

In New Zealand, R. G. Marsh did not advertise the title player in *The Naiad Queen*, but commentators reveal that Hattie Johnson assumed the part formerly played by Louise Arnot. Hattie, remembered by one spectator as "demure," had been listed among the troupe's players for quite some time, but Marsh rarely accorded her featured billing.[91] A description of her portrayal of Queen Lurline as "coquettish or love-struck" contrasts sharply with reports of Louise's robust presence in the role.[92]

While earlier news stories reported that Jenny Arnot had stayed with her sister in Australia, other evidence suggests that she rejoined the troupe in New Zealand. A May 1863 ad for Dunedin's Princess Theatre says that "Miss Eliza" will enact Mrs. Toodles. One month later, ads for the same theatre state that "Little Jenny Arnot" will play Mrs. Toodles, "her original character with the Troupe."[93] A subsequent ad listed both a dance by "Miss Jennie" (presumably Jenny Gourlay) and an upcoming benefit for "Little Jenny" indicates that there were two girls with this name and suggests that Jenny Arnot returned to the company.[94]

In New Zealand, as he had in other places, Marsh worked to ingratiate his company with the public by aligning with local politics. He added the words "Vivat Regina" in large letters to the end of his advertisements, and the evening's performance on Queen Victoria's birthday began with a full company rendition of "God Save the Queen."[95] He won the favor of the governor, His Excellency Sir Henry Barkly, and thus advertised performances "by Vice Regal desire."[96] The wedding of Albert, Prince of Wales, provided ample opportunities to generate publicity and good feeling for the troupe. Marsh managed the exhibition of the "English Standard," reported to have been sold recently for £180 sterling and urged the public to "Be Prepared with your Flags, Banners & Transparencies," which he conveniently sold.[97] At a ceremony where two royal oaks were planted in honor of the regal couple, Marsh had the troupe sing two verses of the national anthem. They performed the anthem again at a ceremony on the marriage day, dressed "in evening costume" that attracted the admiring attention of the soldiers on parade.[98] Mr. Marsh easily adapted to local as well as imperial politics. While in New Zealand, the troupe performed a song written "in honor of the 70th regiment and *apropos* of the departure of the detachment." The *Hawk's Bay Herald* reported that when Georgie Marsh sang the last verse solo, finishing with the words, "'Put your trust in Providence, but keep your powder dry,' there was a united burst of applause such as had never before been heard within the walls."[99] R. G. Marsh expertly used children to mix politics with sentiment.

By the end of the tour in July 1863, R. G. Marsh had become an esteemed member of the Dunedin community. The *Otago Daily Times* printed an offer of a benefit in his honor, signed by over two dozen "friends desirous of testifying their appreciation of [his] many excellent qualities, not merely as an actor, but as a man foremost in every good enterprise, and respected in private as well as public life."

The troupe left Dunedin and set sail for home, but it was ninety-five days later before they reached San Francisco. According to Louis Aldrich, they stopped in Tahiti, performing for Queen Pomare IV, who walked barefoot to the playhouse. Pomare IV (1813–77), whose portrait hangs in the Bibliothèque Nationale, was a figurehead ruler in a French protectorate but held her title for fifty years.[100] Aldrich claimed the Queen was "much taken with the acting of the juveniles."[101]

In October 1863 the Marsh Troupe disembarked from their Pacific tour into the arms of Tom Maguire (1820?–96), the "Napoleon of the San Francisco Stage."[102] Maguire, born poor in New York, had followed the gold rush to California and set up businesses, running a gambling saloon and then a series of theatres. With a seemingly "occult power in judging character" and a "lavish touch," Maguire had made himself into a cultural force.[103] At Maguire's Theatre, San Franciscans welcomed the company back with three weeks of "very fine business."[104]

Commenting on their return, the *Clipper* wrote that "the principal artists retain[ed] their relative positions occupied" in their last California visit; however, the writer contradicted that clearly inaccurate statement a few sentences later by declaring, "The leading lights of the troupe are George W. Marsh, Miss Hattie and Jennie [*sic*] Arnot."[105] Hattie and Jenny had never received prominent billing during the troupe's heyday. The original leads were gone: Mary, burned to death; Alfred Stewart, off in a storm of litigation; and Louise Arnot, a married woman in Australia. Only Georgie remained.

"The Marsh troupe are 'children' no longer," announced the *Clipper*'s San Francisco correspondent.[106] A spectator who may have seen them shortly after their arrival complained of seeing, "Young girls of 17 or 18, many of them dressed as small girls of 12, which did not agree at all with their womanly development."[107] Published rumors that "some half dozen of the troupe" would secede and "enter into matrimonial engagements" proved prophetic.[108] Within weeks of landing, Louis Aldrich, a mainstay during the Pacific tour, married fellow Marsh trouper Clara Shropshire and left the company.[109] Aldrich, Shropshire, and three other Marsh children were hired into Tom Maguire's stock company as adults.[110]

Officially, the juvenile company disbanded, although the phrase "Marsh Troupe" would continue to pop up in advertisements over the next half decade, associated primarily with the Marsh family men and the Arnot women. In early 1864, the *Sacramento Daily Union* advertised a "Re-Engagement of the Marsh Troupe."[111] In addition to George Marsh, the small casts listed include only three names: Miss Katy, Miss Hattie, and Jenny Arnot. In April, George played "Diggory" in a San Francisco benefit production of *The Blacksmith of Antwerp* led by Lotta Crabtree at the Metropolitan Theatre. Lotta, born the same year as Mary Marsh, had begun her professional career about the same time but on the opposite side of North America. Nine years later, in 1864, Lotta was well established as a West Coast favorite, on her way to becoming one of the highest paid stars in the nation; she would retire a millionaire. George, just a few years younger, was billed here as "little George Marsh," although nearly a man by nineteenth-century standards.[112] There is no record that he ever worked with Lotta again.

George continued working with his father, who moved north to Canada. By the spring of 1866, Robert Guerineau Marsh had established himself in Victoria, British Columbia, where he would remain for two years as the lessee of "the New Idea." The theatre was a "plain building" that had been "converted out of an old fort of the Hudson Bay Company."[113] By May, he had done several months of successful business managing a company consisting of Tom LaFont, Jenny Arnot, Sam Ramous, "and a number of local celebrities."[114] In addition to Georgie, Jenny Arnot is the only name familiar from the juvenile troupe. A notice six months later in the *Daily Dramatic Chronicle* indicates a marginal professional status, noting that "R. G. Marsh and Jennie [*sic*] Arnot . . . occasionally assist in dramatic entertainments given by the Amateur Association.[115] In 1867, a dozen years after the founding of the Marsh Juvenile Comedians, Robert, George and Jenny assisted the amateurs in a "localized burlesque of *Shylock*" that played to a full theatre and grossed six hundred dollars.[116] Although younger than Georgie Marsh, even Little Jenny was growing up. A spectator who visited Victoria in 1868 wrote that Jenny had married "a young man in good business" and that George "still stands by the stage" as a member of his father's company.[117] Robert Guerineau Marsh was not finished yet, although the only original player left was little George, now eighteen years old.

CHAPTER 5

TOMBOYS RULE

Louise Arnot remained in Australia when the Marsh Troupe sailed to New Zealand in 1863. This text takes up her narrative, not only because she will re-enter the Marsh story, but also to avoid tacitly subscribing to the ideology of protected childhood. That mode of thinking mythologizes childhood as a state wholly separate from adulthood with clear chronological borders, and labels those who leave it as somehow disfigured or, as James Kincaid writes, extinct. An alternate view is that childhood is an oozy, chaotic continuum through which individuals necessarily proceed in irregular spurts. Philippe Ariès approvingly presents the medieval (or traditional) view of childhood as an apprenticeship for adulthood. In this model, childhood, like apprenticeship, is a transitional state whose entire goal is forward thinking, and whose value can only be judged at its culmination, based on whether the apprentice has gained the skills necessary for sustaining a livelihood. To ignore Louise Arnot's journeyman phase would be to buy into the idealized childhood paradigm. To assess her childhood career in traditional terms, it is necessary to test the effectiveness of her apprentice years in forming the master adult. Louise Arnot, at the time of her marriage, was both a journeyman adult and a journeyman actor. Her success as a woman claiming considerable agency in a patriarchal society and as an actress who continued performing regularly into her seventies illustrates the importance of the child actor/apprentice model that challenges the protected childhood ideal.

Louise Arnot's career, viewed in its totality, also provides a canvas for a discussion of several concepts or trends present in nineteenth-century theatre and culture in the United States, including the professional craft and talent of children, the tomboy, juvenile and adult cross-dressing, shifts in popular entertainment genres, and female agency.

Arnot's professional longevity serves as a testament to her early training. By the age of twelve she had the skills that equipped her for life: acting, adaptability, and resilience. Coached to be competent as a child, Arnot became a woman capable of developing and exploiting professional contacts, managing a company, and obtaining a legal divorce in a foreign country during an age when most women had limited legal rights and were often confined helplessly within the domestic sphere. While Arnot's sixty-year career was buttressed by her personal strengths, the training and structure of the Marsh Troupe provided the foundation to develop those considerable strengths. Arnot's trajectory during and after her time with the Marshes makes this clear.

Louise Arnot's childhood career demonstrates both the talent and craft that children can bring to their profession. From the company's very beginning in 1855, Louise played large roles and received featured billing—equal to or greater than that of George and Mary, the biological Marsh children. Her privileged status was justified by the response of the critics who routinely singled her out, such as a St. Louis writer who wrote that, within an excellent cast, she should receive "special merit."[1] A Boston writer enthused, "She has fire, energy and spirit in her acting."[2] A commentator in the *Los Angeles Herald* would later write that at this time Louise was "the best 'lead' in the world of her age."[3] Critics frequently observed that young Arnot had the craft of a mature actress, insisting that she played every part in a manner "creditable to a veteran stager,"[4] or that "a large number of leading ladies might take a few lessons from her."[5] At sixteen, she was "designated an accomplished actress and fully acquainted with stage business."[6] For her benefit she received, "such demonstrations of applause as have rarely vouchsafed to maturer [*sic*] performers."[7] In Australia and New Zealand Louise earned good notices and was considered one of the Marsh Troupe's major attractions, just as she had been in the United States. The *Argus* (Melbourne) reported that Louise and Georgie were the "great popularities" of the troupe.[8] Another Melbourne writer referred to her as the troupe's "leading actress" while the *Otago Daily Times* (Dunedin, New Zealand) named her the "leading favorite" of the Marsh troupe.[9] There is no record of any professional training Louise may have had before joining the troupe, but she certainly flourished under Marsh's tutelage. Her professional competence was acknowledged and respected by her contemporaries.

Louise's stage acclaim did not depend on romanticized ideals of girlhood. In the Marsh company Louise played the leading men and often villains to Mary's dainty, feminine heroines. The Batemans utilized a similar structure, placing their younger, more talented, daughter Ellen in the male roles opposite their older, prettier daughter Kate. When Mary Marsh played in *Beauty and the Beast*, her "Beast" was Louise.[10] In the farce of *Nan, the Good for Nothing*, Mary was "Nan" and Louise was "Harry Johnson." In *Black-Eyed Susan*, the title role again went to Mary while Louise enacted "William," the swashbuckling sailor and husband. Louise played Capt. Murphy Maguire in *The Serious Family* and Duke Aranza in *The Honeymoon*. And so it went. Louise's title roles were strong, heroic men in *The Brigand* and *Ingomar, the Barbarian*.[11]

Audiences were familiar with these plays and readily compared performances. For example, during the 1850s when the juvenile troupe had several long engagements at Boston's Howard Athenaeum, spectators could have seen "Louise's roles" played by a variety of grown men. The role of Claude Melnotte in *Lady of Lyons* had been played by Mr. W. Marshall (opposite Mrs. Mowatt), W. R. Goodall (opposite Miss Davenport), R. H. Sedley (opposite Anna Cruise), J. G. Hadley (opposite Laura Keene), Mr. Neafie (opposite Miss Davenport), Mr. McFarland (opposite Mrs. Farren), and Mr. J. Anderson.[12] Yet, Louise's performances were always well received. When Mr. Marsh gave a curtain speech, the Athenaeum audience "called clamorously for 'Louise,'" whose "popularity was palpably manifested."[13] A Boston critic raved, "Louise's William [in *Black-Eyed Susan*] is an extraordinarily clever performance."[14] Spectators compared her to adult performers, and critics praised her craft, rather than simply the novelty of the entertainment. Through the lens of the antebellum definition of childhood, Louise was an adept professional artist.

Gender in children is not clearly marked, and the theatre has often made use of children's androgyny. The most familiar example of this practice is seen in boy apprentices who played Shakespeare's women. In the 1850s a circus entrepreneur/promoter gained attention by costuming and billing his young daredevil-riding protégé as a Mademoiselle, although it was quickly an open secret that Mademoiselle was actually Monsieur Omar Kingsley.[15] Blackface minstrel troupes regularly included a cross-dressed man as a "yellow gal" singer. Most cross-dressed actors in the nineteenth century, however, were female. The convention of cross-dressing was "at its peak on the American stage in terms of the practice's critical acceptance and its audience appeal."[16]

Many of the young girls who made their names in breeches roles felt ambivalent about impersonating men in an age that glorified femininity. Ellen Bateman, born the same year as Louise Arnot, earned most of her renown playing powerful men like Richard III and Macbeth. In spite of significant critical praise and a strong family tradition, Bateman chose not to pursue an adult career, retiring at age twelve. Perhaps the onset or approach of menarche made the continued suppression of girlhood uncomfortable. Amy Roselle and Marie Wilton, British actresses noted for playing breeches roles as children prior to adult stage careers, both had reservations about this experience. Marie Wilton "complained to her mother about her continued success in boys' roles."[17] Roselle, born one decade after Louise, "particularly loathed" playing boys' parts; "I think it was partly because I often had to wear a boy's dress," she told an interviewer.[18] Videotaped discussion between two former child actresses in the late twentieth century, Jeannie Russell, who played Margaret on the *Dennis the Menace* television show (1959–63), and Alison Arngrim, who played Millie on *Little House on the Prairie* (1974–81), revealed similar discomfort. Both actresses talked about their childhood experiences playing characters that did not fit the feminine ideal.[19] While neither played a male, each found it painful to represent a polar opposite of idealized sweetness while developing a personal female identity offstage. Clearly, there are many significant differences between the nineteenth and twentieth centuries, and playing a tomboy or a pest is not the same as portraying a male, but both eras idealized womanhood, girlhood, and femininity. Indeed, demure purity and perfection were part of the appeal of child actresses like Mary Marsh and Kate Bateman, but their costars, Louise and Ellen, shared no part of this identity. Ellen Bateman's early retirement may be partly attributable to the discomfort described by other cross-dressing girl actresses. Louise Arnot, who played "barbarians" and "brigands," has not left us any reflections about her experiences in breeches roles. It's impossible to know the options she faced in 1857 (or what job her mother might have arranged if the abduction had succeeded), but on the verge of puberty at age thirteen, Arnot made a conscious choice to continue playing men for Marsh.

Much has been written about the purpose and reception of nineteenth-century cross-dressed performances by actresses—adults as well as children. Among the multiple factors complicating this question, the age of the performer is certainly paramount. Ellen Bateman portrayed Richard III with her tiny, prepubescent body draped in thick, ermine robes, her face often blotted with a fake mustache or goatee. It seems unlikely that many spectators would have eroticized the body under the robe, as a few scholars have argued.[20] Images of Clara Fisher (1811–98) and Anna Marie Quinn in the same role look similar.[21] Jim Davis, acknowledging the craft of the young actresses, has argued that spectators who projected "their own fantasies or desires" upon cross-dressed child actresses may have mistaken "precocity embedded in premature adulthood, social maturity, and professionalism for sexuality, even though this was neither acknowledged nor intended by the performer."[22] These girl performers were mature and professional, qualities some spectators do not readily connect with girls. In contrast, Adah Isaacs Menken (1835?–68), who assumed her first breeches roles when she was around twenty-five years old, deliberately invited the sensual gaze, posing as Mazeppa or sailor William in *Black-Eyed Susan*.[23] However, Charlotte Cushman (1816–76), one of the most prominent cross-dressing actresses of the era, was entirely different. Her male characters radiated masculine strength rather than female sensuality. As Lisa Merrill and others have shown, Cushman's cross-dressing may have been her most natural role.[24] Both Menken and Cushman began cross-dressing as adults, whereas Louise performed in male clothing both as a child and during her early years as an adult performer.

The eroticization that often defined cross-dressing is notably absent from the framing and reception of Arnot's roles. Discussion of her legs, figure, and alluring appeal is virtually nonexistent in all extant criticism. There is very little overlap between Louise's repertory and those roles Elizabeth Reitz Mullenix has catalogued as most commonly played by breeches actresses.[25] This may be one reason that Louise generally escaped the harsh or dismissive comments that Mullenix reports were often targeted at cross-dressing actresses.[26]

Accounts of Arnot's acting consistently emphasize her power on stage; even when playing women, she radiated authority, distinguishing herself, for example, as a female sovereign. At the St. Louis Theatre, young Arnot "looked the Queen of the Naiads and performed as the Queen of the stage."[27] In Boston, "Louise play[ed] the queen as well as it need be played" and "'marshal[ed] her clan' with a precision and tact which might be envied by any young officer."[28] As a teenager, Arnot took on new breeches roles such as King Arthur, Alessandro Massaroni, and the title character in *The*

Drunkard, a role that several adult male actors had leveraged "as a way to advance significantly in their profession."[29] Australian and New Zealand audiences responded positively to Louise's cross-dressed performances in these powerful and demanding roles. In Sydney, her performance as Claude Melnotte elicited "unbounded admiration."[30] As an adult, however, Louise abandoned breeches roles after her twenties, although her career extended several more decades.

Cross-dressing has sometimes been adopted by performers animated by same-sex sexual desire. Scholars have argued that knowledge of the role of same-sex sexual desire in actors' lives and performances is central to understanding their historical contributions and theatrical careers.[31] Arnot's cross-dressing and descriptions of her acting prompt examination. She did not leave any private papers, and the visual record of her life is slight. There are no images of her as a child, aside from the 1857 collective sketch of the "Marsh Children" (see figure 1.1). In extant adult photos, she poses unsmilingly with arms crossed or akimbo, dressed as a queen or an ancient Roman. Arnot is womanly rather than pretty, and her broad shoulders and expressive eyes communicate strength. While biographical information is scant, there do not seem to be any "signs of concealment or erasure" in the historical record.[32] Arnot did not seem to cultivate a circle of female companions in the manner of other famous nineteenth-century cross-dressing performers. Instead, she married three men and raised a daughter, continually entwining personal and professional relationships. Rather than a personal expression of her sexuality, Arnot's cross-dressing was a function of Marsh's theatrical needs.

The initial assignment of Louise's line of business is probably attributable to a single physical feature, "a deep contralto voice of the most astonishing power."[33] This trait—along with the fact that the manager's daughter was precast as the troupe's leading lady—placed eleven-year-old Louise in breeches. The roles seemed to suit her well, however; according to the *Clipper*, Louise skillfully managed her voice to "closely resemble the other sex."[34] Thirty years later, reviewers still remarked on her "masculine baritone voice."[35] While Louise clearly had a naturally deep voice, as a consummate professional, she probably accentuated her masculinity by speaking primarily in her lower register (or chest voice). The nineteenth century had an imperfect understanding of the voice, but as several critics remarked on probable damage, it's possible that Louise may have pushed from her throat when projecting to large houses. When Louise was

Figure 5.1. Louise Arnot as an adult actress in ancient period costume. TCS 2, Harvard Theatre Collection, Houghton Library, Harvard University.

twenty-three, one critic reported that her voice had not recovered from the "injury done . . . by her too early training."[36] A writer for the *Argus* said her voice sounded "artificial" and "by no means pleasant to listen to."[37] Viewing her career in its totality, a much later commentator concluded, "Louise Arnott [*sic*] ruined her voice by excessive use, and for that reason did not, when she grew to womanhood, attain anything like the distinction in the theatre to which her early promise seemed to entitle her."[38] Like other trades, childhood apprenticeships in theatre did have the potential to cause harm. While Louise probably had a much more vibrant career than a protected childhood would have given, it is also clear that too much use may have damaged her still-developing vocal system.

Louise Arnot's swashbuckling childhood persona may seem like the antithesis of Victorian girlhood, but the audacious or rebellious girl appeared frequently in nineteenth-century American theatre, art, and popular fiction.[39] Susan Burns writes that the "presence of the nineteenth-century tomboy in life and art is beyond dispute."[40] Lithographs and engravings by Lilly Martin Spenser published during the 1850s and 1860s frequently depicted female mischief makers. Eastman Johnson's paintings from the 1870s show girls climbing in haylofts or ice skating. Jo March, the heroine of Louisa May Alcott's *Little Women* (1868), is rough and strong and loves boys' games. Similar traits are seen in the lead characters of novels by Mary J. Holmes (*Meadow Brook*, 1869) and Susan Coolidge (*What Katy Did*, 1872). Anne Scott MacLeod found counterparts of these imagined girls in the autobiographies of women who grew up in the nineteenth-century United States before 1875.[41] Many of these women recalled an "unfettered and vigorous" outdoor life.[42] As girls, they enjoyed "physical and psychic freedom." Given the chance, this type of adventurous girl would certainly have identified with Arnot's audacious characterizations.

For most nineteenth-century girls, however, impending womanhood cut short the days of free-spirited romping. MacLeod writes that the girlhood freedom enjoyed by her subjects was "unmatched by anything in their later life."[43] MacLeod calls this the "Caddie Woodlawn Syndrome," after the title character of a novel set in the 1860s. Caddie Woodlawn resists the pressure to give up the freedoms of girlhood and accept her inevitable imprisonment in a woman's sphere.[44] Such resistance or ambivalence is seen in many of the fictional heroines of the period and depicted in paintings such as Johnson's *The Party Dress* (1872) or Eakins's *Elizabeth Cromwell with a Dog* (c. 1871). These works acknowledge the loss of freedom that maturity brought to most nineteenth-century girls.[45] Unlike her contemporaries, Louise Arnot's ascent to adulthood did not abruptly curtail her freedom. Because her childhood training equipped her with both confidence and skills, she maintained her autonomy as an adult.

After her marriage, Louise left the Marsh Troupe to be with her new husband, the daring Bartine, a master of both trapeze and slack rope, and, from contemporaneous reports, a handsome and ambitious man proficient at self-promotion. One news writer declared "that the man is more than a mere acrobat—in fact, that he is not deficient of good manners and education."[46] In Australia advertisements, Bartine likened his own performance to that of Charles Blondin, the French acrobat who crossed Niagara Falls on a tightrope in 1859.[47] The similarity is exaggerated, given that Bartine performed indoors and descriptions of his act more closely resemble a slightly simplified version of William Hanlon's "Zampillaerostation" than Blondin's waterfalls exploit.[48] A witness in Sydney described his task: "Reaching a stand at the extreme end of the stage from the upper tier of boxes, by a series of flying springs or leaps, aided only by three sets of cords rigged at equi-distance from the starting point to the goal."[49] The configuration of William Hanlon's apparatus was similar, but Hanlon began atop a fifty-foot-high pillar and somersaulted between the trapezes. While Mark Cosdon writes that the Zampillaerostation was "widely thought to be the nineteenth-century's most daring aerial feat," Australian audiences seemed sufficiently thrilled by the danger Bartine courted.[50] In smaller venues, Bartine eliminated the trapezes and walked "on a single wire from the back of the stage to the gallery."[51]

Following her marriage, Louise Arnot launched her independent career in New Zealand in July 1863. Her success as an adult actress testifies to the skills she attained as a child, as well as to her personal fortitude and versatility. She began moderately, appearing in a benefit production of Tobin's *The Honeymoon*. Louise took the small role of Rolands rather the major role of Duke Aranza that she performed in the Marsh productions.[52] During her marriage, Arnot often performed on the same bill with her husband in the type of varied program typical of the time. For example, a benefit for Bartine at Dunedin's Princess Theatre in 1863 included acrobatics, Bulwer Lytton's *Richelieu*, and a poetry recital. Bartine did his slack rope routine with "grace and daring" while Arnot performed the breeches role of De Maupras in *Richelieu*.[53] On this occasion, Louise's performance was met with the disapproval of the local critic, dismayed that she would attempt "such a part" with the adult company. While acknowledging her talent and prior success with the Marsh troupe, the writer for the *Otago Daily Times* found the effect of the cross-dressing "unpleasant, because unnatural in the extreme."[54] Although Dunedin served as a busy cultural center, the critic's desire for verisimilitude could indicate unfamiliarity with the convention of cross-dressing. It could also signal a shift in reactions to cross-dressed performers—even among spectators accustomed to the convention—that occurred during the 1860s.

One year later, after "a temporary absence from the stage," Louise reassumed her career in Sydney. The absence was likely due to the birth of a daughter, Jennie Bartine, who is listed in the 1870 U.S. census as age six, born in Australia.[55] Louise appeared in Sydney with a "small but most effective dramatic company" at the Royal Victoria. Apparently undaunted by the New Zealander's prior disapproval, Louise performed one of her old breeches roles—William in *Black-Eyed Susan*—and received positive notice.[56] With the same company, she played two characters in *The Bottle, Or, The Drunkard's Doom*, after which Bartine did his feat of walking on a single wire "from the back of the stage to the gallery."[57] Now twenty years old and clearly a grown woman, her assumption of male clothing could have had erotic appeal, but contemporary notices indicate that she played against that possibility. None is suggested by the review, which praises her performance of William as "replete with dramatic feeling and intensity," but makes no mention of her appearance.[58]

Louise remained in Sydney for the last two months of 1864, but she switched back to women's parts and moved to the Prince of Wales Theatre. Here she played new roles in plays never produced by the Marsh Juveniles, appearing as Oceania in *Metamora* and Desdemona in *Othello*. Unfortunately, there is no extant critical comment on these performances; however, Arnot's comic abilities were praised as Mrs. O'Trot in *Ireland as It Was* and Columbine in the Christmas pantomime.[59] Comic Irish women became a mainstay of Arnot's late career, suggesting that she had profited from her close contact with "Irish comedian" Alfred Stewart.

The Price of Wales company also performed *Lady of Lyons*. The reviewer mentions no role for Louise, although as a child she won kudos playing Claude Melnotte. It must have been frustrating to watch her new colleague, Mr. Allen, play the role in a manner "scarcely above mediocrity."[60] She left that company shortly thereafter and six months later joined another cast of *Lady of Lyons* at Mason's Theatre in Brisbane. Here, while

Louise played the minor role of the Widow, at least Mr. Younge, the actor who played Claude Melnotte, "represented it admirably."[61] At the close of the engagement, Louise made arrangements to present the play again at the same theatre, finally reclaiming her old part of Claude Melnotte. She made a "great hit" and "a very large audience stamped an approval" of her acting.[62] Emboldened perhaps, she next revisited another of her old signature roles, playing Don Caesar de Bazin "to perfection."[63] Australian audiences praised the cross-dressed twenty-two-year-old actress in the same roles she had played a decade earlier. For her benefit in Brisbane's Victoria Theatre, Arnot chose *The Rough Diamond*, another Marsh standby.[64] In 1867 she took on *Mazeppa*. The *Argus* noted that Menken's success in the play had inspired a number of revivals, but made no critical comment on Arnot's portrayal, merely noting that she'd "sustained the part of the hero" in this "novelty."[65]

Louise continued to intersperse cross-dressed roles with her old and new female repertory, even dancing an occasional hornpipe.[66] In Boucicault's *Grimaldi*, she played "an accomplished actress, the worshipped of London loungers and acted, as usual, very charmingly."[67] One of her biggest artistic stretches might have been playing ingénue leads in plays like Foote's comedy *The Liar*, produced at the Haymarket in August 1867. The plot concerns the complications that ensue when an heiress pretends to be her own best friend in order to avoid marrying the man her father intends. The lightweight intrigue and "sparkling and brilliant" dialogue of this sort of comedy were far removed from the language of queens or brigands. It was in this role that Louise's voice was criticized as suffering from injury due to too-early training.[68] It may be that the strain detected by the spectator was the result of her efforts to force her naturally low, masculine voice to sound sweetly feminine in the unaccustomed style of the comedy.

Louise may also have felt out of place in the Haymarket's *Rumplestiltskin*. Australian British audiences loved Christmas pantomimes, but Louise was not native to the tradition, and these plays were far different from the fairy extravaganzas of her youth. She was cast once again as the love interest, Princess Superba, to whom the king wished to marry his "scapegrace son Prince Poppet," played by Miss Alice Wiseman.[69] Louise, who had spent most of her career as the cross-dresser, now played the female role opposite a cross-dressed actress. The production also included "twenty little children dressed as sailors," who might have been young Louise Arnots as they "danced hornpipes and went through cutlass exercises with great gravity." It would have been easy to project herself into any number of roles other than the one she was playing.

Arnot accomplished everything on her own. Clearly confident in her own abilities, Arnot moved from colony to colony and from company to company, reclaiming and enlarging her repertoire. Comments about Louise during this period were generally quite positive, reflecting the high esteem she had earned as a professional with the Marsh Troupe. When she joined Mr. Mason's Dramatic Company in 1865, the *Brisbane Courier* called her "a most talented and clever actress," and congratulated the manager on the acquisition of such an "accomplished artiste."[70] When she took a benefit in Brisbane in 1866, the same paper predicted large attendance because she was "well-known to the people of Brisbane as a clever and deserving actress, and one of the best members of the present company."[71] The *Argus* predicted she would be a "very useful addition" when she joined that city's Haymarket Company in 1867.[72] The following year, Arnot starred with Mr. Walter T. Airey in a "song-and-dance show" that spent six weeks touring Western Australia, with stops in "Perth, Fremantle, Guildford and York."[73] The *Perth Inquirer* declared, "Miss Louise Arnot has earned for herself the reputation of a first class comedienne" and claimed that "her name alone" was sufficient guarantee of superior entertainment.[74]

While Louise Arnot's professional life was successful during this period, her personal life erupted. Bartine was unhappy with the interaction between his wife and some gentlemen who, while "on a visit to the colony," were sitting in the "Prince's suite" at the Haymarket Theatre on the last Saturday of 1867.[75] Monday morning, Mrs. Bartine—as she was referred to in all the news coverage—swore out a complaint against her jealous spouse for threatening her life. Bartine was arrested, though eventually released on his own recognizance. Nineteenth-century men generally had more rights than women. The Australian historian Stuart Macintyre writes of the "continuing legal and economic imbalance between the sexes" during this period and laws that "provided few opportunities for [a wife] to escape an oppressive husband."[76] It seems, however, that Mrs. Bartine obtained a divorce, because after this point, there were no more joint appearances. Perhaps these events explain Arnot's willingness to undertake a tour to the wilds of Western Australia about this time, where, according to one writer, residents had never before had "the pleasure of welcoming a 'troupe' of actors" to their city.[77] She had handled the crisis with courage and competence. Perhaps, as some commentators have suggested, the experience of

Figure 5.2. Louise Arnot dressed in a queen's costume. TCS 2, Harvard Theatre Collection, Houghton Library, Harvard University.

wearing men's clothes somehow endowed her with the independence and competence nominally the province of men.

Louise Arnot returned to the United States in 1869, a twenty-five-year-old mother with her best stage work behind her. By this time, Robert G. Marsh had given up his theatre in British Columbia and was back in San Francisco with his loyal son George. Arnot repartnered with her old associates almost immediately.[78] Surely, Robert Marsh had created a positive experience for the child actress and not oppressed or exploited her. The independent young woman, like the twelve-year-old girl, chose to align with Marsh, although as an adult she now received separate billing.[79] The play was *American Ladies Seen through the English EyeGlass*, written in a "puerile style" according to the local critic, who allowed that Louise managed her part very well. Or, as another writer put it, "the author makes her say a lot of stupid stuff but she manages to make the people laugh."[80] Yet once again, her voice was the issue for one critic, who griped, "Miss Arnot has the false intonation of voice common to all 'infant prodigies,' with a very pronounced style of acting."[81] In the eyes of some spectators, Louise had not surmounted her classification as a child performer.

The February–March engagement at the New Alhambra Theatre also included *The Irresistibles* and *Toodles* from the old Marsh Troupe repertoire. In these pieces, Georgie played the same roles he had done in Boston during the 1850s. Louise took on roles previously performed by Little Mary Marsh and, later, by Louise's sister, Little Jenny Arnot. While the *Daily Morning Chronicle* enjoyed Georgie's performance, it made no mention of Louise, who was probably miscast.[82] Reunited after a six-year separation and immersed in a play from their youth, the feelings of these two young actors can only be imagined.

The company's name still seemed to have some value for at least one local critic who proclaimed, "The management has exhibited great enterprise in engaging the Marsh troupe as an attraction."[83] Ever the promoter, Marsh employed a number of his customarily effective devices. He tied into local interests by making up "in imitation of a well-known politician."[84] He exploited ethnic humor by casting George as a Chinese servant, and he featured a "Corps de Ballet of 20 Young Ladies, in Military Evolutions." Hiring "young ladies" instead of girls, it looked as though R. G. Marsh may have intended to reboot his old ideas with an adult company.

A month later in Nevada, Georgie and Louise were still working together, but there was no mention of the Marsh Troupe. Hired as individuals in a company led by Annette Ince and Harry Edwards, they performed *Love's Sacrifice*, *Ion*, and *Mary, Queen of Scots*.[85] The casting indicates that both young performers had "graduated" to independent adulthood. By August 1869, however, Louise and George had gone separate ways and would not work together again. Georgie Marsh's story is taken up in chapter 6.

Meanwhile, Louise Arnot relaunched herself on the American stage, just as she had relaunched her career in Australia following childbirth. Louise found employment in Sacramento, a theatre-loving town. Sacramento was the site of the "first complete theatrical performance in California" back in 1849 at the beginning of the gold rush.[86] Playhouses, considered as essential as saloons, were among the first public buildings erected there.[87] Now, twenty years later, Sacramento was an established center for performance, and the jumping-off point for a circuit of mining towns to the north.[88] Tom Maguire managed the city's Metropolitan Theatre as well as multiple venues along the circuit. Louise may have been helped by Marsh alumnus Louis Aldrich, now a well-established member of Tom Maguire's stock company.

Louise was featured at the Metropolitan Theatre along with Sue Robinson, supporting the low comedian M. W. Leffingwell in a "short season of comedy, burlesque and extravaganza."[89] Sue Robinson and Louise worked well together, perhaps because they had trod similar paths. Robinson had begun her childhood career even younger than Louise, dancing in California's gold mining camps described by George MacMinn. One of the first of the many little girl performers termed "Fairy Stars," Robinson later moved to the legitimate stage and was thought "a very gifted woman."[90] "An Old Playgoer" recalled that she could sing "operatic music with a verve that was almost incredible." Like Arnot, Robinson had a young child to support. Between 1860 and 1866, Robinson had reportedly earned over eighty thousand dollars, but all of it had been gambled away by an abusive husband.[91] Robinson's domestic trouble, a motif common in nineteenth-century melodrama and fiction, as well as twentieth-century tropes about child actors, accentuates the fortitude and independence of Arnot, who had refused to be victimized by a husband.

Arnot's work continued to earn praise. The Leffingwell company opened with a parody of *Cinderella* in which Louise played Prince Pofetti; Robinson was Dandina, Katy Wilson was Cinderella, and Leffingwell was "the Gushing Clorinda." The local critic felt that "much of the success" of the piece "resulted from the superior impersonations" of the three supporting women.[92] Leffingwell, later remembered as "a great comic, though not a great actor," took his *Cinderella* across the nation to Philadelphia's Walnut Street Theatre, but the three women stayed on in Sacramento.[93]

For *Cinderella*, Louise was back in breeches—or perhaps tights. Referring to Leffingwell's production, Andrew Davis points out that burlesques of this type were not known for sexual connotations, but rather were simple parodies, written in rhyme and heavily reliant on "punning humor, dancing, and musical parodies set to popular songs."[94] That tradition was shifting, however, due largely to performances by Lydia Thompson (1836–1908) and her British Blondes. While Arnot was starting *Cinderella* in California, Thompson was just winding up an astonishing ten-month run at Wood's Theatre in New York City. Thompson had combined her talents as a singer and comedian with daring costuming and clever business strategies to transmogrify old-fashioned burlesque, virtually creating the modern "leg show." The hit of Thompson's repertory was *Ixion*, "a typical, if top-rank, example of the theatrical burlesque of the early Victorian era."[95] Using a mash-up of Greek and Roman gods, the plot involved a human king, played by Thompson, who drew Zeus's ire by flirting with the god's wife. Thompson's production transformed burlesque in America and with it the convention of cross-dressing. Elizabeth Reix Mullenix has argued that it was the "institutionalization of Thompsonian burlesque" that "changed the performance culture" and "altered critical perceptions of the cross-dressed actress."[96] After this period, it was impossible for cross-dressing to appear sexually neutral.

On August 16 Lydia Thompson began an East Coast tour that featured *Ixion* at every stop.[97] Three weeks later, on September 6, 1869, Sue Robinson, Louise Arnot, and Katie [*sic*] Wilson opened in *Ixion* at the Metropolitan Theatre in Sacramento; they would play it in repertory for the rest of the month.[98] Robinson played the Lydia Thompson role while Louise had second billing as Mercury. The timing of this production clearly indicates Maguire's intention to capitalize on the success of the British Blondes, but it is not clear that the costuming or staging of his production was in the Thompsonian mode. The production seems to have drawn very little attention.[99] The theatre writer for the *Sacramento Daily Union* made no qualitative comments about any of the performances, although he did support a joint benefit for Arnot and Robinson at the end of the run. "These ladies have used their utmost exertions to please Sacramento audiences and have been the main attractions of the company," he wrote.[100] Yet, the same column had expressed discomfort with cross-dressed performances by both Arnot and Robinson in other pieces. Robinson had tried the feat of enacting the title twins of *The Corsican Brothers*.[101] The reviewer groused that she "scarcely looked the characters" and did only "as well as ladies generally do when they assume masculine roles." Similarly, praise for Louise in *Lady of Lyons* seemed grudging. "Louise Arnot as Claude [Melnotte] could not, of course, be expected to look the character to perfection, but she certainly read finely, and acted admirably."[102] Mullenix has suggested that in cross-dressed performance, "verisimilitude was not always the central casting requirement."[103] Yet, it seems that the (assumed male) reviewer didn't quite know what to make of the cross-dressed actresses. His comment echoed that of the New Zealand commentator who had complained six years earlier that Louise's performance was "unnatural." There is no suggestion of the appreciative wink that lurks in most positive reviews of cross-dressers such as Lydia Thompson and Adah Isaacs Menken. These performers actively cultivated sexually charged responses. The lack of attention drawn by Arnot and Robinson may indicate that they did not seek or evoke erotic reactions.

Two years later, in 1871, Arnot appeared with Lydia Thompson. Arnot could not appear in this troupe without adapting to the new style of sexualized cross-dressing. Both Louise and her sister Jenny received praise for their performances in Thompson's production of *Lurline*. "Jenny Arnot as Lady Una and Louise Arnot as Count Calmanco were captivating."[104] In *Lydia Thompson: Queen of Burlesque*, Kurt Gänzl reports that the troupe generally traveled with "just eight performers, to be supplemented at each stop by members of the local stock company."[105] It is not clear whether Arnot was an integral troupe member or simply local support; however, an enthusiastic announcement in the *Memphis Daily Appeal* stated that the cast "list embraces Miss Thompson and stars of scarcely less magnitude."[106] Among the "stars," Louise Arnot received first mention, followed by Eliza Weatherby [*sic*], Jennie [*sic*] Arnot, Fanny Wheatleigh, and eight others. According to Gänzl, Eliza Weathersby performed featured roles with the Thompson troupe for years, even substituting for Lydia herself. Weathersby was "Lydia's most effective supporting 'blonde.'"[107] The placement of Louise Arnot's name ahead of Weathersby's certainly argues that Arnot had become an integral member of Thompson's troupe. But whether the Memphis appearance was a brief experiment or the inauguration of a new phase in Arnot's career, any performance with Thompson would have mandated refashioning Arnot's style to suit the tastes of modern burlesque. The old tomboy would have had to dress and move as a sexually alluring woman.

After parting from Lydia Thompson's troupe, Arnot worked steadily during the early 1870s. She briefly managed her own company, the "Louise Arnot Troupe," reportedly drawing full audiences during her time in Victoria, British Columbia, in March 1870.[108] There's a record of an appearance with her sister Jenny in Buffalo the same year.[109] The sisters also appeared together in burlesque in Memphis in 1871. Louise was dubbed a "favorite" during stints at DeBar's St. Louis Opera House in 1872, 1873, and 1874.[110] She played one of Shakespeare's *Merry Wives of Windsor* in Missouri in 1874.[111] These disparate locations and genres demonstrate the itinerant life of a dedicated craftsperson taking the best available parts, not the coherent trajectory that a leading star could commandeer. Tracing Arnot's long path helps us see what life was like for an ordinary theatre practitioner.

In 1870 T. Allston Brown published his *History of the American Stage*, which stated that Louise Arnot was "now the wife of Australian circus manager, John Wilson."[112] Brown's reliability on this point is strengthened by his direct link to the Marsh Troupe. His wife Fanny Beckley (1842–99) performed with the juvenile company in its early years.[113] The *Clipper* would also claim that Arnot and Wilson were married about this time, but Arnot and Wilson are not listed together in the 1870 U.S. Census.[114] That document actually includes two entries for Louise, both in New York City with her sister Jenny and her six-year-old daughter. Apparently Louise moved during the long period in which the survey was in process, so the census counted her in June and then again in December. According to the June report, there were four females living in her household in the city's nineteenth district. All four are listed as actresses. According to a December report, Louise was living in the eighteenth district with just her sister and daughter.[115]

June Record	**December Record**
Louise Arnot, aged 26, head of household	Louise Arnot, aged 26, head of household
Jane Arnot, 26	Jennie Arnot, 20
Jane Bartine, 6, born in Australia	Jennie Barnot [*sic*], 6, born in Australia
Mary Bartine, 49	

The handwriting in both reports is quite clear, but there are some obvious, although easily explainable, errors. Actress "Jane Arnot, 26" in the June report is probably meant to be "Jennie Arnot, 20" as listed in December. And whether her first name was Jane or Jennie, the Australian-born six-year-old girl in both reports must certainly be the daughter Louise conceived with Bartine, an odd name easily misunderstood by a note-taker. (As an adult, Louise's daughter appeared onstage as Jennie Bartine.)[116] The mystery is forty-nine-year-old Mary Bartine, who was part of the household in the summer, but gone before Christmas. The obvious supposition is that Bartine's mother had joined her daughter-in-law but, while grandmothers can be quite devoted, few women bring their mothers-in-law halfway around the world to live with them following a divorce, only to lose them six months later. John Wilson, Louise's supposed husband in 1870, is absent and Louise heads an all-female household.

Beginning in 1875, when Louise turned thirty-one, there is an eleven-year gap, during which only a single record of performance has been found. It is entirely possible that Arnot was traveling with her husband during these years. John Wilson was a Scottish butcher-turned-American-circus-owner who toured all over the world. A "man of great perseverance and energy and a better loser could hardly be found," according to one journalist. "Disagreeably notorious . . . shrewd, smooth, and oily, and . . . very hard to beat," according to another.[117] Arnot and Wilson may have crossed paths in Australia as early as 1866 when Wilson's Circus played there and she had just divorced the trapeze artist.[118] About 1875, Wilson embarked on another long international tour that included Australia, New Zealand, China, and India. Arnot may have taken a hiatus from performing to raise her daughter and travel with the circus manager. Arnot is not listed in the 1880 U.S. Census, but her acting career picks up again in 1886, shortly after the death of John Wilson.

While Louise Arnot's career was in abeyance, her old scene partner, Louis Aldrich, advanced to star status. Having earned respect during a decade with Boston and Philadelphia stock companies, he achieved national fame with *The Danites* in 1876.[119] Aldrich followed this New York and touring success with *My Partner*, which he toured as a star vehicle for six years, becoming the most renowned of all the Marsh children.[120] The prestige accompanying Aldrich's wealth and fame involved him in some contentious public discussions about child actors.

Professional child performers first became the target of protective legislation during the 1870s, although it would be decades before any consensus would be reached about appropriate norms. In New York State, Elbridge Gerry, a cofounder of the Society for the Prevention of Cruelty to Children, successfully lobbied for the passage of 1876's Act to Prevent and Punish Wrongs to Children. Gerry used this law to protect children performing as street musicians, in circuses, traveling shows, and even on Broadway from both real and exaggerated dangers.[121] While some former child actors like Joseph Jefferson actively opposed any protective legislation, Louis Aldrich advocated an odd compromise that would have put the Marsh Juveniles out of business. Addressing the New York State Senate committee in 1897, Aldrich argued that children should be allowed to act legitimate speaking roles (as he had), but agreed with Gerry and the SPCC that the State should bar children from singing or dancing on stage.[122] The California Civil Code passed in 1872 also focused on child workers; however, as Staenberg and Stuart have pointed out, "There was nothing in this statute that sought to offer minors any protection from exploitation." The law stripped away the right of minors to disaffirm contracts made by them or on their behalf.[123] Most other states would not begin to regulate child performers as laborers until after the turn of the century. As late as 1938, with the passage of the Federal Fair Labor Standards Act, basic protections afforded other child workers still exempted young actors. In the second decade of the twenty-first century, government regulation and protection of juvenile performers remains a patchwork of unenforced inconsistency. Louise Arnot's views on child actor protection laws are not part of the public record.

In the mid-1880s, as Arnot hit her forties, her independence and audacity were again on display. She toured as a star attraction, "Supported by her own Excellent Company."[124] Despite the proud billing, however, her status had declined. When she had headlined for the Marsh Troupe, admission cost a dollar a ticket. During this period, Arnot made many appearances at the Dime Museum in Washington, D.C., where spectators paid only ten cents. In these lower-class venues she utilized new repertoire and hyperbolic advertising. In December 1885, an ad in the *National Republican* boasted of "A Glorious Success!"[125] The following year the same paper acclaimed the forty-two-year-old Arnot "America's Brilliant Young Actress."[126] She now worked, apparently, "Under the control of the manager of the Barnum Show."[127] In addition to paid advertising, Arnot also reaped praise from the *Washington Critic*, who termed her "one of the brightest little women on the stage" and "an actress of most winning ways."[128]

Although the venues were not first class, Arnot was comfortable enough to contemplate retirement. In 1888, she purchased "a beautiful farm in Chester County, PA."[129] And then she kept on working. Arnot finally banished the old Marsh pieces from her repertoire. Instead, she copied a Lotta Crabtree technique as a protean comedian, playing five different characters in a single piece, such as *The Little Detective*.[130] She took on *Leah, the Forsaken*, a role made famous by Kate Bateman, a model for successful transition from infant prodigy to respected actress. Arnot varied her program nightly. For example, in a single week at the Fulton Opera House in Lancaster, Pennsylvania—a frequent stop—Arnot presented *Hidden Hand*, *M'Liss*, *Child Stealer*, *Two Orphans*, *Fun on the Potomac*, and *Leah, the Forsaken*.[131] In 1887, she revived George Fawcett Rowe's *Fun on the Bristol* at Jacob's Third Avenue Theatre in New York where admission was twenty, thirty, or fifty cents.[132] The *Evening World* deemed her "effectively amusing" as the Widow O'Brien.[133] The *Sun* observed that she had "traveled the circuits widely" and seemed "to have been liked."[134] She specialized in comic Irish roles and received generous applause from good houses when she added *Ireland as It Is* to her repertoire in Richmond, Virginia.[135] In January 1891 she continued touring her company in minor cities such as Leighton, Pennsylvania.[136] These performance spots exemplify the life of a touring actor.

During this time, vaudeville replaced stock companies. In her study of Louise's contemporary Clara Morris (1846/8–1925), Barbara Wallace Grossman writes that a large number of "legitimate" actors were "lured to the vaudeville stage" during the 1890s, "in part to bring more 'class' to the popular entertainment form, in part to provide an endless array of attractions."[137] Certainly the changes in genre and production structures could not have made finding work easy for actresses of a certain age, and the incident at Mary's grave indicates that Louise did conceal her true age, in an era before the Internet would make that impossible. Although Louise continued working, she no longer appeared as the star comedienne, but as a member of the cast in a series of long-touring vehicles. As a master of her craft since childhood, Arnot adapted and worked.

Arnot spent two years touring the West and Northwest with *Ole Olsen*, playing another comic Irishwoman in a play that poked gentle fun at Swedish immigrants. Arnot played Mrs. Bridget O'Flanagan, "on the warpath for husband No.2" and "brought the house down" in Montana.[138] Arnot apparently based her characterization on Mary E. Lease, a nationally famous stump speaker of the Populist Party who supported prohibition and women's suffrage and was an easy target for satire. Louise's oft-criticized voice worked to her advantage as an "exact duplicate."[139] As usual, however, there were some critics who found fault with her vocal work. While a Los Angeles critic found her "very acceptable," he commented that she had "acquired a masculine baritone voice" since leaving the Marsh Troupe.[140] In the nineteenth century, vocal mastery provided the foundation of an actor's craft, yet throughout Arnot's career, critics kept vacillating on whether her voice was natural or affected, vibrant or injured, an asset or a detriment.

In 1893, at the age of fifty, Arnot continued acting, touring to less-developed towns for steady work. These comments from a writer in Butte, Montana, give some impression of how she was viewed at the time:

> Louise Arnot has too many admirers throughout the West and is too widely known to need praise. It would be hardly fair to her youthful appearance and sprightliness to say that she made a hit when many other actresses now on the stage were yet in the nursery. Miss Arnot has played and played them well, probably more characters in her time than any other actor or actress on the stage.[141]

While the last claim is perhaps overstated, it does give a sense of Arnot's aura, as well as the respect paid to her professional longevity.

Despite her advancing age, Arnot continued touring; perhaps she could not envision another life or perhaps she simply enjoyed it. She played generally in smaller markets but did succeed in a few populous centers as well. In 1894 Arnot appeared in New York City in *A Romance of Coon Hollow*, a play to which the *Evening World* paid this faint praise: "Its characters are human; its scenic effects are not cheap or exaggerated, and the cast is certainly admirable." However, Arnot and her scene partner "cover[ed] themselves with glory."[142] In the same role in 1896, a Washington, D.C., critic described her as "a most engaging ingénue of forty or thereabouts" who "not only won 'a man' but also the good graces of the audience."[143] In 1898, she began touring in H. A. Du Souchet's *My Friend from India* for the Smyth and Rice company. Louise played yet another Widow, but with "a snap that made her very popular with the audience."[144] Arnot proved that even in a small role she could still "bring down the house" with her comic timing.[145] One brief stop on the tour was Macon, Georgia, where she squeezed in a visit to Rose Hill Cemetery and wept at Mary Marsh's grave.

Louise was still performing at the turn of the twentieth century, most often on the same bill with Tom Gunn, to whom she was married at the time of her death in 1919. Significantly, she never used a married name professionally. Many actresses utilized the title "Mrs." to bolster their respectability, although Tracy C. Davis, J. K. Curry, Renée Sentilles, and others have pointed out how theatrical employment also empowered actresses in ways not generally available to other women.[146] Arnot, like other actresses, exercised an autonomy from which Victorian society generally barred middle-class wives. However, Arnot's decision to use her own name and rely on her own well-earned reputation conveys her profound self-respect and professional pride as a master of her craft.

Arnot and Gunn performed the "exciting melodrama" *Under Southern Skies* at New York's Fourteenth Street Theatre in 1903.[147] They made their vaudeville debut together at Pastor's in 1904 in a new farce called *Regan's Luck*.[148] Whatever damage might have been done to her voice earlier was not obvious to the writer for the *New York Dramatic Mirror*, who found Arnot's Irish dialect to be "almost flawless" and her brogue to be "rich, natural and unexaggerated." Potentially sowing marital discord, the critic found fault with Gunn's performance and suggested that if the actor "would just take a few points from Miss Arnot's natural method his performance would be just right."[149] A 1903 photograph of Louise Arnot shows short hair, dark calm eyes, and an expression that seems to focus inward, almost indifferent to the viewer. Sporadic listings for the Arnot-Gunn vaudeville team appear during 1906 and 1908. When Louise Arnot died in 1919, her obituary hailed her as "the last of the famous Marshes," and indeed she was. By that time, her old master Robert G. Marsh had passed away, as well as both his children George and Mary.

Arnot's actions throughout her career demonstrate confidence and strong personal preferences. At age twelve, she defied her parents and chose to continue touring under Marsh. At sixteen, she left Marsh—and her sister—to marry, and then boldly relaunched her career as an adult artist. After performing a female role in a poorly received production of *Lady of Lyons* in Brisbane, she took the initiative to reproduce the play in the same theatre with herself as the male lead. Arnot never seemed to lack the courage to take a risk—or the talent to back it up. Whatever method Marsh used to train his actors, it imbued at least a few of them with skill and confidence.

Figure 5.3. Fifty-nine-year-old Louise Arnot in costume for *Beggar's Luck*, Arcade Theatre, New York City, 1903. Her career would last another decade. Billy Rose Theatre Division, the New York Public Library for the Performing Arts, Astor, Lenox and Tilden Foundations.

Arnot's generation was perhaps the last to benefit from the apprenticeship and stock company style of education and professional training. Living before exploitive industrialization would exhaust young workers, giving them little in return but subsistence wages, her childhood epitomizes the perfect *quid pro quo* of a trade apprenticeship. Even as Arnot helped Robert G. Marsh earn a profit during her childhood, the education he provided enabled her to support herself through a long adulthood and buy a rural retirement. Although never a major star, Arnot lived the life of a working professional— not an easy feat in the entertainment business of any age. Just getting work requires talent, chutzpah, and perseverance. She had an advantage not afforded to many girls of her era, because most apprentices were male. Boys grew up to be self-supporting master craftsmen. Girls who were bound out generally trained either in housewifery or garment making.[150] These limited skills relegated a girl to menial positions or dependency upon a husband. Far from being exploitive, Arnot's childhood training in the Marsh troupe laid the foundation for a life far more free than the lives of most of her female contemporaries.

Arnot's working years coincided with first-wave feminism. She joined the Marsh Company a few years after the Seneca Falls Convention, and died just a year before passage of the Nineteenth Amendment gave women in the United States the right to vote. Arnot left no political statements and may never have self-identified as a feminist, yet her life defied normative expectations for nineteenth-century females. As a child, she didn't act the role of a helpless angel—on stage or in life. As a woman, she exercised agency in the public sphere. Even while collaborating with her husbands professionally, Arnot remained independent of them, receiving her own billing and, presumably, her own paycheck. The confidence required for such a life must surely have sprung in part from her childhood experiences as a valued, competent, and useful professional.

CHAPTER 6

FATHERS AND SONS

On May 21, 1870, Georgie Marsh appeared with the Zavistowski Sisters in *Cinderella* at the Metropolitan Theatre in Sacramento; it was his last credited performance.[1] Georgie got rave reviews during his fourteen years with the Marsh Troupe. His individual career extended slightly further on both ends, from touring as a tyke with the adult Marsh company in *Uncle Tom's Cabin* in 1853 to his days as an independent young man on California stages in 1870. The roles he played and the critical response to his performances were remarkably consistent throughout his career. Working practically nonstop for nearly two decades, he traveled through most of the United States as well as Australia and New Zealand, witnessed his sister's horrific death, and saw the break-up of the company and departure of his childhood companions—all while delighting audiences and taking daily direction from his father. This chapter considers both the professional and personal life of George Washington Marsh in order to examine the legacy of his professional childhood. Considering his career in its social and historical context illuminates the questions of whether childhood work experiences function adequately as a craft apprenticeship to provide the foundation for a lifelong trade, and whether child actors can act—that is, whether their performances require learned skill and craft. Robert Marsh invested intensely in the professional development of his only son and sole surviving child, and thus bequeathed a personal, as well as a professional, legacy to Georgie. Like most traditional fathers, Robert Marsh had sought to bestow on his son a name and a trade. This chapter explores how both aims failed.

George Washington Marsh served as the featured comic performer for the entire life of the Marsh Troupe. Like any member of a stock company, he had to play a large number of supporting roles, but his most prominent parts—Schnapps in *The Naiad Queen*, Aminidab Sleek in *The Serious Family*, Jem Baggs in *The Wandering Minstrel*, and especially, the eponymous Toodles—were all drawn from the personal repertoire of William E. Burton. At mid-century, British-born Burton was perhaps the greatest comic actor and theatre manager working in the United States. One of the busiest as well as most successful theatre men in America during the mid-1840s, Burton simultaneously managed three theatres in two cities, appearing continuously as a star performer while embellishing a reputation as an editor and man of letters.[2]

Burton had two sons. He abandoned his first son, William Shakespeare Burton, along with his mother in 1834 when he fled Britain with his seventeen-year-old neighbor, Carolina Glessing. Without bothering to divorce his first wife, Burton took Carolina as his second. She bore him three daughters and one son, Harry, who fell ill and died at the age of eight.[3] Burton reportedly doted on his daughters—Joseph Jefferson declared that the "little tyrants" managed their father "quite as well as he managed his theatres"—but women were generally relegated to separate spheres, and few men looked on their daughters as professional heirs.[4] Most crafts were transferred from father to son, and a man could be proud knowing that his legacy and name would carry on; but through a death and a desertion, William Burton missed that chance.

Burton probably never guessed that a minor actor he hired in Philadelphia would be the conduit to the boy who would ultimately carry on the Burton theatrical legacy. Master George Washington Marsh not only played Burton's signature roles, but precisely replicated Burton's performance. In his most famous role, for example, Georgie presented "a miniature copy of Burton's *Toodles*, in which all of the business and many of the gags—even to the profanity at the mention of Thompson—were retained."[5] It is unlikely, however, that Georgie Marsh ever saw Burton perform before assuming the roles himself. Conflicting evidence about the year of Georgie's birth sets it between 1848 and 1851.[6] Although Robert Marsh appeared frequently in Philadelphia between 1845 and 1848, acting first at the National Theatre and subsequently at the Arch Street under Burton's direction, during 1851 he acted in New York City.[7] The Marsh family's *Uncle Tom's Cabin* tours began in 1853. Therefore, during Robert

Marsh's years in Philadelphia, Georgie was either not born yet, or under three years old—certainly too young to study Burton's technique directly.

As a member of the Arch Street Theatre Company, however, Robert Guerineau Marsh had ample opportunity to study Burton's management as well as his acting.[8] During an extended 1847–48 holiday season that lasted through February, Burton successfully presented *The Naiad Queen* at the Arch Street Theatre. "Mr. Marsh" performed with Burton onstage, playing Sir Rupert, while Burton enacted the knight's page, Schnapps.[9] Later, as a theatre manager himself, Marsh would copy Burton's practice of installing *The Naiad Queen* for a long run each holiday season. Other repertory that R. G. Marsh chose for his troupe also mimicked Burton's choices. In addition to *The Naiad Queen*, Marsh performed in, or performed on the same bill with, *The Honeymoon* and *Black-Eyed Susan*. During Marsh's years at Arch Street, Burton also produced *Wandering Minstrel*, *Our American Cousin*, *Lady of Lyons*, and Planché's fairy extravaganzas *Beauty and the Beast* and *Aladdin*. All of these plays would become standard fare for the Marsh Children. Like Burton's company, the Marsh Troupe tended to produce the same short farces and light musical pieces over and over again, performed by a stable stock company.

Most significantly, acting opposite Burton afforded Robert Marsh the opportunity to memorize every detail of Burton's performances in his signature roles. Night after night, Robert Marsh watched Burton, internalizing every line reading, gesture, and grimace of the portly, middle-aged comic, which he would later transfer to a boy just past toddlerhood. Lawrence Hutton accurately raved that Georgie Marsh's "powers of imitation were marvelous," but the imitation was not of Burton, but of Robert Marsh imitating Burton. Never renowned as an actor himself, R. G. Marsh's real talent was shaping performances and promoting them. As a conduit for Burton's legacy, Robert excelled.

Clearly, Georgie Marsh learned to mimic, but Jim Davis has pointed out that although mimicry was "at the root of the appeal of [nineteenth-century] child actors" in Shakespearean roles, mimicry was also a "term of critical abuse."[10] Nineteenth-century opinion was divided. While child actors drew audiences, rants abusing their acting were not uncommon. After seeing young Rowena Grace perform in California in 1856, one viewer compared her voice to a "diseased cow" and her dancing to a bear, insisting, that children "should not be forced into parrots—to repeat language they cannot understand, and perpetuate gestures forced and unnatural."[11] Another writer also embraced animal imagery to describe his reaction to the Marsh Troupe's efforts in 1860 California, and to child performers in general:

> To seriously criticize these youngsters is out of the question. The stronger emotions and passions that animate men and women in the drama of the stage, as in real life, cannot be supposed to fill their minds; and they must often necessarily repeat their parts as the parrot speaks. One views their acting with something of the same feeling he has when gazing on dancing dogs, Icarnod pigs or performing monkeys.[12]

An audience member who watched an early Marsh Troupe performance also advanced the argument that child performers simply could not understand the material. An 1855 *Putnam's Magazine* writer asserted that child actors were capable of being only "ineffectual parodies of adult actors and actresses" because the plays written for adults had "their foundations in the experience of life," and thus were "sadly ill-suited to these young, inexperienced children.[13] These writers tended to generalize about all child performers and rarely aimed specific criticisms at the individual performers in the Marsh troupe, which, according to *Frank Leslie's Popular Monthly*, "made a very favorable impression *even* upon people not predisposed to be attracted by any exhibition of prodigies."[14] Negative commentators often disregarded the reality of the audience's pleasure in order to make a philosophical argument against the possibility of children creating successful characterizations.

This prejudice would carry through the twentieth century as well. Child performers who hit their marks and got their laughs were frequently described as simply parrots, as if those accomplishments were not skills. For example, the press repeatedly attributed the success of silent film star Baby Peggy to her strict obedience to her father's commands rather than to her own comic talent.[15] Later in the century, a film called *The Last Emperor* featured a very young boy and won an Academy Award; yet its director, Bernardo Bertolucci, feels that children have no craft and can only portray themselves.[16] The ability of some young performers to deliver successful performances again and again undercuts such assumptions.

Lawrence Hutton's writing about the Marsh Troupe in the 1880s is ambivalent. While rhapsodizing about Little Mary, Hutton dismissively described Georgie as "clever in his way, although not original in his impersonations."[17] Hutton had to admit, however, that in general the acting of the

Marsh children confounded rather than confirmed negative expectations. Their acting did not seem forced or unnatural; on the contrary, he observed

> a perceptible absence of that familiar, parrot-like, mechanical repetition of incomprehensible words, and those studied and artificial attitudes so painfully marked in juvenile players generally. Their impersonations were spirited and exact, and evinced unusual mental aptitude and training, their audiences being sometimes startled by the extraordinary precocity with which some of the leading parts were filled.[18]

Hutton had to acknowledge that his general assumption didn't apply.

Whatever method R. G. Marsh had used to train Georgie, Louise, and the other children surely involved more than mimicry. Under Marsh's coaching, the children's individual talent shone through the familiar characters. Dickens had made child actors famous with his caricature of Ninetta Crummels, an image that reviewers frequently used as a touchstone. Most Dickensian references to the Marshes, however, cited them as a counterexample. Referring to Georgie and Louise, a New Zealand reporter announced, "Two enfant [*sic*] phenomena, not of the type sketched by Dickens, are the chief elements of the Troupe's success."[19] Another reviewer went even further, claiming that either of them, "would have been a fortune to Mr. Vincent Crummels, and would have thrown that proud father's 'infant phenomenon' completely into the shade."[20] Other writers also stressed the quality of the juvenile actor's craft.

> To those who know anything of the difficulties incidental to the theatrical profession, the performances of these young people—many of them mere children in years—must be a source of unalloyed delight. . . . One thing is certain, that if every night does not produce a bumper house, it cannot be from any want of genius in the actors.[21]

This writer's view that knowledgeable spectators would recognize the talent of child performers is reflected in numerous critical comments regarding the Marsh Troupe.

Several modern scholars, including Jim Davis, Marah Gubar, Ann Varty, and Gillian Arrighi have made some effort to recognize the acting craft and talent that earned some nineteenth-century juvenile performers success and respect from their contemporaries.[22] Obviously, consciously making an audience laugh requires craft and talent as a performer. Anyone who's ever tried to interpolate material from a joke book into a social performance knows what it feels like to flop. From a very early age, George W. Marsh had the ability to make people laugh. Spectators continually praised his comic abilities.

> The comicality and humor of Master George W. Marsh are really surprising.[23]
>
> . . . he literally convulses his audience with laughter.[24]
>
> . . . remarkably clever in low comedy . . . never failing to elicit the most rapturous applause.[25]
>
> . . . is irresistibly droll,[26]
>
> Young George Marsh never fails to excite the risibles of every auditor.[27]

Significantly, many critics specifically compared him to adult professionals.

> He introduces an amount of by-play that would do credit to many an experienced professional.[28]
>
> He stands without an equal even of mature years.[29]
>
> He has an innate drollery an older comedian might envy.[30]
>
> . . . perfectly competent to teach several low comedians the elements of their art.[31]

The spectators who made these comments were acknowledging Georgie's youth, but not making allowances for it. They judged Georgie's craft alongside that of his competition, including the professional adult actors who were often simultaneously playing the same roles at neighboring theatres. Georgie made a lasting impression on spectators. A quarter century after seeing him, an "old playgoer" gave this simple summary: "George Marsh was a born actor, a creator of parts."[32] Many different characters earned Georgie praise, but none more than Timothy Toodles, his signature role.

In 1864 Mark Twain saw Georgie's Toodles in Carson City. A man with a keen ear for humor, Twain wrote in the *Territorial Enterprise* that Georgie "performed it as only cultivated talent, or genius, or which you please, or both, could enable him to do it."[33] Burton had crafted Toodles as *his* signature role expressly to exhibit his own talents as a clown.[34] Using Burton's business, Georgie not only made his own performance funny, but made it seem fresh as well. An admiring viewer tried to puzzle out this paradox.

Figure 6.1. George Marsh as "Young Toodles." *Frank Leslie's Popular Monthly* 21 (January–June 1886): 445.

> The Toodles of the little boy is an extraordinary display of histrionic ability, with nothing automatic about it, but with all the appearance of being as much the result of natural intelligence as of acquired instruction. Were the acting merely mechanical, it would be almost painful to witness; but there is so much verve and spontaineousness [*sic*] in it that the effect, is eminently amusing.[35]

The acknowledged fact that Georgie presented "Burton's Toodles" and the common bias about mimicry simply could not be reconciled with the live experience of Georgie's natural performance.

Admittedly, Georgie worked with very good material. One scholar describes some of the business in

> the best-known scene . . . Timothy Toodles, quite drunk and absorbed in his drunken thoughts, mumbles a confused and associative monologue while he acts out other stage business: trying to light his pipe and failing, trying to put on his thumbless glove, dropping it, and falling when he tries to pick it up, and so on.[36]

Standard low comedy business, but not foolproof. Georgie's accomplishment is confirmed when juxtaposed against the efforts of an adult actor called Mr. Florence. Shortly after Burton's death in 1860 his costumes were auctioned. Florence, a "gifted comedian" according to one of his peers, purchased the "Toodles" outfit for $5.75 and one week later appeared in the role.[37] The press castigated poor Florence: "Beyond the dress he wore, there was no more resemblance between the separate impersonae by the two actors than could have been expected—and about as littler merit in that of Mr. Florence as anybody acquainted with his specialty could have hoped."[38] As the old saying goes, dying is easy; comedy is hard.

Many low comedians attempted Toodles and reviewers often compared versions. For example, the *Quebec Colonist* of 1856 commented on Georgie's portrayal, "We have rarely seen this difficult character better performed, even by those by far his senior in years."[39] Reviewing an 1869 Toodles performed by J. T. Raymond, a San Francisco writer criticized that actor's tendency to "overdo" the drunken business, when he wrote, "In this scene we greatly prefer young George Marsh."[40] By 1886, Lawrence Hutton had watched numerous imitators but concluded that Georgie's performance "was certainly better than many of the Toodles that have been seen since

Burton's day."[41] In Hutton's view, Georgie's performance "was almost as funny in its uproariousness as was Burton's Toodles itself."[42] As John Kendall wrote, "Those who were familiar with Burton's famous rendition of this character did not hesitate to compare the work of this child to that of the veteran comedian."[43] According to one report, Georgie's performance pleased even Burton, who gave the boy a gold watch to prove it.[44]

The Romantic ideal of childhood held that children were natural. Observers of child performers from all eras often rave about the unstudied, natural quality of the acting, sometimes insisting that children on stage are simply playing. Heather McMahon argues that the popularity of child actors partially relied on audience belief that the children were untrained—even when that was not only unlikely, but impossible.[45] Given a context that almost universally derided parroting, the career of George Washington Marsh is an anomaly. His performance contained not the slightest pretense of native, unstudied talent. Audiences cheered Georgie *because* of the precision of his craft. Without a hint, or a chance, that the performance was natural, Georgie reaped praise year in and year out. Nineteenth-century critics and audiences were able to accept at least some stage children as skilled professionals.

According to Marsh Troupe lore, Georgie loved performing from his earliest days in *Uncle Tom's Cabin* as the child famously carried over the frozen Ohio River by his fleeing mother in one of the play's most sensational scenes. A story constructed in the style of sentimental fiction and published in the *Marsh Juvenile Era* recounts how on one occasion in 1853, sister Mary fell ill and couldn't perform.

> The father, in great anxiety, went to him and asked him, "George, do you think you know enough of Eva to play the part tonight? Can you get through with it?" "Yes, sir," said the little stripling boldly, "Just let me try and see!" He was at once dressed for the character, —the audience uninformed as to who he was—and he played it to perfection; enacting his own character of Little Harry, besides. Such was the enthusiasm felt throughout the house that he was called out, and then only was it announced to the audience that the Eva of the evening was no other than Little George.[46]

If Georgie did actually substitute for his sister, it means that he played three different roles in *Uncle Tom's Cabin*, Harry, Eva, and Topsy—two in blackface and two cross-dressed.

More objective reports also testify to Georgie's comfort with audiences. A Boston writer described seeing six-year-old Georgie called before the curtain at a time when Edwin Forrest was playing at the Boston Theatre. The little fellow "advanced confidently to the footlights, gracefully acknowledged the applause after the manner of the veterans of the stage" and delivered a speech with perfect aplomb.[47] On another occasion, Georgie engaged his fans even more directly, when he "stationed himself in the lobby and gave a photograph of himself to every lady."[48] The idealized boy actor who emerges from these anecdotes is confident and plucky, more Mickey Rooney than Little Lord Fauntleroy (a character hatched by Romantic childhood that would become a frequent role for many working boy actors in the late nineteenth and twentieth centuries). Georgie seemed to possess personal agency and ownership over himself as well as his craft. To observers, Georgie seemed always to be having fun.

George first performed Toodles in 1856, at about six years old.[49] He continued to perform this role throughout boyhood, puberty, and early manhood in 1869. Although the part is the same and the reviews are consistent, two elements of the performance did not remain static: the body of the performer and his acting partners. The body of a six-year-old differs greatly from that of a twelve-year-old, which in turn is very different from a young man of eighteen or twenty. Georgie's performance could not have remained the same through the years, yet, as if they were rewatching a beloved and classic film, commentators almost never noted any change. Like much low comedy, the role of Toodles relied heavily on the actor's physicality. As we age, our dexterity changes, yet George continuously adapted his performance to his changing body. He also adapted to changing scene partners. For four years, as George grew from age six to ten, he played Toodles opposite his sister Mary.[50] In the summer of 1860, following Mary's death, Jenny Arnot took over as Mrs. Tabitha Toodles.[51] In the spring of 1863, during Jenny Arnot's temporary desertion, "Miss Eliza" took over the role.[52] By June, Jenny Arnot reclaimed "her original character with the troupe," still playing it when the Marsh Troupe played their opening engagement back in the United States that fall.[53]

"George Marsh is at present in California," announced T. Allston Brown, in his 1870 *History of the American Stage*.[54] After that year, no further performances by George are mentioned in the *San Francisco Chronicle*, *New York Clipper*, or other papers that had regularly reported on his work over the previous fifteen years. What had happened to him? In an

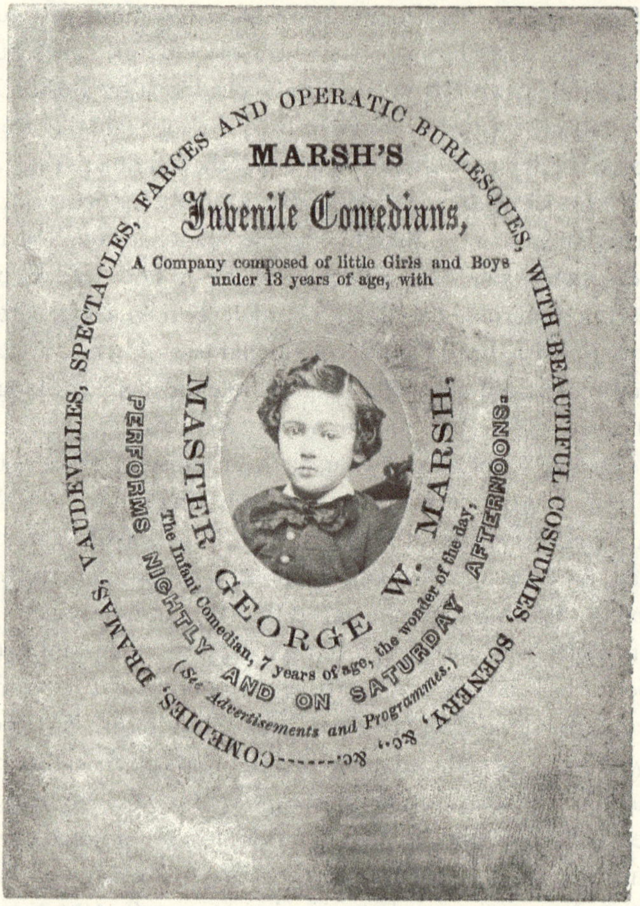

Figure 6.2. Georgie Marsh, Boston, 1857. On closing night, Georgie gave this photo of himself to every lady in the audience. TCS 44, Harvard Theatre Collection, Houghton Library, Harvard University.

1886 article for *Leslie's Magazine*, Lawrence Hutton wrote a retrospective of the Marsh Troupe. Hutton goes into detail about the passing of Little Mary Marsh but speaks only in general terms about the fates of the other children: "As they died—and the mortality among them was remarkable—or as they grew too large for the troupe, their places were filled by other precocious infants." [55] When Hutton republished the essay in his 1901 book, he provided no further details about George Washington Marsh. In a 1952 volume, John S. Kendall wrote flatly, "Georgie, as everyone called him—dies of overwork when still in his teens."[56]

The sacrificing of the life of a second Marsh child to a father's ambition handily fits both nineteenth- and twentieth-century tropes. Nineteenth-century melodrama and sentimental fiction abound with the deaths of children and the greed of adults. Shifting notions of childhood and particular cultural views about child performers influenced twentieth-century writing. Sociologist Jane O'Connor has argued that twentieth-century press coverage "facilitate[d] and perpetuate[d] a certain image of the child star as powerless, pitiful, and cursed."[57] Kendall's mid-twentieth-century history postdated the public spectacle of former child star Jackie Coogan being first robbed by his family and then blacklisted by Hollywood for taking his parents to court. Press coverage transformed Coogan in the public mind from a star to a victim. Firmly grounded in the belief that all child labor is exploitive, twentieth-century readers could understand that Georgie's "overworked" childhood had brought him to an early grave.

The absence of news stories or critical comment about George after 1870 seems to support Kendall's construction of the facts, but cemetery records in Troy, New York, suggest a different story—a story of reinvention. Metamorphosis "is the epitome of the theatrical," as Daniel Gerould has written.[58] The art of transformation is also integral to America, where broad expanses invite fresh beginnings and blur pasts. Steeped in the theatre all his life, and by 1870 a grown man in a newly reunited United States of America, George Washington Marsh was master of his fate. Faithfully following his father's dream, Georgie had played his part, witnessed his sister's incineration, and seen the compatriots of his childhood move away to marriages and adult careers. George had watched all of the other leading players leave, perhaps waiting for his own turn to go. Commenting on the future of the now-grown "children," the *Clipper* called the Marsh troupe an "experiment" and wondered how it would pay off for Georgie. "If any man is entitled to a rich reward for the exhibition of patience, for being up against the 'slings and arrows' of untoward fortune, George Washington Marsh is that man."[59] Apparently, the rich reward desired by George did not include the legacy so painstakingly bequeathed to him by his father.

About 1870, George W. Guerineau took up residence in Watervliet, New York, a small town near Troy. His obituaries, published forty years later in the *Troy Times*, *Troy Record*, and *Troy Daily Press* memorialized him as "a well-known resident" of the city, a "member of the First Avenue Methodist Church" and "a printer by trade."[60] The papers gave George W. Guerineau's age at death as fifty-eight years, twenty-three days, indicating a birthdate of December 26, 1851. There is a slight discrepancy between this date and December 25, 1848 or 1850, which were indicated by advertisements for the boy performer Master George W. Marsh. However, one of the Troy papers explicitly connects George W. Guerineau to Robert Marsh. The *Troy Times* reported, "Mr. Guerineau was the son of Robert Guerineau, who was a well known actor under the stage name of Robert Marsh." The obituary in the *Troy Times* is longer than those in the other papers and includes mention of the fact that Guerineau had worked for a time in that newspaper's printing department. Because Guerineau was a former employee, it stands to reason that the *Troy Times* would have the most accurate and detailed information about him. If this is the case, George Washington Marsh did not die "of overwork when still in his teens," as has been reported, but lived a full adult life span. In this respect, Guerineau's life is oddly parallel to that of his professional role model, William E. Burton, who also reinvented himself. As a young man, comedian Burton had begun "in the printing trade, but left it in 1825 to pursue a stage career."[61] For George, the printing trade provided an alternative to the stage and his father's (and Burton's) legacy.

The *Troy Times* obituary writer, who may well have known George W. Guerineau personally, makes no mention of a childhood stage career in spite of identifying George as the son of Robert Marsh, the "well-known actor." This suggests George W. Guerineau intentionally buried his childhood persona while reinventing himself as a citizen of his father's old home town.

Throughout the history of the Marsh Troupe, the public record is almost silent about George's mother, Jane C. Dutcher Guerineau. Prior to the founding of the juvenile troupe, Jane acted, along with Robert and both her children, in the Marsh production of *Uncle Tom's Cabin* with G. C. Germon in 1853–54. Credited as "Mrs. Marsh," Jane played the minor role of Aunt Ophelia. Although her name is not included on any of the *Naiad Queen* cast lists, many reports of Mary's death state that Mrs. Marsh was on stage at the time of the 1860 accident and sustained burns trying to rescue her daughter. Mrs. "Guerineaux" is given credit for the costumes in a *Naiad Queen* playbill from the same year.[62] Two mentions of Jane appear during the Pacific tour. In the newspaper account of sisters sneaking off to be with Louise following her marriage to Bartine, Mrs. Marsh is minding the children and comes out of the house in time to see the escapee. In New Zealand, an 1863 advertisement for *Naiad Queen* lists "New, beautiful, and appropriate costumes by Mme Guraineux [*sic*]."[63] It may be that Jane had created new costumes, or Marsh had glamorized the billing to promote the show. What emerges, however, is a sketch of a woman who served as needed—whether utility player, dorm matron, or seamstress—rather than a full partner sharing an ambitious vision. This image contrasts with those of the mothers of contemporaneous child performers such as Cordelia Howard, the Batemans, and Lotta Crabtree. Carolina Fox Howard and Sydney Cowell Bateman were theatre professionals in their own right and integral to their daughters' careers. Maryann Crabtree had no background in the theatre but managed every aspect of Lotta's bookings, finances, and personal life. By contrast, Mrs. Marsh is barely visible.

If Jane C. Guerineau had accompanied the Marsh Troupe on all its tours—and there is no evidence to suggest that she hadn't—she had been on the road continuously for almost twenty years. Perhaps she yearned for stability and time with her only living child. The 1872 *City Directory* of Troy lists "Mrs. Robert Marsh" as the owner of a home at 191 Green Street.[64] The city directories for 1878 and 1879 list "Mrs. Jane Guerineau" as the owner of a home at 54 Federal Avenue.[65] It appears that in the 1870s both Jane and George chose to withdraw from the theatre, the Marsh name, and perhaps from R. G. Marsh as well.

On October 15, 1872, George W. Guerineau, "of West Troy," married Sarah Wood at the First Avenue Methodist Church.[66] By the time his name first appeared in the *Troy City Directory* two years later, George owned a home.[67] No residence is listed for 1878 and 1879, but the young couple may have lived in the house owned by Mrs. Jane Guerineau, who had dropped her husband's stage name but retained his legal surname. Beginning in 1880, George W. Guerineau is listed in the *Troy City Directory* every year until his death in 1909. The records suggest a stable life. Guerineau maintained home ownership, a marriage, and a trade for over a quarter century. George and Sarah Guerineau had five children, beginning in 1875 with twins named after George and his sister Mary.[68] In a sadly common occurrence, one of the children died young—a boy called Georgie Frederick—succumbing to neuralgia when he was only eight years old.[69] His twin sister, Mary, survived and was living with her parents in 1900. The other three children, Arthur, Nellie, and Charles outlived both their parents. Arthur's descendants were still living in Troy in 2012.[70] George Guerineau worked with a series of partners in his printing business, becoming a sole proprietor in 1885. George's son Arthur worked with him in the business and continued it, joined by his brother Charles, after their father's death.

George's sons carried on their father's professional legacy, unlike George himself, who had rejected even his father's professional name.

When his young son Georgie Frederick died in 1883, George W. Guerineau bought a large plot in Albany Rural Cemetery and erected a tombstone for his lost child. Although the stone was not as large or as grand as the one in Macon honoring Little Mary Marsh, the act of memorializing the lost child echoed Robert and Jane's behavior twenty-three years earlier. Both acts were atypical for the times. In her study of Victorian tombstones, Susan Buckham found that children who predeceased their parents were often buried without a tombstone. The children's names would be added to a tombstone that would not be purchased until the death of the parent, "with children's deaths commemorated retrospectively."[71] Guerineau's purchase of the stone and the large plot testify to the family's relative prosperity as well as to parental grief. George W. Guerineau, who had led a nomadic childhood and lost his only sister in a hideous accident, invested in a permanent memorial to his attachment to his child. Little Georgie Frederick's headstone is the only monument ever erected on the family plot where George W. Guerineau himself was buried in 1909. The cemetery plot now holds the remains of half a dozen members of George's family—but not his own father.

Robert G. Marsh's history parallels George's in some ways. His record of performance thins following the disbanding of the Juvenile Troupe. In 1870, T. Allston Brown places R. G. Marsh in California.[72] In 1877, the *Clipper* reports, "Robert Guerineau, professionally known as Marsh, and organizer of the once noted troupe of children headed by Little Mary and George Marsh, is in San Francisco."[73] Indeed, the 1880 U.S. census reports a Robert Marsh living in San Francisco, who would be about the right age, but no profession is listed and positive identification is impossible; there is no census record for Robert Guerineau.

An undated, unsigned, unidentified clipping in the Marsh files of the Harvard Theatre Collection tells a chatty tale of a reunion between George and his father, "whom he had not seen since his childhood days, thirty years [ago]."[74] The article gives Robert's age as seventy-nine, which would place the reunion in about 1901. According to the article, Robert had been living in Long Island, but hastened to visit when he learned that his son George, whom he thought dead, was still alive. According to the piece, a warm reunion took place and plans were made for Robert to move into the Guerineau home in Troy. However, Robert sent his regrets a few days later,

Figure 6.3. Georgie F. Guerineau's gravestone, Albany Rural Cemetery. When his eight-year-old son died in 1883, George W. Guerineau purchased a large cemetery plot and erected a gravestone in the boy's memory. By 2012 the stone had fallen off its base. Photo by author.

writing that he had signed a one-year contract to serve as stage manager at Madison Square Garden. Unfortunately, there are a number of factual errors in the piece which call its reliability into question. For example, it states that the Marshes returned to Troy for the years following Mary's death, when their Australian tour during that period is fully documented.[75] In any event, little is known about Robert Marsh's life during the four decades that George Guerineau built his life in Troy.

During those same decades, Louis Aldrich had garnered more fame than that of any other Marsh Juveniles alumnus. Retiring from acting after sustaining injuries in a hotel fire in 1890, Aldrich gave his best energies to his profession, as an active member of the Actors' Society, a group concerned with "wages and working conditions," and as president of the Actors Order of Friendship.[76] In 1897, he became the fourth president of the Actors' Fund of America and launched a campaign to establish a retirement home for needy actors and actresses. Despite opposition and competing ideas, Aldrich "worked tirelessly on the project" and pushed it through.[77] The Actors Fund Home, located in West Brighton, Staten Island, opened on May 8, 1902. Louis Aldrich did not live to see its success, however, as he passed away eleven months before the official opening. Aldrich's motivation is unknowable, but one speculates that it had something to do with his old manager. Robert Guerineau Marsh was one of the original fifteen residents who moved into the Actors' Fund Home when it opened in May 1902.[78]

In two years before the home opened (1897 and 1900), "Robert Guerineau" is listed in the *Troy City Directory*. It appears that R. G. Marsh followed his son's lead by dropping his stage name and moving back to Troy. Unlike George, however, Robert did not own a home and is listed as a boarder at various addresses. Whatever the relations between father and son, in 1902 Robert relied on the charity of his profession to provide him with a home. Robert Marsh lived in the Actors Fund Home on Staten Island for four years, but then returned again to Troy. The *City Directory* lists "Robert Guerineau" as a boarder at 25 Fifteenth Street, Watervliet for 1905, 1906, and 1907. Robert died of "odema of lungs" on December 30, 1907.[79] None of the street addresses recorded for Marsh match that of his son, George W. Guerineau, and, although buried in Albany Rural Cemetery, Marsh was not interred in the Guerineau family plot. Marsh's grave, a single plot never marked with a stone, lies in a different section of the 467-acre cemetery. Robert Marsh's remains lie unmarked, among strangers.

Speculating on the relations between father and son is tempting. George may have felt that Marsh's demands as manager took precedence over his duties as father. Psychologists Lisa J. Rapport and Matthew Meleen studied twentieth-century child actors and noted that issues arise when parents function as agents or business managers. Parents who acted in dual capacities were later evaluated by their adult children as less caring and more overcontrolling.[80] While there is no comparable nineteenth-century study, a desire by George to separate from his father would be consistent with Rapport and Meleen's findings.

The last two survivors of the Marsh family troupe, whose lives were so intensely entwined during almost two decades of nonstop touring and training, died two years apart in the same town. George's apparent renunciation of his stage name and stage persona indicates a rejection of Robert's mission, and possibly of Robert himself. That Robert needed to rely on the charity of his profession for a home in his old age and that he was excluded from a large family cemetery plot further support a theory of estrangement. However, Robert's Watervliet address and his internment in Albany Rural Cemetery suggest some connection to his son. The dubious newspaper clipping suggested warmth on both sides, but George may have refused to have anything to do with his father. Perhaps he could never forgive Robert for sacrificing Mary. None of the accounts of Mary's death mention her ten-year-old brother George, but given the number of scenes they had together in *The Naiad Queen*, he was probably on stage at the time of the accident. George would have watched Mary's dress catch flame and heard the screams. He would have been nearly forgotten in the tumult that followed as spectators and actors made frantic efforts to rescue his doomed sister. Soon after, George would have been pressed into urgent rehearsals when R. G. Marsh recast the role; when the show reopened, George had to make people laugh.

Years later, George would create his own memorial to his lost sister by bestowing her name on his firstborn daughter. George's son followed suit, naming his daughter Mary as well.[81] The preservation of Mary's name through three generations may be an attempt to continue a legacy for one whose lifeline had been so abruptly severed. The naming of his daughter, the memorializing of his son, and his care for all his children demonstrate that George cherished family. George's behavior contrasts with Robert's, whose pursuit of professional success, undeterred by the loss of his child, may illustrate a conflicting set of values. Perhaps, late in his life, Robert saw and envied what George had created, and moved back to Watervliet, unbidden, in hopes of winning from George some acceptance of his rejected legacy or at least forgiveness for the sacrifices of his demanding dream.

AFTERWORD

Since a crooked figure may
Attest in little place a million . . .
—*Prologue, Henry V*

A year after college, when I was lingering around town, I agreed to help out my neighbor Mike, a grad student in environmental science. Each day, he went out on the lake in a small rowboat. At various pre-designated spots, we lowered a bucket on a long rope and waited thirty minutes. Then we pulled the bucket back up and Mike would inspect and record its contents. After counting the number of each kind of fish and recording the time, he would seal a small amount of water in a jar before dumping the bucket and moving on. This memory came back to me as I was reading Richard D. Brown's essay about "Microhistory and the Post-Modern Challenge." Defending microhistory to those who prefer subjects of larger scope, Brown compares the latter to a biologist who would "judge the cleanliness of a lake by looking over the side . . . rather than dipping an ounce of water for microscopic and chemical analysis." Brown writes, "Yes, gross visual inspection, like grand narrative, tells you some important things that you could never learn by dipping an ounce of water—but it also conceals important realities. A lake that looks pure may harbor dozens of organic and inorganic materials that are perceptible only through close analysis."[1]

My study of the Marsh Troupe of Juvenile Comedians is like that jar of water Mike took back to his lab. This company of performing children is a perfect vehicle for exploring the world of nineteenth-century actors and examining the societal construction of childhood, just as both were changing. Over the course of the nineteenth century, our image of the child gradually transmuted, emerging in the twentieth century as that of an idealized and vulnerable angel. The American theatre industry also changed significantly between the middle and end of the century. While, as Brown notes, "there is no way to demonstrate that the microcosm is a miniature version of the macrocosm," each jar of lake water allows us to test some assumptions. These microhistories of ordinary players elucidate nineteenth-century culture.

The company undoubtedly impacted the nineteenth-century theatre industry. The Marsh Troupe trained dozens of professional actors and dancers who continued performing during the 1870s and 1880s. Especially valuable for those who came of age as the traditional stock company system deteriorated, this coaching process ensured the company a far-flung legacy. Over sixty names are recorded as Marsh company members, and many more children performed with the troupe as local auxiliaries in various cities along the tour route. The company served as a valuable apprenticeship for these young performers, providing the professional training so necessary to an adult livelihood before the era of universal academic education.

The Marsh Troupe also created a model for the next generation of theatrical managers who copied Marsh's seminal idea of combining child performers with the day's hottest hits. In the 1880s, when a middle-aged Louis Aldrich was gaining national fame on stage and George W. Guerineau was establishing his printing business and his family in Troy, New York, juvenile *Pinafore* companies were all the rage. Crisscrossing the nation, acting, singing and dancing just as the Marshes had done a quarter century before, these touring troupes presented Gilbert and Sullivan operettas performed entirely by children. The adults organizing these groups and the adults who came to see them continued the tradition that many probably enjoyed as child spectators at Marsh Troupe shows before the Civil War.

Robert G. Marsh deserves mention among American theatrical innovators for developing a number of staging and promotional techniques that later became widespread. Uniformed girls marched in formation for Marsh years before the Zouave drills became popular in the early 1860s and were interpolated into *Black Crook* and Fox's *Humpty Dumpty*. Photography was still in its infancy in 1857 when Marsh had little Georgie handing out copies of his image to fans exiting the theatre. The famed Sarony Photography studio for the stars was not even established until 1867 and *cartes de visite* would not commonly be used by celebrities until after the Civil War.[2] Robert Marsh innovated in numerous ways, exploiting the myth of the idealized child for greater publicity. Ambitious managers who followed perpetuated many of these techniques.

Beyond highlighting the Marsh Troupe's specific contributions to the nineteenth-century American theatre, its history sheds light on three large nineteenth-century groups to which its members belonged. The Marsh Children exemplify the lives of touring professionals, child performers, and antebellum children in all walks of life. The daily work lives of these professional children reveal realities of the antebellum theatre. The rise of the impresario, the commodification of family values and idealized children as a bid for respectability, the repertoire and touring regimen of a stock company, professional actor training, the deep influence of melodrama, and the shift to a wage-based economy—all these appear under the microscope.

The story of the Marsh Troupe challenges stereotypes and limited beliefs about the skill levels and professional capabilities of all child actors. As a productive unit in the nineteenth-century theatre industry, the Marsh Children traveled the same routes as Edwin Booth and Harry Watkins, competed head to head on two continents with Joseph Jefferson, and shared repertoire with Barney Williams, Chanfrau, Menken, and Laura Keene. Documenting the rigor of their work, the respect earned from their professional peers, and the admiration of their audiences proves that nineteenth-century child actors had more to offer than preciousness. Their history should refocus the modern lenses through which child actors have often appeared as mere parrots or freaks. When theatre scholars acknowledged the enormous popularity of nineteenth-century entertainments such as melodrama and minstrelsy, we rightly reevaluated these genres. And yet, the construction of powerless childhood has resulted in some theatre historians entirely discounting nineteenth-century reactions to child performers. Our picture of the theatre industry changes if we acknowledge juvenile performers as talented and skillful professionals who exercised agency in the practice of their craft and the direction of their careers. Theatre scholars need to extend this revisioning to child performers of every era.

The individual stories of the Marsh Troupers display distinct models of childhood. Georgie Marsh and Louise Arnot represent the paradigm theorized by Ariès: as children, they daily presented a professional-quality product while simultaneously developing skills they would use as adults. Louise exercised agency as her role changed from a child, to a teenager, and finally to a professional woman displaying considerable autonomy. Her choice to leave a marriage and subsequently rejoin the Marshes disrupts assumptions of childhood exploitation. Arnot's early experiences equipped her with the confidence and expertise to manage an impressive sixty-year career in the theatre. Similarly, Georgie continually adapted his performance to his own changing body. When he rejected a stage career, he had what he needed to establish himself in a new profession almost immediately. Young Marsh had the interpersonal skills, literacy, confidence, and independence necessary to succeed as a small-business owner. He functioned effectively within social communities as a husband, father, and church member to create a legacy that his own children cherished. A generation later, his family members were still attending the church he had joined and working in the business he had started. Louise and George each made a transition from productive apprentice to autonomous adult. Their stories as working children illustrate an effective educational model in an age before mandatory schooling isolated children from the adult world.

Mary Marsh and Alfred Stewart show the flip side; they are exemplars of the modern paradigm of protected, infantilized childhood. The Romanticization of helplessness camouflaged the labor in Mary's performances, so her death incited little outrage about working conditions. Sentimentality provided an easy shortcut to inaction. In death, she is "preserved" by nostalgia and cloaked in an angelic identity devoid of agency. Her postmortem treatment is emblematic of middle-class girls taught that their primary duty is to remain cute and appear innocent. Alfred Stewart's voice, like Mary's, is absent from the historical record. The press followed his mother's lead by framing him as a vulnerable child in need of protection, yet his contract deprived him of the master's paternal guidance provided by traditional apprenticeship. Like Mary, Alfred seems to have passively abdicated agency while adults fought over him. Exhibiting some traits of the modern helicopter parent, Mrs. Stewart attempted to micromanage her son's life. Ironically, or perhaps inevitably, Alfred Stewart, the Marsh child most "mothered," was perhaps the least successful as an adult.

How do the paradigms epitomized by these nineteenth-century child actors compare with the career patterns for young performers of the twentieth and twenty-first centuries? For modern child actors, the transition to young adulthood precipitates a professional crisis. Unlike Louise Arnot, many modern child actors fail to make successful transitions to adult careers, even after many years of experience. Rather, they are frozen like Mary Marsh in perpetual immaturity. Audiences hate to see them grow up, and the performers themselves, so saturated with the value of their child personae, cannot imagine an adult identity. Before "childhood" became enshrined, life simply flowed. Children, like rivers, sunsets, and other natural phenomena, evolved almost imperceptibly over time. Then life was broken into blocks, creating artificial stages that seem more like locks than flowing rivers. From infant to toddler, to child, to tween, to teen, to boomerang child, the spectrum is minutely divided to better market and control. It is easy for performers—or other children—to get stuck, letting one moment in time define them. The gulf between childhood and adulthood is seen as a chasm, too broad too cross. Too many young performers, unable to make the leap, have chosen suicide instead.[3] Sometimes the only way for young performers to break free of a childhood persona is through extreme behavior that radically violates their earlier image. Thus Miley Cyrus demolishes her Disney-girl aura through sexualized, near-naked dance with a wide open mouth and a too-active tongue. Dream-boy Justin Bieber enacts raucous neighborhood pranks and public drunkenness, performing almost a parody of manhood.[4]

The concretization of performers within childhood is buttressed by film, which captures children at a moment in time and holds them there forever. Even more potent, however, is the prevailing construction of childhood devoid of agency and competence. Children's sentimental value is marketed, while their personal competence is denied. Modern child performers are rarely depicted or described as either workers or apprentices training for a trade. Rather, the distance between character and actor collapses and the actor's labor is obscured in the creation of a theatrical persona, as it was with Mary Marsh. Everything conspires to convince young professionals that their entire value derives from their status as a child rather than from talent or skill. This meaning is reinforced by a public that glorifies and sentimentalizes childhood and by an immense marketplace that capitalizes on it. Disneyworld, Nickelodeon, children's specialty stores, clothing lines, and millions of products created for minutely graded sectors of the populace continually fortify the rigid segmentation of childhood. Endless advertising hammers home the special needs of each stage of childhood as a unique consumption opportunity.

Modern audiences choose to ignore that professional children are workers because child work is socially unacceptable. Within contemporary mores, useful child work is deemed exploitative. Thus, acknowledging the labor of performing children would tend to undermine our enjoyment. Just as the antebellum public consumed Mary Marsh's constructed sentimental persona and failed to see her also as a vulnerable worker, contemporary audiences often fail to credit today's juvenile performers for their labor, or to acknowledge the toll that labor takes. Their work is camouflaged. Thus, *Billy Elliot* has "camps" rather than worker training, and nontheatrical young people have internships rather than jobs.[5] Employers or handlers have little motivation to consider their employees' futures because the public wants to ossify their favorites within childhood. A more fluid construction of childhood would allow us to acknowledge the skilled child working at a craft and yet still enjoy the performance.

For scholars of childhood, young performers provide an ideal subject because they encapsulate our society's inconsistent, and somewhat schizoid, view of childhood. Unlike most children in the United States, professional actors spend their days with adults and are expected to produce a polished product on schedule. Even in this setting, however, children's labor is sometimes overlooked. When a break is called on a film or television shoot, adult actors relax while children are sent to do academic lessons as if their professional exertions were not tiring.

The example of the Stewart-Marsh litigation has numerous sad echoes. The management model epitomized by Mrs. Stewart is frequently seen in modern parents who manage, depend on, or are prominent in their children's careers. The parents of Michael Jackson, Macaulay Culkin, and Lindsey Lohan were publicly conspicuous if not notorious. Throughout the twentieth century, child actors were legally swindled of financial agency and literally robbed of their earnings. Squabbles over income or potential income marred the professional lives of Jackie Coogan in the 1920s, Freddie Bartholomew in the 1930s, Gary Coleman in the 1980s and 1990s, and Taran Noah Smith in the early twenty-first century, and the list goes on. The state of New York did not grant child actors legal ownership of their own earnings until 2003.[6] Some child actors have gained control of their finances through legal emancipation before the age of eighteen. In these cases, a court awards an individual child rights of agency that are routinely denied to minors. Unfortunately, the results of this action have sometimes been disastrous for the child's financial security. Unlike the Marsh Troupers who successfully transitioned to adulthood and seemed to manage their financial affairs responsibly, modern child performers are often infantilized and thus lack the needed maturity when abruptly launched on their own.

Robert Marsh's last years might serve as a cautionary tale for parents of young performers today. Shunned by his son George, whom he had mentored and managed for nearly twenty years, Robert lived in a charity home and was buried in an unmarked grave, excluded from the family plot. In a 1998 study, psychologists Rapport and Meleen concluded that parents of child actors may injure their familial relationship by acting as managers. The former child actors interviewed in their study viewed their mother-managers as "less caring and more controlling than did performers whose parents were not their managers."[7] No psychologist interviewed young George Marsh but his actions seem to tell a similar story.

In looking at these cultural patterns, questions emerge about the disparity between the construction of childhood in the antebellum United States and the way it is constructed today. Many of today's laws and regulations—about media, pornography, statutory rape and sexual activity with adults, guardianship, internships and working papers, financial authority, privacy, and other subjects—deny children agency. Yet Allison James rightly asks, "Do all children have the same capacity for agency? What might inhibit or prevent particular children from exercising it, and under what kinds of circumstances?"[8] The childhood experiences of the Marsh Children enhanced their capacity for agency. Whether the childhood experiences of actors and other young people in the twentieth and twenty-first centuries enhance or inhibit these children's capacity for agency needs further exploration.

The four child members of the Marsh Troupe profiled here each demonstrate extraordinary capacities. On a personal note, as a mother and a teacher, I have learned that the cliché is true: every child is extraordinary. In the United States, we often affirm that children are our most important resource, the treasury of our personal and collective culture and our future. Like Robert Marsh, each one of us hopes somehow to see our children carry on and expand what we have bequeathed them. Despite the near mantra-like status of this truth, children are often not taken seriously in the United States today. Unlike Robert Marsh (who was certainly far from a perfect parent), most of us do not train our children in our craft. Individually and collectively, most of us do not recognize in our children the ability to execute complex tasks competently.[9] While early nineteenth-century parents took children's aptitude for granted and late nineteenth-century employers exploited it, many late twentieth-century parents seem never to have even considered it. We seldom depend on our children—which is another way of saying that their actions don't matter. In our attempts to protect children from abusive practices, we have too often also robbed them of competency, agency, and—perhaps most importantly—a pathway toward successful adulthood.

In the twenty-first century, commentators have lamented how childhood—generally defined as a state of dependency—often extends for twenty, twenty-five, thirty, or even more years. When this happens, the pattern may have arisen not in the later years, but in the early ones. The seventeen-year-old is helpless because the seven-year-old was not empowered to act responsibly. We have stereotyped humans by age, strictly reserving proficiency and agency for adults. Only when young people regain the agency and respect they lost with the enshrinement of "childhood" will they grow naturally into the responsible citizenhood upon which American society is ostensibly based.

Appendix

Notes

Bibliography

Index

APPENDIX

ACTORS REPORTED TO HAVE PERFORMED WITH THE MARSH TROUPE

Actors Identified by First and Last Name

Aldrich, Louis
Ames, Cora
Ames, Rosa
Arnot, Jenny
Arnot, Louise
Bates, Marie
Beckley, Fanny, aka Fanny Clifford*
Christine, Julia
DeAngelis, Jonny†
Gorenflo, Amelia
Gorenflo, Mary
Gourlay, Jennie
Gourlay, Jenny
Gourlay, Maggie
Graham, Bob
Hawk, Harry†
Henry, Josephine
Ingles, Lizzie
Johnson, Harriet

---

* Later the wife of T. Allston Brown.

† These actors were probably adults, as they appeared under Robert G. Marsh's management after the juvenile troupe had officially disbanded.

Kruger, Selma
LaFont, Tom†
Laurens, Josephine
Leaceaux, Francis
Maddern, Minnie‡
Mann, Clara
Marsh, George W.
Marsh, Mary
Melville, Julia
Monk, Minnie
Mousely, Georgiana
Mousely, Helen
Ramous, Sam†
Rand, Olivia†
Secor, Salome
Shaw, Wallace
Shropshire, Clara
Stewart, Alfred
Todd, Waldo
Webb, Ada
Willett, Maggie

Actors Identified by First Name Only

Miss Adelaide
Miss Anna
Miss Carrie
Miss Charlotte
Miss Christine
Miss Henrietta
Miss Jeannie
Miss Julia
Miss Leila
Miss Matilda
Miss Sallie
Master Charles§

‡ Minnie Maddern Fiskee's connection is drawn from a late-life comment by Lotta Crabtree; there is no mention of Maddern contemporaneous with March Troupe performances.

§ It is possible that these represent surnames.

Master Frederick[§]
Master Henry[§]
Master Horatio[§]

Actors Identified by Last Name Only

Miss Maline, aka Meline
Miss Perry
Miss Prowler
Miss Rableaux/Rabauz
Miss Secord[¶]

Master Ames
Master Defitt
Master Welsh
Master Wilet
Master Wiley
Mr. Morrison[†]

¶ This may be a variant spelling for Harriet Melissa Secor, the first wife of Harry Watkins; he records in his diary that she performed with the Marsh Troupe.

NOTES

Introduction

1. Benjamin McArthur, *The Man Who Was Rip Van Winkle*, 196.
2. *Sydney Morning Herald*, January 24, 1863, 7, National Library of Australia, hereafter NLA, accessed June 20, 2010.
3. Richard D. Brown, "Microhistory and the Post-Modern Challenge," 11.
4. Jill Lepore, "Historians Who Love Too Much," 141.
5. Daniel Thomas Cook, *The Commodification of Childhood*, 2.
6. Neil Postman, *The Disappearance of Childhood*, 67.
7. Philippe Ariès, *Centuries of Childhood*, 26.
8. Margaret King expressed her opinion on a panel at a conference of the Society for the History of Childhood and Youth at Columbia University, June 2011.
9. For a good summary of these arguments see Daniel Thomas Cook, *The Commodification of Childhood*. There is also debate, which does not concern me here, about the forces that contributed to this change including literacy and the printing press. See Neil Postman, *The Disappearance of Childhood*, and the theories of Jean-Jacques Rousseau (*Emile*, 1762) and John Locke (tabula rasa).
10. Steven Mintz, *Huck's Raft*, viii.
11. Anne Higonnet, *Pictures of Innocence*; see also, Holly Pyne Connor, *Angels and Tomboys*.
12. Viviana A. Zelizer, *Pricing the Priceless Child*, 94.
13. Robin Bernstein, *Racial Innocence*.
14. Jared Diamond, *The World until Yesterday*, 175.
15. *Ibid.*, 189, 204.

16. Jens Qvortrup, William A. Corsaro, and Michael-Sebastian Honig, eds., *The Palgrave Handbook of Childhood Studies*, 21.
17. *Ibid.*, 21; Allison James and Alan Prout, *Constructing and De-Constructing Childhood*, 8.
18. Allison James, "Agency," in Qvortrup, et al., *The Palgrave Handbook of Childhood Studies*, 34.
19. Steven Mintz, *Huck's Raft*, 383.
20. Nan Mullenneaux, "Our Genius, Goodness, and Gumption," 281.
21. Laurence Hutton, *Curiosities of the American Stage*, 245–46.
22. "Comedians Past and Present," *Los Angeles Herald*, February 26, 1893, California Digital Newspaper Collection, hereafter CDNC, www.cdnc.ucr.edu, accessed May 17, 2012.
23. Karen Sánchez-Eppler, *Dependent States*; Jane C. Hunter, *How Young Ladies Became Girls.*
24. Miriam Forman-Brunell and Leslie Paris, *The Girls History and Culture Reader*, 9.
25. Cecelia Guerineau, widow of George W. Guerineau's son Arthur, telephone interview with author, January 16, 2011.

1. Beginnings and Success

1. The entire incident is recounted in "An Old Tragedy Recalled: Burning of Mary Marsh on the Ralston Hall Stage," *Macon Telegraph*, December 9, 1898, p. 6, col. 1, Galileo, University of Georgia in Athens; accessed June 13, 2012.
2. Bridges Smith, "All aboard for the Seeing-Macon Car," *Macon Telegraph* December 16, 1917, http://rosehillcemeterymacongeorgia.blogspot.com/2010/07/all-aboard-for-seeing-macon-car.html, accessed December 13, 2011.
3. Some performing "families" were actually nonrelatives performing under the same surname, but they typically included only two to four children. This was especially common in the circus.
4. *New York Times*, December 11, 1855, ProQuest, http://search.proquest.com.central.ezproxy.cuny.edu:2048/hnpnewyorktimes/docview/95883115/fulltextPDF/B6455D07D6C44B87PQ/1?accountid=26979, accessed March 29, 2015.
5. Emphasis added. Internal references to the Howard Athenaeum and the children's ages indicate that the clipping probably dates from early 1857.
6. On Children's *Pinafore* companies, especially in the UK and Australia, see Marah Gubar, *Artful Dodgers* and "Who Watched *The Children's Pinafore*?"; and Gillian Arrighi, "D'Oyly Carte's Pantomimes," 31–44.

7. Eddie Cantor with Jane Kesner Ardmore, *Take My Life*, 33; Cantor and George Jessel played with the act in 1912.
8. *New York Daily Tribune*, December 8, 1856, *Chronicling America*, Library of Congress, http://chroniclingamerica.loc.gov/, accessed May 9, 2011.
9. *New York Daily Tribune*, February 13, 1856, *Chronicling America* Library of Congress, accessed May 9, 2011.
10. *Cincinnati Enquirer*, July 12, 1857, Public Library of Cincinnati and Hamilton County, hereafter PLCHC.
11. *Picayune*, March 22, 1858, Billy Rose Theatre Collection of the New York Public Library, hereafter NYPL.
12. *Marsh's Juvenile Dramatic Era*, 1857, Harvard Theatre Collection, hereafter HTC.
13. *Cincinnati Enquirer*, July 10, 1857, PLCHC.
14. Howard Athenaeum playbill dated September 11, 1857, HTC.
15. *Star*, October 21, 1861, 1; December 16, 1861, NLA, http://trove.nla.gov.au/ndp/del/title/189, accessed June 27, 2012.
16. *Marsh's Juvenile Dramatic Era*, HTC.
17. Maud Otis Skinner, *One Man in His Time*, 100, 155.
18. George Odell, *Annals of the New York Stage* 5:596, 6:140, 191, 229.
19. Sam Wilson was locally referred to as "Uncle Sam." Troops who saw the beef he delivered to the army marked "U.S." made the connection, according to George Baker Anderson, "History of Troy, New York (As a Village)," *From Landmarks of Rensselaer County, Syracuse* (New York: D. Mason & Co., 1897).
20. Birth year calculated by counting back from age given in his obituary.
21. Stacy Pomeroy Draper, "History of Second Street and its Surroundings," in John Waite Associates, *The Marble House in Second Street*, 17.
22. *Troy Post*, May 7, 1846, p. 2, col. 5, as recorded in *Vital Records—Troy Newspapers* 1812–85, 2:16, Troy Public Library, Troy Room, hereafter TPL.
23. William G. B. Carson in *The Theatre of the Frontier*, esp. chap. 8, lists among the company for 1839–40 "the new 'heavy man' one Marsh," but gives no further clues to his identity and it is impossible to prove this to be Robert Guerineau Marsh. The possibility is tantalizing though as twenty-two-year-old Hezekiah L. Bateman was also in the company.
24. George Odell, *Annals of the New York Stage*, 5:596.
25. Arthur Herman Wilson, *A History of the Philadelphia Theatre 1835–1855*, 314, 342, 697.
26. Debut on September 4, 1846, *Clipper*, May 31, 1866.

27. *North American* LXV, no. 16205, December 31, 1847, advertisement, p. 3, col 5; *Philadelphia Public Ledger* XXIV, no. 133, February 26, 1848, 2; J. S. Dalrymple, Esq., *The Naiad Queen* (Boston: William V. Spencer, n.d.) University of California library, pdf lists "Mr. Marsh" as Sir Rupert in Burton's 1848 production, accessed May 15, 2011.
28. Information published during George's career conflicts with dates given in his obituaries in 1909. He was born between 1848 and 1851.
29. David L. Rinear, *Stage, Page, Scandals, and Vandals*, 144.
30. *Ibid.*
31. George Odell, *Annals of the New York Stage*, 5:596; 6:140, 191, 229.
32. *Ibid.*, 6:229.
33. Harriett Beecher Stowe, *Uncle Tom's Cabin*, 70, Google Books, accessed October 10, 2011.
34. The Aiken script is included in Don B. Wilmeth, ed., *Staging the Nation*, as well as in other anthologies. The Conway script is quoted in Sarah Meer, *Uncle Tom Mania*, 123. For more on the Conway script, see Bruce A. McConachie, "H. J. Conway's Dramatization of *Uncle Tom's Cabin*," 149–54.
35. *Sydney Morning Herald*, November 29, 1862, NLA, June 27, 2012.
36. *Ibid.*, Saturday, January 24, 1863, 7, NLA.
37. *Otago Daily Times* 487, July 13, 1863, 4, NLA, accessed September 6, 2011.
38. *Sacramento Daily Union*, July 21, 1860, CDNC.
39. T. Allston Brown, *History of the American Stage*, 126; *New York Times*, August 13, 1857, advertisement with cast list; *St. Louis Leader*, June 10, 1857, State Historical Society of Missouri, hereafter SHSM.
40. On May 13, 1858; John S. Kendall, *The Golden Age of the New Orleans Theatre*, 480.
41. Helen Huff, "The Haunting of Celebrity and the Construction of Nationalism."
42. T. Wood Clark, *Utica for a Century and a Half*, 42.
43. Effie Ellsler Weston, ed., *The Stage Memories of John A. Ellsler*, 94; "Early History of 'Uncle Tom,'" *Chicago Tribune*, April 28, 1907, *Uncle Tom's Cabin* and American Culture website, accessed January 30, 2012.
44. On the Howard family, see Laurence Senelick, *The Age and Stage of George L. Fox.*
45. *Cincinnati Enquirer*, November 26–December 10, 1853, PLCHC.
46. *Ibid.*
47. *Cincinnati Gazette*, December 2, 1853, col. 20, PLCHC.
48. Cordelia Howard Macdonald, "Memoirs of the Original Little Eva," 268 fn.; Whittle was also known as Charles W. Barry. *Clipper*, February 17,

March 3, 1877, *Uncle Tom's Cabin* and American Culture, accessed January 30, 2012. The production was also joined temporarily by Gary Hough as Gumption Cute, a role created by Aiken.

49. Effie Ellsler Weston, ed., *The Stage Memories of John A. Ellsler*, 99. Ellsler refers to Marsh's son as "little Bob Marsh." Rice's presence suggests a pro-slavery slant.
50. At Cincinnati's National Theatre with Wesley Barmore, *Cincinnati Gazette*, December 21, 1853, PLCHC.
51. *Marsh's Juvenile Dramatic Era*, HTC.
52. Eric Lott, *Love and Theft*, 212.
53. See Eric Lott, *Love and Theft*; Robert C. Toll, *Blacking Up*; Sarah Meer, *Uncle Tom Mania*; John Frick, "Uncle Tom's Cabin on the Antebellum Stage."
54. "Early History of 'Uncle Tom,'" *Chicago Tribune*, April 28, 1907, *Uncle Tom's Cabin* and American Culture, accessed January 30, 2012.
55. For example, Howard Athenaeum playbill, February 11, 1857, HTC; National Theatre advertisement for "Colored Boxes," *Cincinnati Enquirer*, July 28, 1857, p. 1, col. 3, PLCHC.
56. Ellsler writes that Marsh ran out, abandoning his financial responsibilities to the company and his partner; Effie Ellsler Weston, ed., *The Stage Memories of John A. Ellsler*, 100.
57. [1857] clipping, HTC.
58. Robin Bernstein, *Racial Innocence*, 4.
59. *Marsh's Juvenile Dramatic Era*, HTC; *Clipper*, February 19, 1859.
60. *Marsh's Juvenile Dramatic Era*, HTC.
61. David Grimsted, *Melodrama Unveiled*, appendix I, "Popularity of Particular Plays, 1800–1851," 249–56.
62. T. Allston Brown, *History of the American Stage*, 235. There is no mention of this performance in Andrew Davis's *America's Longest Run*; *New York Daily Tribune*, January 14, 1856, *Chronicling America*, Library of Congress, accessed September 26, 2012.
63. *New York Times*, December 11, 1855, ProQuest, http://search.proquest.com.central.ezproxy.cuny.edu:2048/hnpnewyorktimes/docview/95883115/fulltextPDF/B6455D07D6C44B87PQ/1?accountid=26979, accessed March 29, 2015.
64. *Clipper*, August 23, 1856, NYPL.
65. *New York Daily Tribune*, February 13–May 16, 1856, *Chronicling America*, Library of Congress.
66. *Frank Leslie's Popular Monthly*, April 1886, 439.
67. *Clipper*, December 11, 1855.

68. "Dramatic and Other Sketches," *Clipper*, May 31, 1862.
69. *Marsh's Juvenile Dramatic Era* states, "Mary and George are the only children." In its files on the Marsh Children, the Harvard Theatre Collection includes two photographs of "Master William Marsh the Infant Drummer." This boy was the son of Joseph Y. Marsh who presented him in two performances in the spring of 1852 (*New York Times*, April 21 and June 16, 1852). William Marsh was never associated with the Marsh Troupe, and does not appear to have maintained a professional career.
70. *Picayune*, March 5, 1858, NYPL.
71. When the Theatre Royal at Bury St. Edmonds was restored and reopened in 2007, *Blackeye'd Susan* (*sic*) was chosen as its inaugural production as an exemplar of a Georgian melodrama. The Theatre Royal, Bury Street St. Edmunds, http://secure.theatreroyal.org, accessed October 21, 2011.
72. David Grimsted, *Melodrama Unveiled*, 254; Marvin Carlson, "He Never Should Bow Down to a Domineering Frown," 151, 158.
73. They performed it in Boston in 1853 and St. Louis in 1855, only two years before the Marshes would arrive there. Robert Samuel Badal, "Kate and Ellen Bateman: A Study in Precocity" (PhD dissertation, Northwestern University, 1971), 159–68; September 9, 1853 Howard Athenaeum playbill, HTC.
74. Claudia Johnson, *American Actress: Perspectives on the Nineteenth Century* (Chicago: Nelson-Hall, 1984), 155. Renée M. Sentilles, *Performing Menken*, 183; photo in Elizabeth Reitz Mullenix, *Wearing the Breeches*, 88.
75. Ellen and Kate Bateman played the smaller roles of Jacob Twig and Dolly Mayflower, respectively; Howard Athenaeum playbill, September 9, 1853, HTC.
76. *New York Daily Tribune*, September 16, October 20, November 8, 1856, *Chronicling America*, Library of Congress.
77. David L. Rinear, *Stage, Page, Scandals, and Vandals*, 72.
78. *Ibid.*, 127.
79. The phrase is borrowed from an anonymous admirer of Kate Bateman, quoted in Jim Davis, "Freaks, Prodigies, and Marvelous Mimicry," 190.
80. *Boston Post*, December 12, 15, 17, 1856, BPL; Howard Athenaeum playbill, HTC.
81. Howard Athenaeum playbill for *Naiad Queen*, January 13, 1857, HTC.
82. Unidentified, undated clipping in the "Marsh Children" file, HTC; it is possibly from a subsequent tour.
83. Unidentified, undated clipping in the "Marsh Children" file, HTC.
84. *Clipper*, January 10, 1857, NYPL.

85. Lawrence H. Officer and Samuel H. Williamson, "Purchasing Power of Money in the United States from 1774 to 2005."
86. Howard Athenaeum playbills and programs, February 10, 11, 12, 13, 1857, HTC.
87. Bluford Adams, *E Pluribus Barnum*, 58.
88. "Saturday's Dramatic Gossip," [February 1857], unidentified clipping in the Marsh Children folder, HTC. On photography, see William C. Darrah, *Cartes de Visite in 19C Photography* (Gettysburg, PA: W. C. Darrah, 1981), esp. 1–4, and Ben L. Bassham, *The Theatrical Photographs of Napoleon Sarony* (Kent, OH: Kent State University Press, 1978).
89. The rare salt print by Cutting and Turner is in the collection of the Louisiana State Museum (Object #07159) but the image is severely degraded.
90. Howard Athenaeum playbill, February 10, 1857, HTC. The bill lists them as "Louise & Mary Marsh," an inaccuracy that will be discussed in chapter 3.
91. Howard Athenaeum playbill, HTC.
92. Howard Athenaeum program, February 13, 1857, HTC.
93. The troupe closed on February 13, 1857. Although undated, the clipping very likely refers to this engagement because of its reference to "Friday." During the troupe's early period, 1857 was the only year in which February 13 fell on a Friday.
94. "Note to the Public," Howard Athenaeum programs, February 10, 11, 12, 13, 1857, HTC.
95. *Clipper*, March 28, 1857, NYPL. *St Louis Missouri Republican*, June 8, 1857, p. 3, col. 2, SHSM.
96. Charles Van Ravenswaay, *Saint Louis*, 328, 342, 353, Google Books, http://books.google.com/books?id=rMBVmdUygRMC&q=marsh#v=onepage&q=theatre&f=false, accessed August 5, 2013.
97. *St. Louis Leader*, June 9, 1857, SHSM.
98. David L. Rinear, *Stage, Page, Scandals, and Vandals*, 59.
99. John S. Kendall, *The Golden Age of the New Orleans Theatre*, 198.
100. June 8, 1857, *St. Louis Leader*, p. 1, col. 7, SHSM; Benjamin McArthur, *The Man Who Was Rip Van Winkle*, 124; De Witt Bodeen, *Ladies of the Footlights* (Pasadena, CA: The Logan Printing and Binding Co., 1937; repr. Whitefish, MT: Kessinger Publishing Rare Reprints, 2005), 68, www.kessinger.net, accessed May 15, 2011.
101. J. S. Dalrymple, *The Naiad Queen*, pdf.
102. In Dalrymple's text the character is "Baptiste."
103. *St. Louis Missouri Republican*, June 8, 1856, p. 3. col. 1, SHSM.
104. *St. Louis Leader*, June 9, 1857, SHSM.

105. *St. Louis Leader*, June 10, 1857, SHSM.
106. *Picayune*, March 19, 1858, NYPL.
107. *St. Louis Leader*, June 8, 1857, p. 1, col. 7, SHSM.
108. Gerald Bordman, *American Musical Theatre* 3rd. edition, 2001, 20, 25. Kendall reports, Mrs. John Wood performed *The Zouaves* in New Orleans in May 1862, and "Owens supplied her with forty young women who wore the appropriate costumes, and sang and danced to great applause." The *Clipper* records dozens of Zouave performances during 1861–62. Renée Sentilles has written on their American reincarnation.

    In late 1859 a volunteer militia from Chicago named "The United States Zouave Cadets" trained by Elmer Ellsworth, began traveling around the Northeast performing drills and marching in parades. Their display of skills earned the Zouaves celebration in the national press and enormous crowds gathered to watch their rather flamboyant drill, inspired by the original Berber Zouave battalions of the French Army.

109. *Cincinnati Enquirer*, July 22, 1857, PLCHC.
110. *San Francisco Daily Morning Chronicle*, February 28, March 2, 1869; ProQuest Historical Newspapers, accessed July 12, 2011.
111. Unidentified, undated clipping in the "Marsh Children" file, HTC; it is possibly from a subsequent tour.
112. *St. Louis Missouri Republican*, June 12, 1857, SHSM.
113. *St. Louis Missouri Republican*, June 17, 1857, SHSM.
114. Letter to Joseph Jefferson, quoted in Nora Titone, *My Thoughts Be Bloody*, 170.
115. Maud Otis Skinner, *One Man in His Time*, 158.
116. *Cincinnati Enquirer*, July 21, 1857, PLCHC.
117. *New York Daily Tribune*, July 30, 1857, *Chronicling America*, Library of Congress.
118. *Clipper*, July 27, 1857, NYPL; *New York Daily Times*, August 1, 1857, ProQuest, http://search.proquest.com.central.ezproxy.cuny.edu:2048/hnpnewyorktimes/docview/95944918/fulltextPDF/66CBDCA147ED4B37PQ/2?accountid=26979, accessed March 29, 2015; *New York Daily Tribune*, July 30, 1857, *Chronicling America*, Library of Congress, accessed September 26, 2012.
119. *Clipper*, August 8, 1857, NYPL.
120. *New York Daily Times*, August 17, 19, 24, 1857, NYPL.
121. The Marsh-Stewart contract can be found in the Louisiana Archives, docket 12246, housed in the Louisiana Division of the New Orleans Public Library. The contract is in a file relating to a suit brought before the Third District Court of Louisiana in 1858. All of the Marsh-Stewart documents discussed in this chapter are in the same location, henceforth designated as LA Archives.

122. *New York Daily Tribune*, August 26, 1857, *Chronicling America*, Library of Congress.
123. *New York Daily Times*, August 17, 19, 24, 1857, NYPL; *Picayune*, 27 February 1858, NYPL.
124. *Clipper*, 5 September 1857, NYPL.
125. HTC.
126. Nora Titone, *My Thoughts Be Bloody*, 159.
127. Throughout this text the title of Tobin's play has been regularized as *The Honeymoon* although in playbills and newspapers it was variously called *Honeymoon*, *Honey Moon*, or *The Honey Moon.*
128. David Grimsted, *Melodrama Unveiled*, 108, 127.
129. Howard Athenaeum clippings file, HTC.
130. *Clipper*, October 24, 1857, NYPL.
131. Howard Athenaeum program, January 8, 1857, HTC.
132. Howard Athenaeum playbill, HTC. The clipping is hand labeled "January 8, 1857" but this is clearly an error since Stewart did not sign a contract with the troupe until July 1857. Fall 1857 was the only season that Stewart played with the troupe at the Howard.
133. *Clipper*, January 23, 1858, NYPL.
134. David Carlyon, *Dan Rice*, 100.
135. Spaulding was a druggist turned theatre entrepreneur and circus owner. He had various partnerships with Charles P. Rogers, David Bidwell, and Dan Rice, among others. See John S. Kendall, *The Golden Age of the New Orleans Theatre*, 477–79; and David Carlyon, *Dan Rice*, especially chapter 6, "Spaulding and Spicy Rice."
136. *New Orleans Picayune*, March 28, 1858, NYPL.
137. *New Orleans Picayune*, February 27–April 1, 1858, NYPL.
138. *Clipper*, April 20, 1858, NYPL.
139. Scott Gac, *Singing for Freedom*; Mark Cosdon, *The Hanlon Brothers.*
140. *Clipper*, April 11, 1857, NYPL.
141. *Clipper*, August 15, 1857, NYPL.
142. *Ibid.*
143. *Clipper*, August 29, 1857, NYPL.
144. *Clipper*, November 14, 1857, NYPL.
145. *Clipper*, December 5, 1857, NYPL.
146. Quinn was the same age as Georgie Marsh. At six years of age, Quinn had made front-page news in San Francisco playing Hamlet and other Shakespearean roles. See Nicole Anae, "An Infant Phenomenon in Colonial Australia," 55–78; Barbara J. Griffith, "All the Lovely Sisterhood," 7–10; George MacMinn, *The Theatre of the Golden Era in California*, 102.

147. *Clipper*, November 28, 1857, NYPL.
148. *Clipper*, December 5, 1857, NYPL.
149. Andrew Davis, *America's Longest Run*, 112.
150. *Boston Sunday Record*, October 3, 1886: "An Actors' Career: Louis Aldrich's Reminiscences of 31 Years of Stage Life," Aldrich clippings file, Billy Rose Theatre Collection, NYPL.
151. *Clipper*, November 14 and 21, 1857, NYPL.
152. *Clipper*, May 15, 1858, NYPL.
153. *Marsh's Juvenile Dramatic Era*, HTC.

2. First Losses, and a Battle Won

1. See Shauna Vey, "An American Antebellum Child-Actor Contract," in Gillian Arrighi and Victor Emeljanow, eds., *Entertaining Children*," 33–50.
2. *St. Louis Missouri Republican*, June 5, 1857, SHSM.
3. The timing makes it entirely possible this is the same man who organized Nagle's Juvenile Comedians, which had a short life in the summer and fall of 1857, the period just following the separation of Nagle from the Marsh Troupe, but the identity cannot be confirmed.
4. *St. Louis Leader*, June 5, 1857, p. 1, col. 4. The same story was covered in *St. Louis Missouri Republican*, June 5, 1857, p. 3, col. 1, SHSM, and *New York Herald*, June 14, 1857, 2, http://fultonhistory.com/Fulton.html/, accessed August 24, 2011.
5. T. Allston Brown, *History of the American Stage*, 235.
6. Missouri State Archives, Missouri's Dred Scott Case, 1846–1857 (2007–12), Missouri Office of the Secretary of State, Missouri State Library, SHSM, accessed June 25, 2012.
7. Although Mr. Scott was denied his freedom by the court decision in March, Scott was freed by his owner on May 26, 1857.
8. Nora Titone, *My Thoughts Be Bloody*, 159.
9. *Ibid. St. Louis Leader*, June 5, 1857, SHSM.
10. *St. Louis Leader*, June 5, 1857, p. 1, col. 4; *New York Herald*, June 14, 1857, 2, SHSM.
11. *Frank Leslie's Popular Monthly*, April 1886, 439.
12. T. Allston Brown, *History of the American Stage*, 236.
13. John S. Kendall, *The Golden Age of the New Orleans Theatre*, 477.
14. T. Allston Brown gives her birth year as 1844; *Clipper*, May 31, 1862. Her obituaries give her age as seventy-six in August 1919. "Obituary 1—no Title," *New York Times (1857–1922)*, August 16, 1919, http://central.ezproxy.cuny.edu:2048/docview/100456397?accountid=26979, accessed August 28, 2011.

15. *Ibid. St. Louis Leader*, June 5, 1857, SHSM.
16. Rick Altman, *The American Film Musical*, 5.
17. *St. Louis Leader*, June 5, 1857, SHSM.
18. *St. Louis Missouri Republican*, June 5, 1857, SHSM.
19. See Barbara Welter, "The Cult of True Womanhood," 151–74.
20. Similar events would trouble child actor Freddie Bartholomew in the 1920s when he was brought to Hollywood by an aunt. After his success in films, various relatives sued for a piece of his earnings, undermining his career and depleting his profits.
21. Viviana A. Zelizer, *Pricing the Pricing Child*, 85–112.
22. T. Allston Brown, *History of the American Stage*, 347–48.
23. *Cincinnati Enquirer*, December 21, 1853, PLCHC.
24. Siobhan Fitzpatrick, ed., *Orphan to Apprentice*, 1.
25. *Picayune*, March 18, 1858, NYPL; Howard Athenaeum playbill, HTC. The clipping is hand labeled "January 8, 1857," but this is clearly an error since Stewart did not sign a contract with the troupe until July 1857. Fall 1857 was the only season that Stewart played with the troupe at the Howard.
26. *Picayune*, March 26, 1858, NYPL.
27. LA Archives.
28. *Ibid.*
29. Marc R. Staenberg and Daniel K. Stuart, *Children as Chattels*. Retrieved from *A Minor Consideration*, www.minorcon.org, accessed June 1, 2012.
30. Laurence Senelick, *The Age and Stage of George L. Fox*, 63. An adult member of the same company earned $18 per week. As a young actor in 1842, Cordelia's father had been paid $8 per week (18). For actors salaries after 1880 see Benjamin McArthur, *Actors and American Culture*. He cites an average player's salary in 1894 as $35 per week, more than double the average manufacturing job at that time (24). There is no comparable study for the antebellum period.
31. W. J. Rorabaugh, *The Craft Apprentice*, 141; Nina E. Lerman, "Preparing for the Duties and Practical Business of Life," 42.
32. Lawrence H. Officer and Samuel H. Williamson, "Purchasing Power of Money in the United States from 1774 to the Present."
33. The term "apprenticeship" has been used to describe a variety of situations including indentured servitude and the binding out of paupers and foundlings. Apprenticeships varied drastically relative to the economic and social class of the individuals involved. I use the term to refer to a class of boys who were bound out for the express purpose of learning a craft. See W. J. Rorabaugh, *The Craft Apprentice*; Nina

E. Lerman, "Preparing for the Duties and Practical Business of Life," 31–59; Brian P. Luskey, "What Is My Prospects?"; Richard D. Stott, *Workers in the Metropolis*; Ian Quimby, *Apprenticeship in Colonial Philadelphia*.

34. Nina E. Lerman, "Preparing for the Duties and Practical Business of Life," 41–42.
35. Quimby identified sixty-eight different crafts in eighteenth-century Philadelphia (30).
36. See W. J. Rorabaugh, *The Craft Apprentice*, passim.
37. *Ibid.*, 99.
38. Specifically, the Children of the Queens Revels, Edel Lamb, *Performing Childhood in the Early Modern Theatre*, 57, 56. Andrew Gurr asserts that arrangements were not so formal: "There was no set pattern, and nothing quite like the seven-year apprenticeships that youths in the guilds went through before rising to the status of journeyman." *The Shakespearean Stage 1574–1642*, 113–14. In practice, not all apprenticeships led to careers, although Gurr mentions Nathan Field, Joseph Taylor, William Ecclestone, and Stephen Hammerton as positive examples.
39. Edel Lamb, *Performing Childhood in the Early Modern Theatre*, 56–57. Lamb views the Children of the Queens Revels as a derivative of the Children of the Chapel and antecedent of the Children of Blackfriars and the Children of Whitefriars who performed until 1613 (11).
40. Robert J. Myers and Joyce Brodowski, "Rewriting the Hallams," 1. See also Don B. Wilmeth with Tice Miller, *Cambridge Guide to American Theatre*, 182.
41. Robert J. Myers and Joyce Brodowski, "Rewriting the Hallams,"5.
42. Nina E. Lerman, "Preparing for the Duties and Practical Business of Life," 41.
43. Laurence Senelick, *The Age and Stage of George L. Fox*, passim.
44. Cordelia Howard Macdonald and George P. Howard, "Memoirs of the Original Little Eva," 281. Cordelia made the decision to retire from the stage at age thirteen; her parents continued to act.
45. Five generations of Cowells were actors, and several were memoirists as well including Joe Cowell, *Thirty Years Passed Among the Players in England and America* (New York: Harper and Bros., 1844); Mrs. Sam (Emilie Marguerite Ebsworth) Cowell, *The Cowells in America: Being the Diary of Mrs. Samm Cowell*, ed. M. Willson Disher (London: Oxford University Press, 1934). See also Heather M. McMahon, "Profit, Purity,

and Perversity"; Robert Samuel Badal, "Kate and Ellen Bateman: A Study in Precocity" (PhD dissertation, Northwestern University, 1971).

46. While Quimby and Luskey aver that the erosion had begun as early as the American Revolution, other scholars including Rorabaugh and Lerman point to many examples of the practice continuing up to the Civil War. I am not concerned here with pinpointing the beginning of the decline or prioritizing among the factors that have been identified as contributory. My argument relies on the results of the change, about which there is general agreement.
47. For example, an early shoe factory in Lowell, Massachusetts, stopped taking in apprentices. Boys tended machines but did not learn how to make an entire shoe. W. J. Rorabaugh, *The Craft Apprentice*, 60.
48. Rorabaugh explains:

> This new system of manufacturing products did not necessarily mean the use of machinery; it did mean the concentration of capital, available for the first time through the new financial system, under the leadership of selected master craftsmen in order to use skilled labor more efficiently. . . . An economy based on cash-wage jobs threatened apprenticeship. In a society without much money a youth sacrificed little in lost wages by becoming an apprentice. The free room and board that the apprentice received in return for learning a trade was compensation enough. In that kind of society no true alternative existed. (*Ibid.*, 68–69)

49. *Ibid.*, 73
50. *Ibid.*, 38.
51. *Ibid.*, 139.
52. The content of this paragraph and all of the quotations are taken from *Ibid.*, 60, 73, 74, 139, and 209.
53. Quimby found terms ranging from under two to twenty years. Ian Quimby, *Apprenticeship in Colonial Philadelphia*, 37.
54. *A Father's Gift to His Son on His Becoming an Apprentice* (New York: Samuel Ward & Sons; Baltimore: Samuel S. Ward & Co., 1821), quoted in Ian Quimby, *Apprenticeship in Colonial Philadelphia*, 7.
55. Ian Quimby, *Apprenticeship in Colonial Philadelphia*, 52.
56. Christine A. Adamec and William L. Pierce, eds., "Introduction," in *The Encyclopedia of Adoption*, 2nd edition (NY: Facts on File, 2000), xxi, quoted in Carol J. Singley, "Neither Indentured nor Adopted," in Siobhan Fitzpatrick, ed., *Orphan to Apprentice*, 19.
57. LA Archives.

58. Emphasis added; *New York Times*, December 5, 1855.
59. Emphasis added; *Picayune*, March 18, 1858.
60. Emphasis added; *Argus*, November 4, 1860, http://nla.gov.au/nla.news-page 201194, accessed June 20, 2010.
61. *Picayune*, March 18, 1858.
62. Edwin G. Burrows and Mike Wallace, *Gotham*, 817.
63. The statement from Dr. Warren Brierhill certifying Alfred's health and billing Marsh fifty dollars is dated April 2, 1858, after the court had decided in Marsh's favor. However, the judge's opinion in the appeal states that the question of Alfred's health was determined by the initial court. Therefore, the examination was probably conducted several days before the statement was signed. Another possibility is that Mrs. Stewart had arranged for a different doctor to examine Alfred prior to March 30, 1858, but no documentation exists to support this thesis.
64. *Picayune*, April 22, 1858.
65. *Clipper*, May 1, 1858. The item seems to indicate that she is an actress but no record of her performing career has been located. If this was the case, Alfred Stewart, like Cordelia Howard and the Bateman children, was following the family craft.
66. The documents in the Louisiana Archives indicate a different outcome from that announced in the newspapers.
67. The judge's opinion uses the term "relator" here. Both "plaintiff" and "relator" are used throughout the LA Archive documents to indicate Mrs. Stewart.
68. *Clipper*, May 29, 1858.
69. Miriam Forman-Brunell and Leslie Paris, *The Girls' History and Culture Reader*, 11.
70. *Richmond Enquirer*, May 28 and June 1, 1858; *Richmond Dispatch* June 2, 3, 4, and 5, 1858; *New York Times*, July 9, 1858; *Clipper*, June 5 and 9, July 3, 10, and 17, 1858.
71. Kurt Gänzl, *Lydia Thompson*, 84.
72. *Clipper*, June 5, 1858.
73. Emphasis in original; *Clipper*, June 26, 1858.
74. "Mirror Interviews Louis Aldrich," *New York Dramatic Mirror*, June 9, 1894; "Life and Death of Louis Aldrich," *New York Dramatic Mirror*, June 29, 1901; "Louis Aldrich," in Louis M. Simon, *A History of the Actors' Fund of America*, 111–14; Franklin Graham, *Histrionic Montreal*, 251; "An Actor's Career: Louis Aldrich's Reminiscences of 31 Years of Stage Life: His Opinion of Modern Drama," *Boston Sunday Record*, October 3, 1886, Louis Aldrich file, Billy Rose Theatre Collection, NYPL; John Bouvé Clapp and Edwin Francis Edgett, *Players of the Present*.

75. Benjamin McArthur, *The Man Who Was Rip Van Winkle*, 108–9; Barbara Wallace Grossman, *A Spectacle of Suffering*, 35–56. Ellsler may have been Morris's lover as well as mentor. Aldrich was already with the Marsh Troupe by the time Morris joined Ellsler in 1861, although they met later. Clara Morris was born the same year as Mary Marsh, but by the time Morris began her career, Mary Marsh was already dead.
76. Daniel Thomas Cook, *The Commodification of Childhood*, 15–16.
77. *Clipper*, May 28, 1858.
78. Aldrich later bemoaned the combination company's rise over the stock company that had provided young actors with such excellent opportunities for training. *Boston Sunday Record*, October 3, 1886.
79. On May 11, 1859, Aldrich received a benefit in New Orleans on the fiftieth night of the troupe's residence at the Spaulding and Rogers Amphitheatre, *Clipper*, May 28, 1858.
80. *Cincinnati Enquirer*, July 11, 1857, p. 1, col. 5, PLCHC.
81. *Cincinnati Enquirer*, October 21, 1858, PLCHC.
82. *Cincinnati Enquirer*, September 26, 1858, PLCHC.
83. At the Quebec Music Hall, *Quebec Colonist*, August 23, 1856, Google News Archive.
84. *New York Daily Tribune*, December 8, 1855.
85. *Cincinnati Enquirer*, July 9, 1857, October 12, 1858, PLCHC.
86. *Picayune*, February 27, 1858, NYPL.
87. Marar Gubar argues that children were the intended audience for most performances; "Entertaining Children of All Ages," 6.
88. *Marsh's Juvenile Dramatic Era*, HTC.
89. *Cincinnati Enquirer*, September 9–October 21, 1858, PLCHC. It is interesting that Marsh chose the word "Union" at this point in time.
90. Emphasis added; *New York Daily Tribune*, July 30, 1857, *Chronicling America*, accessed September 22, 2011.
91. *Clipper*, January 22, 1859, NYPL.
92. James H. Dorman Jr., *Theatre in the Antebellum South*, 119.
93. *Ibid.*, 154–55.
94. *Clipper*, April 9, 1859.
95. *Ibid.*
96. *Clipper*, May 7, 1859.
97. *Ibid.*
98. If Mrs. Stewart had a written contract with Spaulding, it remains undiscovered. None of the documents examined for this chapter enlarge upon the terms of their agreement.
99. *Clipper*, May 7, 1859.

100. *Cleveland Plain Dealer*, February 8, 1859, quoted by Stephanie Lincecum, Rose Hill Cemetery blog, http://rosehillcemeterymacongeorgia.blogspot.com, accessed October 28, 2011.
101. *Clipper*, May 7, 1859, NYPL.
102. *Cincinnati Enquirer*, January 30, 1859, p. 1, col. 4, PLCHC.
103. *Clipper*, February 19, 1859, NYPL.
104. *Ibid.*
105. Emphasis added; *Clipper*, February 26, 1859, NYPL.
106. *Clipper*, March 5 and 12, 1859, NYPL.
107. "Theatricals in General," *Cincinnati Enquirer*, April 3, 1859, 3, PLCHC.
108. "Music and Drama. Theatrical. New Orleans," *Cincinnati Enquirer*, April 24, May 22, 1859, 3, PLCHC.
109. *Richmond Enquirer*, May 28, and June 1, 1858; *Richmond Dispatch*, June 2, 3, 4, and 5, 1858; *New York Times*, July 9, 1858. *Clipper*, June 5 and 9, July 3, 10, and 17, 1858.
110. T. Allston Brown, *History of the American Stage*, 347–48.

3. A Perfect Angel—Forever

1. *Marsh's Juvenile Dramatic Era* 1, no. 7 (October 5, 1857), Marsh Children folder, HTC. Possibly the only issue ever produced.
2. *Clipper*, 1855, NYPL.
3. Laurence Hutton, *Curiosities of the American Stage*, 245.
4. *Cincinnati Enquirer*, November 26, 1853, PLCHC.
5. *Clipper*, February 19, 1859, NYPL.
6. *Ibid.*
7. HTC. The *Era* promises a biography of a leading player in each issue. Unfortunately, subsequent issues of the *Era* are not extant, if in fact they ever existed.
8. James Kincaid, *Child-Loving*, 223.
9. Scholars have used various terms in their discussion of childhood including Romantic, ideal, idealized, sentimental, and Racial Innocence. These terms interchangeably here as they all refer to the same phenomena and my concern is less with terminology than the relationship between the social construct of childhood and the lived experience of the members of the Marsh Juveniles.
10. Laurence Hutton, *Curiosities of the American Stage*, 245–46.
11. James Kincaid, *Child-Loving*, 72.
12. Anne Higonnet, *Pictures of Innocence*, 9, 8.
13. Neil Postman, *The Disappearance of Childhood*, 51.
14. Anne Higonnet, *Pictures of Innocence*, 24.

15. Robin Bernstein, *Racial Innocence*, 4.
16. The verb is Bernstein's; *ibid.*, 34.
17. Viviana A. Zelizer, *Pricing the Priceless Child*, 95.
18. *Ibid.*, 95.
19. See Benjamin McArthur, "'Forbid Them Not,'"; Shauna Vey, "Good Intentions and Fearsome Prejudice."
20. Ann Douglas, *The Feminization of American Culture*, 50.
21. Marah Gubar, "Entertaining Children of All Ages," 7.
22. Jared Diamond. *The World until Yesterday*, 2012.
23. Barbara Welter, "The Cult of True Womanhood," 160; Sara Jane Clarke, *Greenwood Leaves* (Boston: Ticknor, Reed, and Fields, 1850), quoted in *ibid.*, 160.
24. Ann Douglas, *The Feminization of American Culture*, 51–52.
25. *Ibid.*, 74.
26. "This role of the child as the antithesis to the marketplace was rooted in the unbreakable early association of children with the home." Ellen Marie Snyder, "Innocents in a Worldly World," in Richard E. Meyer, ed., *Cemeteries and Gravemarkers*, 13.
27. This ideal ignored the reality in which increasing numbers of girls and young women labored in household service, factories, and other trades outside of the home. The ideal was only available to the middle and upper classes.
28. Jane H. Hunter, *How Young Ladies Became Girls*, 12.
29. HTC.
30. Robin Bernstein, *Racial Innocence*, *Figure I.2*, p. 5; Harriet Beecher Stowe, *Uncle Tom's Cabin or Life Among the Lowly*, edited by David S. Reynolds (Oxford, UK: Oxford University Press, 2011).
31. Robin Bernstein, *Racial Innocence*, 5; Jill Weitzman Fenichell, cited in Amy Hughes, *Spectacles of Reform*, 102.
32. Jane O'Connor, *The Cultural Significance of the Child Star*, 105.
33. James Kincaid, *Child-Loving*, 220.
34. John W. Frick, *Theatre, Culture and Temperance Reform in Nineteenth-Century America*, 57.
35. Robin Bernstein, *Racial Innocence*, 24.
36. Rosemarie K. Bank, *Theatre Culture in America*, 110.
37. Christopher B. Balme, "Playbills and the Theatrical Public Sphere," in Charlotte M. Canning and Thomas Postlewaite, eds., *Representing the Theatrical Past*, 42.
38. October 5, 1857, Howard Athenaeum Register: *Marsh's Juvenile Dramatic Era* 1, no. 7.

39. Mullenneaux points out that all of Cordelia Howard's characters were "ultra-virtuous"; "Our Genius, Goodness, and Gumption," 291.
40. Anne Varty, *Children and Theatre in Victorian Britain*, 137.
41. James Kincaid, *Child-Loving*, 220.
42. "Art Matters," *Putnam's Monthly* 7, no. 37 (January 1856): 111–12.
43. Anne Varty, *Children and Theatre in Victorian Britain*, especially chap. 2, "Looking Glass Children: The Performing Child as Erotic Subject"; James Kincaid, *Child Loving*; Marah Gubar, *Artful Dodgers*, and "Who Watched *The Children's Pinafore*?," 411.
44. James Kincaid, *Child Loving*, 374. On similar practices in visual art, see Anne Higonnet, *Pictures of Innocence*.
45. See Gubar's discussion in *Artful Dodgers*, chap. 3, "Reciprocal Aggression: Un-Romantic Agency in the Art of Lewis Carroll."
46. Laurence Hutton, *Curiosities of the American Stage*, 246.
47. Marah Gubar, "Who Watched *The Children's Pinafore*?," 421.
48. *Cincinnati Enquirer*, July 5–25, 1857, PLCHC.
49. *Cincinnati Enquirer*, July 7, 8, 9, 10, 11, 12, 14, 16, 17, 18, 19, 21, 22, 23, 24, 25, 1857, PLCHC.
50. *Boston Post*, December 12, 15, 17, 1856, BPL.
51. *Cincinnati Enquirer*, July 9, 1857, PLCHC.
52. Weymss, *Twenty-Six Years* (New York: Burgess, Stringer and Co., 1847), 344, quoted in David Grimsted, *Melodrama Unveiled*, 105.
53. See Meredith Henne, *The Richmond Theater Fire*.
54. John Campbell Butler, *Historical Record of Macon and Central Georgia*, 216.
55. *Cleveland Plain Dealer*, February 8, 1859, Rose Hill Cemetery blog, accessed December 12, 2011.
56. Alisa C. Roost, "Melodrama or Tragedy? The United States Worldview since 9–11."
57. *Clipper*, February 19, 1859, NYPL.
58. October 5, 1857, Howard Athenaeum Register: *Marsh's Juvenile Dramatic Era* 1, no. 7.
59. John W. Frick, *Theatre, Culture and Temperance Reform in Nineteenth-Century America*, 135.
60. Cynthia Eagle Russett. *Sexual Science*, 12, 51, 132.
61. *Ibid.*
62. Viviana A. Zelizer, *Pricing the Priceless Child*, 85–96.
63. John Campbell Butler, *Historical Record of Macon and Central Georgia*, 216.
64. *Ibid.*

65. *Cincinnati Enquirer*, January 30, 1859, p. 1, col. 4, PLCHC.
66. Mary Grace Swift, "Dancers in Flames." On the 1861 death of the five Gale sisters and others in Philadelphia, see also *Clipper*, September 14, 21, 28, 1861, NYPL.
67. Ann Douglas, *The Feminization of American Culture*, 12.
68. Robin Bernstein, *Racial Innocence*, 24.
69. J. M. Barrie, *Peter Pan* (1911; Project Guttenberg, 1991), accessed February 10, 2012.
70. James Kincaid, *Child-Loving*, 226.
71. Diana Serra Cary, *Whatever Happened to Baby Peggy?*, 249; interview with the author.
72. Diana Serra Cary, *Whatever Happened to Baby Peggy?*, 280.
73. James Kincaid, *Child-Loving*, 82.
74. Stanley French, "The Cemetery as Cultural Institution," 53; Margaretta J. Darnall, "The American Cemetery as Picturesque Landscape," 252. Other examples are Mt. Auburn (founded in Boston 1831), Laurel Hill (Philadelphia, 1836) Greenwood (Brooklyn, 1838), Bellefontaine (St. Louis, 1849), Mt. Hope (Rochester), Allegheny (Pittsburgh, 1844), Spring Grove (Cincinnati, 1845), Cave Hill (Louisville, 1848), Hollywood (Richmond, 1849), and Magnolia (Charleston, 1850).
75. Thomas J. Craughwell, *Stealing Lincoln's Body*, 128, quoted in Seth Mallios and David M. Caterino, "Mortality, Money and Commemoration," 432.
76. Lynn Rainville, "Hanover Deathscapes," 559.
77. Ann Douglas, *The Feminization of American Culture*, 212.
78. *Macon Telegraph*, January 15, 1907, 4, Georgia Historic Newspapers, Digital Library of Georgia, Georgia Public Library Service, hereafter GHN, accessed April 5, 2011.
79. Blanche Linden-Ward, "Strange but Genteel Pleasure Grounds," in Richard Meyer, ed., *Cemeteries and Gravemarkers*, 317.
80. *Ibid.*, 318.
81. J. C. Louden, *On the Laying Out, Planting and Managing of Cemeteries, and on the Improvement of Church Yards* (London: Longman, Brown, Green, and Longman, 1843), 66, quoted in Margaretta J. Darnall, "The American Cemetery as Picturesque Landscape," 264.
82. Stanley French, "The Cemetery as Cultural Institution," 54.
83. Heather McKillop, "Recognizing Children's Graves in Nineteenth-Century Cemeteries," 81.
84. *Ibid.*, 90.
85. *Cleveland Plain Dealer*, February 8, 1860, Rose Hill Cemetery blog, accessed December 12, 2011.

86. Aubrey Cannon, "The Historical Dimension in Mortuary Expressions of Status and Sentiment," 440, fig. 1, "Popularity trends for selected monument shapes." Also see Frederick Burgess, *English Churchyard Memorials*, 133–35.
87. Susan Buckham, "Commemoration as an expression of personal relationships and group identities," 165.
88. *Ibid.*, 161.
89. Association for Gravestone Studies, "Some Common Symbols/Emblems Found in Nineteenth-Century Cemeteries," accessed for download, April 6, 2012; Douglas Keister, *Stories in Stone*, 62.
90. Lynn Rainville, "Hanover Deathscapes," 572.
91. Karen Sánchez-Eppler, *Dependent States*, 141.
92. Ann Douglas, *The Feminization of American Culture*, 202.
93. Victorian practice included photos of dead children posed as if living, bracelets made out of the deceased's hair, wall-hanging shadowboxes filled with artifacts of the deceased, and mourning cards, but I have found no instances of a reliquary such as Mary's.
94. Kevin Trainor, "*Pars pro toto*," 271.
95. *Ibid.*, 271; Peter Brown, *The Cult of the Saints*, 55.
96. Kevin Trainor, "*Pars pro toto*," 272.
97. John Campbell Butler, *Historical Record of Macon and Central Georgia*, 216. Writing in 1879, Butler saw the wreath in a glass case that he locates at the base of the stone. Bridges Smith ("All aboard for the Seeing-Macon Car," *Macon Telegraph*, December 16, 1917, Rose Hill Cemetery blog, accessed December 13, 2011), mentions a circular metal case, on top of the slab; however, it was missing by that time and he may have confused it with the urn, also missing. John T. Boifeuillet described Mary's grave in his "Caught on the Wing" column (*Macon Telegraph*, January 15, 1907, 4) and made no mention of the case, so it was probably removed prior to 1907.
98. Joseph Roach, *It* (Ann Arbor, MI: University of Michigan Press, 2007), 63.
99. *Ibid.*, 55.

4. Chasing Audiences and Aging Out

1. *Clipper*, June 11, 1859.
2. *Clipper*, July 16, 1859.
3. *Clipper*, August 20, 1859.
4. *Clipper*, September 3, 17, October 1, 1859.
5. *Clipper*, October 8, 1859.
6. *Clipper*, October 18, 1859.

7. Playbill, June 11, 1855, New Concert Hall, Batavia, New York; October 19, 1855, Walnut Street Theatre, Philadelphia; December 30, 1856, Howard Athenaeum, Boston; "Marsh Children" file, HTC.
8. *Clipper*, December 31, 1859. T. Allston Brown confuses the names of the Mousely sisters, writing of "Helen Mousely who afterward married William Henry, a property man, in 1862 and died in New York from the effects of burns received in trying to save Mary Guerineau" (*History of the American Stage*, 235). While both girls acted with the troupe, at the time of the accident, only Georgina was reported injured. It seems likely that Helen's postmarriage death was unrelated to the 1859 stage accident.
9. *Clipper*, February 4, 11, 1860.
10. Grace King, *New Orleans*, 290; *Clipper*, February 18, March 17, 1860.
11. Grace King, *New Orleans*, 300.
12. "Mirror Interview Louis Aldrich," *New York Dramatic Mirror*, June 9, 1894, fultonhistory.com, accessed August 24, 2011; "An Actor's Career: Louis Aldrich's Reminiscences of 31 Years of Stage Life: His Opinion of Modern Drama," *Boston Sunday Record*, October 3, 1886, clipping in Aldrich file, Billy Rose Theatre Collection, NYPL.
13. Nora Titone, *My Thoughts Be Bloody*, 122; Ulysses S. Grant, *Personal Memoirs*, chap. 14. The trip indirectly cost Booth his life, as well as his earnings.
14. "Panama Railroad Completed," *The Western Journal and Civilian* 8, no. 6, M. Carver and T. Cobb, editors and proprietors, St. Louis, Missouri, May, 1855 (The Cooper Collections); *Wikipedia Commons*, accessed August 14, 2013, http://en.wikipedia.org/wiki/File:Panama_RR_Opens_1855.jpg#Transcription.
15. *Clipper*, August 20, 1859; May 12, 1860 (dateline April 4).
16. *Sacramento Daily Union*, July 21, 1860, CDNC.
17. *Sacramento Daily Union*, July 16, 1860, CDNC; Playbill, Forrest Theatre, Sacramento, May 17, 1860, Marsh Children folder, HTC.
18. *Sacramento Daily Union*, July 20, 1860, CDNC.
19. U.S. Census *1870*; *New York Ward 20 District 19 (2nd Enum), New York, New York;* Roll: *M593_1048*; Page: *871A*; Image: *343*; Family History Library Film: *552547*; and *New York Ward 20 District 18 (2nd Enum), New York, New York*; Roll: *M593_1048*; Page: *828B*; Image: *258*; Family History Library Film: *552547*. Ancestry.com. *1870 United States Federal Census* (database online). Provo, UT: Ancestry.com Operations, Inc., 2009, accessed June 12, 2012.
20. *Bell's Life in Sydney and Sporting Chronicle*, August 3, 1861, 2, NLA, accessed June 27, 2012.
21. *Marsh's Juvenile Dramatic Era*, October 5, 1857, HTC.

22. *Clipper*, September 22, 1860.
23. Joseph Jefferson, making the same journey a year later on a faster than average ship, reported a fifty-five-day voyage, departing from San Francisco September 10, arriving at Sydney November 4, 1861; *The Autobiography of Joseph Jefferson*, 176.
24. *Sydney Morning Herald*, September 12, 1864, 1, NLA, accessed April 19, 2012.
25. Benjamin McArthur, *The Man Who Was Rip Van Winkle*, 189.
26. Jane Kathleen Curry, *Nineteenth-Century American Women Theatre Managers*, 44.
27. Louisa (Lane) Drew and Douglas Taylor, *Autobiographical Sketch of Mrs. John Drew*, 109.
28. G. R. MacMinn, *The Theatre of the Golden Era in California*, 178; *Sydney Morning Herald*, September 12, 1864, 1, NLA, accessed April 19, 2012.
29. M. B. Leavitt, *Fifty Years*, 20.
30. *Queanbeyan Age*, April 10, 1868, NLA.
31. M. B. Leavitt, *Fifty Years*, 25–26.
32. *Ibid.*, 34–35.
33. Stuart Macintyre, *A Concise History of Australia*, 87.
34. From "430,000 in 1851 to 1,150,000 in 1861," *ibid.*, 87.
35. *Ibid.*, 109.
36. *Ibid.*, 118.
37. *Ibid.*
38. *Ibid.*, 108.
39. "Comedians Past and Present," *Los Angeles Herald*, February 26, 1893, CDNC, accessed May 17, 2012.
40. *New York Times*, December 11, 1855, ProQuest, NYPL.
41. "Report from the Journals of Australia" of November 26, 1860, *Clipper*, February 9, 1861.
42. Raised to age sixteen in 1885, Marah Gubar, *Artful Dodgers*, 224n4.
43. Rosemarie K. Bank, *Theatre Culture in America, 1825–1860*, 128.
44. Aldrich told an interviewer that he was fifteen when he set sail, but according to his undisputed birth date of 1843, he was actually seventeen. *Clipper*, "Notable Players of the Past and Present," no. 118 (February 13, 1913), Theatre Collection, NYPL.
45. Quoted in the *Clipper*, February 9, 1861.
46. See chapter 1. Quinn's later life was troubled by spousal abuse and accusations of theft, while Arnot seemingly found a worthwhile professional partner in her final mate. Quinn returned to Australia for a third tour, 1864–67, when Louise Arnot was married and touring as an adult.

47. Nicole Anae, "An Infant Phenomenon in Colonial Australia," 62; Barbara J. Griffith, "All the Lovely Sisterhood," 1–7.
48. Nicole Anae, "An Infant Phenomenon in Colonial Australia,"62.
49. *Ibid.*
50. Quoted in the *Clipper*, February, 9 1861.
51. *Argus*, November 14, 1860, NLA.
52. *Sydney Morning Herald*, June 25, 1861, 1, incorrectly reports that the troupe had performed in Victoria for nine months, but they only arrived seven months earlier.
53. Joseph Jefferson, *The Autobiography of Joseph Jefferson*, 176.
54. *Bell's Life in Sydney and Sporting Chronicle*, July 20, 1861, 2, NLA, accessed July 9, 2011.
55. *Sydney Morning Herald*, June 25, 1861, 1, Google News Archive, accessed May 1, 2012.
56. *Bell's Life in Sydney and Sporting Chronicle*, July 20, 1861, 2, NLA, accessed July 9, 2011.
57. *Argus*, November 14, 1860, NLA.
58. *Bell's Life in Sydney and Sporting Chronicle*, July 20, 1861, 2, NLA, accessed July 9, 2011. *Sydney Morning Herald*, July 29 and August 3, 1861, Google News Archive, accessed May 1, 2012. An ad for *Under the Rose* promises appearances by "Misses Louise and Jenny Arnot, and Jennie Gourlay" (*Argus*, August 26, 1862, NLA), making it clear that there were two Jennies in the troupe. It would be simple to assume that the girls could be distinguished by the spellings but there are several occasions that list "Jennie Arnot" and many more that list "Little Jenny." In the absence of a surname, for many dates it is impossible to say absolutely which girl is appearing.
59. *Argus*, August 27, 1861, 6, NLA, accessed 2011.
60. Stuart Macintyre, *A Concise History of Australia*, 111.
61. *Argus*, August 27, 1861, 6, NLA, accessed September 25, 2012.
62. *Star*, September 3, 7, October 12, December 16, 1861, NLA accessed June 27, 2012.
63. *Star*, December 21, 1861, NLA, accessed June 27, 2012.
64. *Star*, January 22, 1862, NLA, accessed June 27, 2012.
65. *Star*, April 1, 1862, 2, NLA, accessed June 27, 2012.
66. *Age*, March–June and October 1862, Google News Archive, accessed May 1, 2012.
67. *Age*, October 2 and 6, 1862, p. 1, col. 5. By 1863 the theatre had reverted to its former name. *Age*, November 21, 1863, p. 1, col. 5, Google News Archive, accessed May 1, 2012.

68. *Age*, March 25, 1862, 1, Google News Archive, accessed May 1, 2012.
69. *Otago Daily Times*, June 3, 1863, p. 3, col. 5, Papers Past, National Library of New Zealand, hereafter NLNZ, accessed May 1, 2012. Marsh may have capitalized on local hostility toward Chinese, the largest non-European immigrant group in Australia.
70. *Star*, October 21, 1861, 14, NLA, accessed June 27, 2012; *Bell's Life in Sydney*, February 14, 1863, 2, NLA, accessed June 27, 2012.
71. *Age*, October 14, 1862, p. 1, col. 5, Google News Archive, accessed May 1, 2012. Joseph Jefferson gave a benefit for the same team. Benjamin McArthur, *The Man Who Was Rip Van Winkle*, 193.
72. Jane Cathleen Curry, *Nineteenth-Century American Women Theatre Managers*, 63. Keene was performing this play at Ford's Theatre the night Lincoln was assassinated.
73. *Bell's Life in Sydney and Sporting Chronicle*, February 14, 1863, NLA, accessed June 27, 2012; Benjamin McArthur, *The Man Who Was Rip Van Winkle*, 196.
74. See John W. Frick, *Theatre, Culture and Temperance Reform in Nineteenth-Century America.*
75. *Otago Daily Times*, June 25, 1863, p. 3, col. 4, Papers Past, NLNZ, accessed May 1, 2012. *Age*, March 26 and October 2, 1862, Google News Archive, accessed May 1, 2012.
76. Amy Hughes, *Spectacles of Reform*, 65.
77. The phrase is from Howard Becker, cited in John W. Frick, *Theatre, Culture and Temperance Reform in Nineteenth-Century America*, 120; *Age*, March 26 and October 2, 1862, Google News Archive, accessed May 1, 2012.
78. *Ibid.*
79. *Otago Daily Times*, July 13, 1863, 4, Papers Past, NLNZ, accessed September 6, 2011.
80. *Sydney Morning Herald*, January 24, 1863, 7, NLA, accessed June 20, 2010; playbill for July 22, 1863, lists Jenny Arnot as "Eva" and Louise Arnot as "Slave, mistress to Legree, HTC.
81. *Sydney Morning Herald*, January 24, 1863, 4, NLA, accessed June 27, 2012.
82. Robin Bernstein, *Racial Innocence*, 50.
83. *Sydney Morning Herald*, February 17, 1863, 4, NLA, accessed December 2, 2011.
84. *Brisbane Courier*, April 30, 1863, NLA, accessed December 2, 2011.
85. Stuart Macintyre, *A Concise History of Australia*, 90.
86. *Otago Daily Times*, issue 487, July 13, 1863, 4, NLNZ, accessed September 6, 2011.

87. *Southland Times*, July 3, 1863, 2, Papers Past, NLNZ, accessed May 1, 2012.
88. *Otago Daily Times*, May 4, 1863, Papers Past, NLNZ, accessed May 1, 2012.
89. *Mercury*, NLA, accessed February 12, 2006.
90. *Otago Daily Times*, May 26, 1863, Papers Past, NLNZ, accessed May 1, 2012.
91. *Marsh's Juvenile Dramatic Era*, October 5, 1857, HTC, lists "Harriet" as among the original nine members; "Theatric Reminiscences—Some account of Sacramento Theatres—The 'Old' Metropolitan," *Sacramento Daily Union* 15, no. 105, June 23, 1882, accessed August 29, 2011. T. Allston Brown recorded Hattie Johnson as a troupe member who married Charles Thorne, who subsequently drowned at sea, and by 1870 she had married Mr. Middleton, an actor (T. Allston Brown, *History of the American Stage*, 235), http://cdnc.ucr.edu/cdnc/cgi-bin/cdnc?a=d&cl=search&d=SDU18820623.2.2&srpos=122&e=——en—20—105—txt-IN-%22george+marsh%22—#.
92. *Otago Daily Times*, May 27, 1862, Papers Past, NLNZ, accessed May 1, 2012.
93. *Otago Daily Times*, May 21, June 19, 1863, Papers Past, NLNZ, accessed May 1, 2012.
94. *Otago Daily Times*, July 2, 1863, Papers Past, NLNZ, accessed May 1, 2012.
95. *Otago Daily Times*, May 25, 1863, p. 3, col. 5, Papers Past, NLNZ, accessed May 1, 2012.
96. *Argus*, June 2, 1862; *Bell's Life in Sydney and Sporting Chronicle*, March 14, 1863, 2, NLA, accessed June 27, 2012.
97. *Otago Daily Times*, June 17, 1863, Papers Past, NLNZ, accessed May 1, 2012.
98. *Otago Witness*, July 4, 1863, 2, Papers Past, NLNZ, accessed May 1, 2012.
99. *Hawk's Bay Herald*, June 10, 1862, Papers Past, NLNZ, accessed May 1, 2012.
100. An oil on canvas by Pierre Loti; portraits by Charles Giraud, hang in the Musée du quai Branly in France and the Musée de Tahiti et des Îles in her homeland.
101. Unidentified magazine clipping in Louis Aldrich clippings file, Billy Rose Theatre Collection, NYPL; *New York Dramatic Mirror*, June 9, 1894.
102. Don B. Wilmeth, ed., *Cambridge Guide to American Theatre*, 245.
103. Constance Rourke, *Troupers of the Gold Coast*, 32.
104. *Clipper*, December 5, 1863, NYPL.

105. *Clipper*, November 28, 1863. NYPL.
106. *Clipper*, December 5, 1863, NYPL.
107. Walter B. Cheadle, *Cheadle's Journal of Trip across Canada, 1862–1863* (Edmonton, Alberta, Canada: M. G. Hurtig, 1971), 236, Google Books.
108. *Clipper*, December 5, 1863, NYPL.
109. Various sources report erroneously that Aldrich married Jenny Arnot. The error began while Aldrich was still alive, as he told an interviewer, "It has been repeatedly published that I married Jennie [*sic*] Arnot, a sister of Louise Arnot. Please correct that impression. I married Clara Shropshire, the eldest of three sisters, all members of the Marsh troupe"; *New York Dramatic Mirror*, June 9, 1894.
110. The company also included Frank Mayo, Junius Booth, and Walter Leman. Aldrich stayed with Maguire until 1866. See also *New York Dramatic Mirror*, June 29, 1901, "Life and Death of Louis Aldrich," Aldrich file, Billy Rose Theatre Collection, NYPL; "Notable Players of the Past and Present," no. 18, Aldrich file, Billy Rose Theatre Collection, NYPL; Louis M. Simon, *A History of the Actors' Fund of America*, 112.
111. *Sacramento Daily Union*, February 10, 18, 1864, CDNC, accessed May 17, 2012.
112. *Daily Alta*, April 19, 1864, p. 1, col. 2, CDNC, accessed May 17, 2012. On Lotta, see David Dempsey with Raymond P. Baldwin, *The Triumphs and Trials of Lotta Crabtree*, 99, 111; Diana Serra Cary, *Hollywood's Children*, 15–28.
113. "A Sketch of British Columbia in 1868 by an Occasional Correspondent of the Lyttelton Times," *Star*, September 8, 1868, p. 3; Papers Past, NLNZ, accessed May 1, 2012.
114. *Daily Dramatic Chronicle*, May 5, 1866, 2, ProQuest, NYPL.
115. *Daily Dramatic Chronicle*, November 3, 1866, 3, ProQuest.
116. *Daily Dramatic Chronicle*, March 9, 1867, 3, ProQuest.
117. "A Sketch of British Columbia in 1868 by an Occasional Correspondent of the Lyttelton Times," *Star*, September 8, 1868, 3, Papers Past, NLNZ, accessed May 1, 2012.

5. Tomboys Rule

1. *St. Louis Leader*, June 10, 1857, p. 1, col. 6.
2. Unidentified, undated clipping in the Marsh Children folder, HTC; probably 1857.
3. "Comedians Past and Present," *Los Angeles Herald*, February 26, 1893, CDNC, accessed May 17, 2012.
4. *St. Louis Missouri Republican*, June 17, 1857, p. 3, col. 3.

5. Unidentified, undated clipping in the Marsh Children folder, HTC; probably 1857.
6. *Clipper*, February 9, 1861.
7. *Bell's Life in Sydney and Sporting Chronicle*, July 20, 1861, 2, NLA, accessed July 9, 2011.
8. *Argus*, November 14, 1860, NLA.
9. *Clipper*, February 9, 1861; *Otago Daily Times* 510, August 8, 1863, 4. Papers Past, NLNZ, accessed September 6, 2011.
10. *New York Times*, August 13, 1857.
11. *Picayune*, March 7, 1858.
12. Howard Athenaeum playbills, HTC. The file yields one example of an adult actress playing Claude Melnotte: Mrs. M. Jones as playing Claude Melnotte, opposite Mrs. Mowatt (September 10 and 19, 1851) and opposite Georgiana Barrett (January 8, 1852), but such mentions were clearly the exception.
13. "Saturday's Dramatic Gossip," unidentified clipping, HTC; external evidence indicates February 13, 1857.
14. Marsh Children folder, n.d., probably 1857, HTC.
15. Shauna Vey, "The Master and the Mademoiselle," *Theatre History Studies* 27 (2007): 39–59; Laurence Senelick, "Boys and Girls Together," in Leslie Ferris, ed., *Crossing the Stage*, 80–95.
16. Elizabeth Reitz Mullenix, *Wearing the Breeches*, 13.
17. Jim Davis, "Freaks, Prodigies, and Marvelous Mimicry," 188.
18. "A Chat with Amy Roselle," *Era*, December 2, 1893, 11, quoted in Tracy C. Davis, "The Employment of Children in Victorian Theatre," 126.
19. *Child Stars: Their Story*, documentary, produced and directed by Henry Schipper.
20. Heather McMahon, "Profit, Purity, and Perversity."
21. The oft-reproduced image of Bateman is on the cover of Anne Varty's book, *Children and Theatre in Victorian Britain*; Fisher's image is found in Elizabeth Reitz Mullenix, *Wearing the Breeches*, 49; Quinn's in Nicole Anae, "An Infant Phenomenon in Colonial Australia," 71.
22. Jim Davis, "Freaks, Prodigies, and Marvelous Mimicry," 189.
23. Mullenix gives Menken's birth as either 1835 or 1836; *Wearing the Breeches*, 68.
24. Lisa Merrill, *When Romeo Was a Woman*; Denise A. Walen, "'Such Romeo as We Had Never Ventured to Hope For': Charlotte Cushman," in Robert A. Schanke and Kim Marra, eds., *Passing Performances: Queer Readings of Leading Players in American Theater History* (Ann Arbor: University of Michigan Press, 1998).
25. Elizabeth Reitz Mullenix, *Wearing the Breeches*, 40.

26. Mullenix mentions *Little Pickle* and Young Norval in *Douglas*, in addition to many Shakespearean roles.
27. *St. Louise Leader*, June 9, 1857, p. 1, col. 8.
28. Unidentified, undated clipping in the Marsh Children folder, HTC; probably 1857.
29. Amy Hughes, *Spectacles of Reform*, 65.
30. *Bell's Life in Sydney and Sporting Chronicle*, July 20, 1861, 2, NLA, accessed July 9, 2011.
31. Billy J. Harbin, Kim Marra, and Robert A. Schanke, eds., *The Gay and Lesbian Theatrical Legacy*, 2.
32. *Ibid.*, 5.
33. *Clipper*, February 9, 1861, NYPL.
34. *Ibid.*
35. This commentator believes that the low voice was acquired after Arnot left the Marsh Troupe. *Los Angeles Herald*, February 18, 1893, "Amusements," CDNC, accessed May 17, 2012.
36. *Argus*, August 27, 1867, 5. NLA, accessed February 22, 2010.
37. *Argus*, November 14, 1860, NLA, accessed June 1, 2007.
38. John S. Kendall, *The Golden Age of the New Orleans Theatre*, 478.
39. Nan Mullenneaux, "Our Genius, Goodness, and Gumption," 286.
40. Sarah Burns, "Making Mischief," 87, and Lauren Lessing, "Roses in Bloom," both in Holly Pyne Connor, *Angels and Tomboys*; Jane H. Hunter, *How Young Ladies Became Girls*, 140–45.
41. Anne Scott MacLeod, "The Caddie Woodlawn Syndrome," in Miriam Forman-Brunell and Leslie Paris, eds., *The Girls' History and Culture Reader*, 199–221.
42. *Ibid.*, 204.
43. *Ibid.*
44. *Ibid.*, 220.
45. These works and this theme were featured in the Newark (New Jersey) Museum exhibit "Angels and Tomboys: Girlhood in Nineteenth-Century American Art," organized by Dr. Holly Pyne Connor, curator of Nineteenth-Century American Art; September 12, 2012, to January 20, 2013.
46. *Sydney Morning Herald*, February 17, 1863, 4, NLA, accessed December 2, 2011.
47. *Sydney Morning Herald*, September 12, 1864, NLA, accessed April 19, 2012.
48. Mark Cosdon, *The Hanlon Brothers*, 18–20.
49. *Sydney Morning Herald*, September 12, 1864, NLA, accessed April 19, 2012.

50. Mark Cosdon, *The Hanlon Brothers*, 19.
51. *Sydney Morning Herald*, September 12, 1864, NLA, accessed April 19, 2012.
52. *Otago Daily Times*, July 16, 1863, accessed May 1, 2012.
53. *Otago Daily Times*, August 8, 1863, 4, Papers Past, NLNZ, accessed September 6, 2011.
54. *Ibid.*
55. U.S. Census Year: *1870*; Census Place: *New York Ward 20 District 19 (2nd Enum), New York, New York*; Roll: *M593_1048*; Page: *871A*; Image: *343*; Family History Library Film: *552547*. Ancestry.com. *1870 United States Federal Census* (database on-line). Provo, UT: Ancestry.com Operations, Inc., 2009, accessed June 12, 2012.
56. *Bell's Life in Sydney and Sporting Chronicle*, August 20, 1864, 2, NLA, accessed February 22, 2010.
57. *Sydney Morning Herald*, September 12, 1864, NLA, accessed April 19, 2012.
58. *Bell's Life in Sydney and Sporting Chronicle*, August 20, 1864, 2, NLA, accessed February 2, 2010. William was among Menken's breeches roles.
59. *Sydney Morning Herald*, November 12 and December 10, 1864, and January 2, 1865, NLA.
60. *Sydney Morning Herald*, November 12, 1864, 5, NLA, accessed December 10, 2010.
61. *Brisbane Courier*, June 12, 1865, 2, NLA.
62. *Brisbane Courier*, June 17, 1865, 10, NLA.
63. *Brisbane Courier*, June 17, 1865, 10, NLA.
64. *Brisbane Courier*, January 30, 1866, 2, NLA.
65. *Argus*, November 26, 1867, 5, NLA. For an excellent detailed discussion of *Mazeppa* as a cultural event, see, Renée M. Sentilles, *Performing Menken*.
66. *Queenslander*, February 3, 1866, 7, NLA.
67. *Brisbane Courier*, January 5, 1866, 2, NLA.
68. *Argus*, November 27, 1867, 5, NLA.
69. *Argus*, December 28, 1867, 5, NLA. This is not the same role as the title character of the 1890 Hanlon Brothers *Superba*, who is a goddess. Mark Cosdon, *The Hanlon Brothers*, 121.
70. *Brisbane Courier*, May 13, 1865, NLA.
71. *Brisbane Courier*, January 30, 1866, 2, NLA.
72. *Argus*, August 26, 1867, 5, NLA.
73. David Hough, "The Playmakers," in Geoffrey Bolton, Richard Rossiter, and Jan Ryan, eds., *Farewell Cinderella*, 16.
74. *Inquirer and Commercial News*, March 25, 1868, NLA.

75. Versions of the story were reported in the *Portland Guardian and Normandy General Advertiser*, January 2, 1868, 2; *Cornwall Chronicle*, January 4, 1868, 3 ; and *Rockhampton Bulletin and Central Queensland Advertiser*, January 23, 1868, 2, which cites *Bell's Life*, NLA.
76. Stuart Macintyre, *A Concise History*, 115.
77. *Inquirer and Commercial News*, March 25, 1868, 2, NLA.
78. *Daily Morning Chronicle*, February 28 and March 2, 1869, ProQuest, accessed May 17, 2012.
79. *Ibid.*
80. *Daily Alta California*, February 17, 1869, CDNC, accessed May 9, 2012.
81. *Daily Alta California*, February 23, 1869; MaritimeHeritage.org, accessed May 1, 2012.
82. *Daily Morning Chronicle*, February 24, 1869, ProQuest, accessed September 13, 2011.
83. *Daily Alta California*, February 17, 1869, CDNC.
84. *Daily Alta California* 21, no. 6909, February 17, 1869, CDNC.
85. *Daily Morning Chronicle*, April 2, 1869, 3, ProQuest, accessed September 13, 2011.
86. Nora Titone, *My Thoughts Be Bloody*, 114.
87. Constance Rourke, *Troupers of the Gold Coast*, 25.
88. *Ibid.*, 96.
89. *Sacramento Daily Union*, August 20, 1869, CDNC, accessed May 17, 2012.
90. Constance Rourke, *Troupers of the Gold Coast*, 54, 153; "Comedians Past and Present," *Los Angeles Daily Herald*, February 26, 1893, CDNC, accessed May 15, 2012.
91. *Ibid.*
92. *Sacramento Daily Union*, August 24, 1869, CDNC, accessed May 17, 2012.
93. "Comedians Past and Present," *Los Angeles Daily Herald*, February 26, 1893, CDNC, accessed May 15, 2012. Andrew Davis, *America's Longest Run*, 143.
94. *Ibid.*
95. Kurt Gänzl, *Lydia Thompson*, 87.
96. Elizabeth Reitz Mullenix, *Wearing the Breeches*, 13.
97. Kurt Gänzl, *Lydia Thompson*, 127–29.
98. *Sacramento Daily Union*, September 6, 7, 9, 20, 23, 24, 1869, CDNC, accessed May 17, 2012.
99. Gänzl writes quite colorfully about efforts by Maguire and Sherry Corbyn to copy *Ixion* in 1870 in San Francisco, but has either mistaken the year or is unaware of this 1869 Sacramento production under the same team.
100. *Sacramento Daily Union*, September 24, 1869, CDNC, accessed May 17, 2012.
101. *Sacramento Daily Union*, September 21, 1869, CDNC, accessed May 17, 2012.

102. *Sacramento Daily Union*, September 25, 1869, CDNC, accessed May 17, 2012.
103. Elizabeth Reitz Mullenix, *Wearing the Breeches*, 133.
104. *Clipper*, May 20, 1871, Illinois Digital Newspapers Collections, hereafter ILL.
105. Kurt Gänzl, *Lydia Thompson*, 127.
106. *Memphis Daily Appeal*, April 30, 1871, *Chronicling America*, accessed May 17, 2012.
107. Kurt Gänzl, *Lydia Thompson*, 125, 130.
108. Special Dispatch to the *San Francisco Chronicle*, March 4, 1870, 1, ProQuest, accessed September 13, 2011.
109. "Theatrical News by the Mail," *Sydney Morning Herald*, November 8, 1870.
110. *Clipper*, October 19, 1872; October18, November 15, 1873; February 21, 1874, ILL.
111. *St. Joseph Daily Gazette*, January 6, 1874, Google News Archive, accessed September 6, 2011.
112. T. Allston Brown, *History of the American Stage*, 236.
113. *New York Times*, January 27, 1899, ProQuest, accessed May 12, 2014. They married in 1861.
114. *Clipper*, August 29, 1885, 12, ILL. The postmortem remembrance sets the marriage "about twenty years" earlier.
115. U.S. Census *1870*; *New York Ward 20 District 19 (2nd Enum), New York, New York; Roll*: *M593_1048*; Page: *871A*; Image: *343*; Family History Library Film: *552547*; and *New York Ward 20 District 18 (2nd Enum), New York, New York*; Roll: *M593_1048*; Page: *828B*; Image: *258*; Family History Library Film: *552547*. Ancestry.com. *1870 United States Federal Census* (database online). Provo, UT: Ancestry.com Operations, Inc., 2009, accessed June 12, 2012.
116. *Clipper*, September 28, 1884; February 13, 1886, ILL; *New York Times*, October 9, 1887. She married Broadway comic actor, David Frank, *Clipper*, September 29, 1888, ILL; *New York Times*, December 3, 1899, ProQuest.
117. *Clipper*, August 29, 1885, 12, ILL; *Australian*, February 20, 1869, article 137563425, NLA.
118. "Theatrical Intelligence," *Empire*, March 5, 1866, article 63244314, NLA.
119. John Bouvé Clapp and Edwin Francis Edgett, *Players of the Present*, 13–14; T. Allston Brown: *A History of the American Stage*.
120. Louis M. Simon, *A History of the Actors' Fund of America*, 112.
121. See Benjamin McArthur, "'Forbid Them Not'"; Shauna Vey, "Good Intentions and Fearsome Prejudice."
122. "Children on the Stage: Mr. Gerry and Mr. Aldrich discuss the subject," *New York Times*, February 18, 1987, ProQuest.

123. Marc R. Staenberg and Daniel K. Stuart, *Children as Chattels.*
124. *Lancaster Daily Intelligencer*, October 23, 1886, *Chronicling America*, accessed May 17, 2012.
125. *National Republican*, December 4, 1885, *Chronicling America*, accessed May 17, 2012.
126. *National Republican*, December 27, 1886, *Chronicling America*, accessed May 17, 2012.
127. *Washington Critic*, December 31, 1886, *Chronicling America*, accessed May 17, 2012.
128. *Washington Critic*, December 24 and 28, 1886, *Chronicling America*, accessed May 17, 2012.
129. *Clipper*, February 11, 1888, ILL.
130. *National Republican*, December 4, 1885, *Chronicling America*, accessed May 17, 2012.
131. *Lancaster Daily Intelligencer*, October 23, 1886, *Chronicling America*, accessed May 17, 2012.
132. *Sun*, December 26, 1887, 9, *Chronicling America*, accessed May 17, 2012.
133. *Evening World*, EXTRA, December 27, 1887, 3, *Chronicling America*, accessed May 17, 2012.
134. *Sun*, December 25, 1887, 9, *Chronicling America*, accessed May 17, 2012.
135. Richmond *Daily Times*, January 13, 1888, *Chronicling America*, accessed May 17, 2012.
136. *Carbon Advocate*, January 24, 1891, *Chronicling America*, accessed May 17, 2012.
137. Barbara Wallace Grossman, *A Spectacle of Suffering*, 232.
138. *San Francisco Call*, February 10, 1893, *Chronicling America*, accessed May 17, 2012. The character's name is spelled differently in almost every ad; I have utilized a consistent spelling.
139. *Los Angeles Herald*, February 15, 1893, 4, *Chronicling America*, accessed May 17, 2012.
140. Critic is assumed male. *Anaconda Standard*, April 5, 1893, 3; *Los Angeles Herald*, February 18, 1893, *Chronicling America*, accessed May 17, 2012.
141. *Anaconda Standard*, March 31 1893, 4, *Chronicling America*, accessed May 17, 2012.
142. *Evening World*, September 1, 1894, 6, *Chronicling America*, accessed May 17, 2012.
143. *Evening Times*, October 20, 1896, 3, *Chronicling America*, accessed May 17, 2012.
144. *Saint Paul Globe*, February 27, 1899, 4, *Chronicling America*, accessed May 17, 2012.

145. *Newport News Daily Press*, November 24, 1898, *Chronicling America*, accessed September 6, 2011.
146. Tracy C. Davis, *Actresses as Working Women: Their Social Identity in Victorian England* (London: Routledge, 1991); Jane Kathleen Curry, *Nineteenth-Century American Women Theatre Managers*.
147. *New York Times*, November 1, 1903, ProQuest, accessed August 30, 2011.
148. *New York Dramatic Mirror*, December 31, 1904, 18, Old Fulton Postcards, accessed August 30, 2011.
149. *Ibid*.
150. Siobhan Fitzpatrick, ed., *Orphan to Apprentice*, 33, 35.

6. Fathers and Sons

1. *Sacramento Daily Union*, May 21, 1870, CDNC.
2. He had previously founded and edited *Burton's Gentleman's Magazine* and was the author/adaptor of numerous plays. Rinear, *Stage, Page, Scandals, and Vandals*, 50.
3. Harry died in 1844. Burton's will mentions a stepson who may have been the son of actress Jane Hill, a woman often advertised as Burton's wife. *Ibid*., 84, 240–42.
4. Joseph Jefferson, *The Autobiography of Joseph Jefferson*, 82.
5. Laurence Hutton, *Curiosities of the American Stage*, 245.
6. Most sources agree that Georgie was born in late December. Col. T. Allston Brown, writing for the *Clipper* May 31, 1862, gives March 4, 1848, as George's birthdate; but he may have confused this with Mary who was born March 4, 1847. Ads in the *New York Daily Tribune*, March 1856, state that he is "only six years of age," indicating an 1850 birth year—consistent with Howard Athenaeum program of January 12, 1857, that states that he is "Seven Years of Age." In Cincinnati, July 1857, he is advertised as "aged 7 years." *Clipper*, August 23, 1856, NYPL.
7. Arthur Herman Wilson, *A History of the Philadelphia Theatre 1835–1855*, 314, 342, 697; playbill of July 29, 1846, in the Theatre Collection, Rare Book Department, Philadelphia Free Library. The company included "Messrs. J. M. Scott, E. Shaw, Spear, J. A. Smith, Marsh, Marshall. Mesdames Mossop, [later Mrs. Louise Lane Drew], Nichols, Shaw, and Marshall." T. Allston Brown writes that "first appearance" of R. G. Marsh who founded the juvenile troupe was at the Arch Street on September 4, 1846; *History of the American Stage*, 235. Rinear confirms *John Jones* (102), but gives a slightly different title, writing that Burton produced Planché's *Charles XII of Sweden* at this time (101); he also lists a new addition to the company as "March" (103).

8. "Mr. Marsh" will play Baron Sternfort in *The Stranger*, advertisement, *Public Ledger*, January 14, 1847, 3, Philadelphia Free Library digital newspaper collection. Mr. Marsh will play Malfort in *Soldier's Daughter*, playbill of January 25, 1857, in the Theatre Collection, Rare Book Department, Philadelphia Free Library. The cast includes Mr. J. Scott, Mr. Howard, Mr. Phillips, Mr. Jefferson, Mr. Jervis, Mr. Hickman, Mr. Fisher, Mrs. Burke, Mrs. Rogers, Mrs. Ribas, Miss Cooper; September 1847, in *Richelieu*, and January 1848 as Edward Wilton in *Man from Manchester*, *Public Ledger*, September 28, 1847, p. 3 col. 5, and January 12, 1848, 3, Philadelphia Free Library, digital.
9. *North American* 65, no. 16205, December 31, 1847, ad p. 3, col. 5; *Public Ledger* 24, no. 133, February 26, 1848, 2; J. S. Dalrymple, Esq., *The Naiad Queen* (Boston: William V. Spencer, n.d.) University of California library, pdf. Also lists "Mr. Marsh" as Sir Rupert in Burton's 1848 production, accessed May 15, 2011.
10. Jim Davis, "Freaks, Prodigies, and Marvelous Mimicry," 190.
11. *Trinity Times* (California), reprinted *Clipper*, October 11, 1856.
12. *San Francisco Bulletin*, April 5, 1860, quoted in Lawrence Estavan, ed., *A Monograph History of the San Francisco Stage and Its People from 1849 to the Present Day, San Francisco Theatre Research, Volume XIV* (San Francisco: Work Projects Administration, Project 10677, 0. P. 665–08–5-167, 1940), 52–53, San Francisco Public Library e-book, accessed November 14, 2011.
13. "Art Matters," *Putnam's Magazine of American Literature, Science and Art* 7, no. 37 (January 1856): 111–12, PLHC.
14. Emphasis in original. Laurence Hutton, "Infant Phenomena," 439, ProQuest, NYPL, 218383501.
15. Diana Serra Cary, *Hollywood's Children*, 172.
16. Conversation with the author, Nepal, 1993.
17. Laurence Hutton, "Infant Phenomena," 439, ProQuest, NYPL, 218383501.
18. *Ibid.*
19. *Southland Times* 2, no. 69, July 3 1863, 2. Papers Past, accessed May 1, 2012.
20. *Argus*, August 26, 1861, NLA, http://nla.gov.au/nla.news-article5703467.
21. *Sydney Morning Herald*, July 15, 1861, 5, NLA, accessed May 1, 2012.
22. See Jim Davis, "Freaks, Prodigies, and Marvelous Mimicry; Anne Varty, *Children and Theatre in Victorian Britain*; Marah Gubar, *Artful Dodgers*; Gillian Arrighi, "D'Oyly Carte's Pantomimes."
23. *New York Times*, December 11, 1855.
24. *Argus*, November 14, 1860, 5, NLA.

25. *Sydney Morning Herald*, July 20, 1861, NLA, accessed 2010.
26. *Sydney Morning Herald*, February 7, 1863, NLA.
27. *Ibid.*
28. *New York Times*, December 11, 1855.
29. Howard Athenaeum program, December 18, 1856, HTC.
30. Unidentified, undated clipping in the Marsh Children folder, HTC; it is possibly from a subsequent tour.
31. *Ibid.*; probably 1857.
32. T. B. M., "Comedians Past and Present . . . ," *Los Angeles Herald*, February 26, 1893, CDNC, accessed May 17, 2012.
33. *Virginia City Territorial Enterprise*, January 13, 1864, accessed July 31, 2012, www.twainquotes.com.
34. "Burton, William Evans," *The Cambridge Guide to Theatre*, 139.
35. *Argus*, August 26, 1861, NLA, http://nla.gov.au/nla.news-article5703467.
36. Randall Knoper, *Acting Naturally*.
37. Maud Otis Skinner, *One Man in His Time*, 183; *Clipper*, July 21, 1860.
38. *Clipper*, July 28, 1860.
39. *Quebec Colonist*, August 23, 1856, Google News Archive, accessed September 22, 2011.
40. *Daily Morning Chronicle*, February 5, 1869, 3, ProQuest.
41. Laurence Hutton, "Infant Phenomena," 446, ProQuest, NYPL, 218383501.
42. *Ibid.*
43. John S. Kendall, *The Golden Age of the New Orleans Theatre*, 478.
44. T. B. M., "Comedians Past and Present. . . ."
45. Heather M. McMahon, "Profit, Purity, and Perversity," 110.
46. *Marsh's Juvenile Dramatic Era*, 1857, HTC. There is no confirmation of the event in the Cincinnati newspapers that covered the tour.
47. Unidentified clipping the Marsh Children folder, HTC, probably from 1857.
48. "Saturday's Dramatic Gossip," [February 1857], unidentified clipping in the Marsh Children folder, HTC.
49. *Clipper*, August 23, 1856, NYPL. *Marsh's Juvenile Dramatic Era*, October 5, 1857, HTC, notes George's age as seven years and two months, and states that the company had been formed twenty months earlier.
50. Playbill, Howard Athenaeum, December 25, 1856, HTC.
51. *Sacramento Daily Union*, July 16, 1860, 1, advertisement, CDNC.
52. *Otago Daily Times*, May 19, 1863, 3, Papers Past, accessed May 1, 2012.
53. *Ibid.* She also plays Little Eva, *Otago Daily Times*, July 12, 1863, 4 review, accessed September 6, 2011.
54. T. Allston Brown, *History of the American Stage*, 236.

55. Laurence Hutton, "Infant Phenomena," 446, ProQuest, NYPL, 218383501; *Curiosities*, 245.
56. John S. Kendall, *The Golden Age of the New Orleans Theatre*, 479.
57. Jane O'Connor, *The Cultural Significance of the Child Star*, 72.
58. Daniel Gerould, ed., *Quick: Essays on Theatre* (New York: Martin E. Segal Center Publications, 2012), xxx.
59. *Clipper*, December 5, 1863, NYPL.
60. *Troy Times*, *Troy Record*, and *Troy Daily Press*, January 18, 1909, TPL.
61. Andrew Davis, *America's Longest Run*, 84.
62. Playbill, May 17, 1860, Forrest Theatre (city unidentified but probably Sacramento) in the R. Marsh file, HTC.
63. *Otago Daily Times*, May 25, 1863, 3; Papers Past, accessed May 1, 2012.
64. *Troy City Directory*, 1872, 97, TPL.
65. *Troy City Directory*, 1878, 190; 1879, 206, TPL.
66. Marriage registry of the First Avenue United Methodist Church of Watervliet, examined May 10, 2012; The witnesses were R. G. Wood and Edward Bartlett; the clergyman was S. W. Brown. *Troy Budget*, cited in *Troy Vital Records* 2, p. 162, compiled by the TPL, 1980.
67. *Troy City Directory*, 1874, TPL.
68. U.S. Census 1900; Watervliet Ward 3, Albany, New York; Roll: *1007*; Page: *7A*; Enumeration District: *105*; FHL microfilm: *1241007*. Ancestry.com. 1900 United States Federal Census (database online). Provo, UT: Ancestry.com Operations Inc., 2004, accessed June 12, 2012. *Troy Times* (p. 6), *Troy Record* (p. 5), and *Troy Daily Press* (p. 8), January 18, 1909, TPL; Albany Rural Cemetery records.
69. Albany Rural Cemetery records. William Burton's son had died at the same age.
70. Cecelia Guerineau, wife of Arthur's son Douglas (deceased), telephone interview with author, January 26, 2012.
71. Susan Buckham, "Commemoration as an expression of personal relationships and group identities," 165.
72. T. Allston Brown: *History of the American Stage*, 235.
73. *Clipper*, Unsigned [Frank Queen], February 3, 1877, University of Virginia. *Uncle Tom's Cabin* and American Culture, accessed July 23, 2007.
74. "An Old Time Minstrel. He Turns Up at Home After Roving About for Many Years," unidentified clipping in Marsh Children folder, HTC.
75. It also states that Robert Guerineau performed under the stage name of George Marsh, which is incorrect.
76. Louis M. Simon, *A History of the Actors' Fund of America*, 110.
77. Cornelia Otis Skinner, "The Actors' Fund Home," in *ibid.*, 178.

78. "A Home for Needy Actors," *New York Times*, May 9, 1902. ProQuest, accessed February 2, 2012. The home was relocated to Englewood, New Jersey, in 1928. The West Brighton, Staten Island residence was demolished in 1938.
79. Albany Rural Cemetery internment record.
80. Lisa J. Rapport and Matthew Meleen, "Childhood Celebrity, Parental Attachment, and Adult Adjustment: The Young Performers Study," *Journal of Personality Assessment* 70, no. 3 (June 1998): 484–504, esp. 499.
81. Cecelia Guerineau, telephone interview with author, January 26, 2012; Albany Rural Cemetery internment record.

Afterword

1. *Journal of the Early Republic* 23 (Spring 2003): 17–18.
2. Renée M. Sentilles, *Performing Menken*, 234–38.
3. Paul Petersen and his advocacy organization, A Minor Consideration, have commemorated a number of these tragedies.
4. See also Jane O'Connor, *The Cultural Significance of the Child Star*, chapter 6 on Charlotte Church.
5. Matthew Gurewitsch, "Flight Training: Building an Army of Billy Elliots," *New York Times*, June 22, 2010, AR22.
6. New York, *Child Performers Education and Trust Act* (McKinney's, 2003), New York Estates, Powers & Trusts Law, art. 7, sec. 7-7.1; New York Labor Law, art. 4-A.
7. Lisa J. Rapport and M. Meleen, "Childhood Celebrity, Parental Attachment, and Adult Adjustment," 499. Oddly, the former child actors did not have the same feeling toward fathers who had acted as managers, only mothers.
8. Allison James, "Agency," 44.
9. See for example, Elizabeth Kolbert, "Spoiled Rotten."

BIBLIOGRAPHY

Included here are sections for newspapers, archives and collections, and books and journal articles.

Newspapers

Anaconda, MT	*Standard*
Ballarat, Victoria, Australia	*Star*
Brisbane, Australia	*Brisbane Courier*
Boston	*Daily Advertiser, Herald, Post, Sunday Record*
Cincinnati, OH	*Gazette, Enquirer*
Chicago, IL	*Tribune*
Cleveland, OH	*Plain Dealer*
Dodge City, KS	*Globe Republican*
Dunedin, New Zealand	*Otago Daily Times, Otago Witness, Southland Times*
Hawke's Bay, New Zealand	*Hawke's Bay Herald*
Hobart, Tasmania	*Mercury*
Lancaster, PA	*Daily Intelligencer*
Launceston, Tasmania	*Cornwall Chronicle*
Leighton, PA	*Carbon Advocate*
Los Angeles, CA	*Herald*
Macon, GA	*Telegraph*
Melbourne, Australia	*Argus, Australian*
Memphis, TN	*Daily Appeal*

New Orleans, LA	*Picayune*
Newport News, VA	*Daily Press*
New South Wales, Australia	*Queanbeyan Age*
New York, NY	*Clipper, Dramatic Mirror, Evening World, Herald, Sun, Times*
Norfolk, VA	*Virginian-Pilot*
Omaha, NE	*Daily Bee*
Philadelphia, PA	*Public Ledger*
Pittsburgh, PA	*Dispatch*
Quebec, Ontario, Canada	*Colonist*
Richmond, KY	*Climax*
Richmond, VA	*Daily Times*
Sacramento, CA	*Daily Union*
San Francisco, CA	*Call, Daily Alta, Era, Daily Dramatic Chronicle, Daily Morning Chronicle*
St. Joseph, MO	*St. Joseph Daily Gazette*
St. Louis, MO	*Missouri Republican, Leader*
St. Paul, MN	*Globe*
Sydney, Australia	*Bell's Life in Sydney and Sporting Chronicle, Morning Herald, Rockhampton Bulletin and Central Queensland Advertiser*
Troy, NY	*Daily Press, Daily Whig, Record, Times*
Virginia City, NV	*Territorial Enterprise*
Washington, DC	*Evening Times, National Republican, Critic*

Archives and Collections

Billy Rose Theatre Collection of the New York Public Library
Free Library of Philadelphia, Rare Book Department, Theatre Collection
Harvard Theatre Collection, Houghton Library
Louisiana Archives, New Orleans Public Library
Public Library of Cincinnati and Hamilton County
Rensselaer County Historical Society
Troy Room, Troy Public Library

Digital Archives

California Digital Newspaper Collection
Chronicling America, Library of Congress
Georgia Historic Newspapers, Galileo, University System of Georgia
Illinois Digital Newspaper Collections

Papers Past, National Library of New Zealand
Trove, National Library of Australia
University of Virginia, "*Uncle Tom's Cabin* and American Culture"

Books and Journal Articles

Adams, Bluford. *E Pluribus Barnum: The Great Showman and the Making of U.S. Popular Culture*. Minneapolis: University of Minnesota Press, 1997.

Altman, Rick. *The American Film Musical*. Bloomington: Indiana University Press, 1987.

Anae, Nicole. "An Infant Phenomenon in Colonial Australia—The Case of Anna Maria Quinn, 1854–1858." *The Historian* 71, no. 1 (Spring 2009): 55–78.

Anderson, George Baker. "History of Troy, New York (as a Village)." In *Landmarks of Rensselaer County*. Syracuse, NY: D. Mason & Co., 1897.

Ariès, Philippe. *Centuries of Childhood: A Social History of Family Life*. Translated by Robert Baldick. New York: Random House, 1962.

Arrighi, Gillian. "'D'Oyly Carte's Pantomimes': Complementarity and Innovation." *Popular Entertainment Studies* 3, no. 2 (2012): 31–44.

"Art Matters." *Putnam's Magazine of American Literature, Science and Art* 7, no. 37 (January 1856): 111–12.

Badal, Robert Samuel. "Kate and Ellen Bateman: A Study in Precocity." PhD dissertation, Northwestern University, 1971.

Baker, Meredith Henne. *The Richmond Theater Fire: Early America's First Great Disaster*. Baton Rouge: Louisiana State University Press, 2012.

Balme, Christopher B. "Playbills and the Theatrical Public Sphere." In *Representing the Theatrical Past*. Edited by Charlotte M. Canning and Thomas Postlewaite. Iowa City: University of Iowa Press, 2010.

Banham, Martin, ed. *Cambridge Guide to Theatre*. New York: Press Syndicate of the University of Cambridge, 1992.

Bank, Rosemarie K. *Theatre Culture in America, 1825–1860*. Cambridge, UK: Cambridge University Press, 1997.

Bordman, Gerald. *American Musical Theatre*. 3rd ed. New York: Oxford University Press, 2001.

Bernstein, Robin. *Racial Innocence: Performing American Childhood from Slavery to Civil Rights*. New York: New York University Press, 2011.

Brown, Peter. *The Cult of the Saints: Its Rise and Function in Latin Christianity*. Chicago: University of Chicago Press, 1981.

Brown, Richard D. "Microhistory and the Post-Modern Challenge." *Journal of the Early Republic* 23, no. 1 (Spring 2003): 17–22.

Brown, T. Allston. *History of the American Stage*. 1870. Repr., New York: Blum, 1969.

Buckham, Susan. "Commemoration as an expression of personal relationships and group identities: a case study of York Cemetery." *Mortality* 8, no. 2 (2003): 160–75.

Burns, Sarah. "Making Mischief: Tomboys Acting Up and Out of Bounds." In *Angels and Tomboys: Girlhood in 19th-Century American Art.* Edited by Holly Pyne Connor. San Francisco: Pomegranate Communications, Inc. and the Newark Museum, 2012.

Burrows, Edwin G., and Mike Wallace. *Gotham: A History of New York to 1898.* New York: Oxford University Press, 1999.

Butler, John Campbell. *Historical Record of Macon and Central Georgia, Containing Many Interesting and Valuable Reminiscences Connected with the Whole State, Including Numerous Incidents and Facts Never before Published and of Great Historic Value.* Macon, GA: J. W. Burke & Co., Printers & Binders, 1879. Google e-book, accessed November 30, 2011.

Cannon, Aubrey. "The Historical Dimension in Mortuary Expressions of Status and Sentiment." *Current Anthropology* 3, no. 4 (August–October 1989): 437–58.

Cantor, Eddie, with Jane Kesner Ardmore. *Take My Life.* Garden City, NY: Doubleday & Co., 1957.

Carlson, Marvin. "He Never Should Bow Down to a Domineering Frown: Class Tensions and Nautical Melodrama." In *Melodrama: The Cultural Emergence of a Genre.* Edited by Michael Hays and Anastasia Nikolopoulou. New York: St. Martin's Press, 1996, 147–90.

Carlyon, David. *Dan Rice: The Most Famous Man You've Never Heard Of.* New York: Public Affairs, 2001.

Carson, William G. B. *The Theatre of the Frontier: The Early Years of the St. Louis Stage.* New York: Benjamin Blom, 1932.

Cary, Diana Serra. *Hollywood's Children: An Inside Account of the Child Star Era.* Dallas, TX: Southern Methodist University Press, 1978.

———. *Whatever Happened to Baby Peggy? The Autobiography of Hollywood's Pioneer Child Star.* New York: St. Martin's Press, 1996.

Child Stars: Their Story. Produced and directed by Henry Schipper. 2000. A&E Television Networks. Television documentary.

Clapp, John Bouvé, and Edwin Francis Edgett. *Players of the Present.* New York: The Dunlap Society, 1899. Google e-book, accessed February 7, 2007.

Clark, T. Wood. *Utica for a Century and a Half.* Utica, New York: Widtman Press, 1952.

Connor, Holly Pyne. *Angels and Tomboys: Girlhood in 19th-Century American Art.* San Francisco: Pomegranate Communications, Inc. in collaboration with the Newark Museum, 2012.

Cook, Daniel Thomas. *The Commodification of Childhood: The Children's Clothing Industry and the Rise of the Child Consumer.* Durham, NC: Duke University Press, 2004.

Cosdon, Mark. *The Hanlon Brothers: From Daredevil Acrobatics to Spectacle Pantomime, 1833–1931.* Carbondale: Southern Illinois University Press, 2009.

Craughwell, Thomas J. *Stealing Lincoln's Body.* Cambridge, MA: Harvard University Press, 2007; Belknap Press, 2009.

Cross, Gary. *Kids' Stuff: Toys and the Changing World of American Childhood.* Cambridge, MA: Harvard University Press, 1998.

———. *The Cute and the Cool: Wondrous Innocence and Modern American Children's Culture.* New York: Oxford University Press, 2004.

Curry, Jane Kathleen. *Nineteenth-Century American Women Theatre Managers.* Westport, CT: Greenwood Press, 1994.

Darnall, Margaretta J. "The American Cemetery as Picturesque Landscape: Bellefontaine Cemetery, St. Louis." *Winterthur Portfolio* 18, no. 4 (Winter 1983):249–69.

Davis, Andrew. *America's Longest Run: A History of the Walnut Street Theatre.* State College: Pennsylvania State University Press, 2010.

Davis, Jim. "Freaks, Prodigies, and Marvelous Mimicry: Child Actors of Shakespeare on the Nineteenth-century Stage." *Shakespeare* 2, no. 2 (December 2006): 179–93.

Davis, Tracy C. "The Employment of Children in Victorian Theatre." *New Theatre Quarterly* 2, no. 6 (1986): 117–36.

Dempsey, David, with Raymond P. Baldwin. *The Triumphs and Trials of Lotta Crabtree.* New York: William Morrow & Company, 1968.

Diamond, Jared. *The World until Yesterday: What Can We Learn from Traditional Societies?* New York: Viking, 2012.

Dorman, James H., Jr. *Theatre in the Antebellum South, 1815–1861.* Chapel Hill: University of North Carolina Press, 1967.

Douglas, Ann. *The Feminization of American Culture.* New York: Knopf, 1977.

Draper, Stacy Pomeroy. "History of Second Street and its Surroundings." In *The Marble House in Second Street: Biography of a Town House and Its Occupants 1825–2000.* Edited by John Waite Associates. Troy, NY: Rensselaer County Historical Society, 2000.

Drew, Louisa (Lane) and Douglas Taylor. *Autobiographical Sketch of Mrs. John Drew; with an Introduction by Her Son John Drew; with Bibliographical Notes by Douglas Taylor.* New York: Charles Scribner and Sons, 1899. Google e-book, accessed June 18, 2007.

Estavan, Lawrence, ed., *A Monograph History of the San Francisco Stage and Its People from 1849 to the Present Day, San Francisco Theatre Research, Volume XIV*. San Francisco: Work Projects Administration, Project 10677, 0. P. 665–08–5-167, 1940. San Francisco Public Library e-book, accessed November 14, 2011.

Fitzpatrick, Siobhan, ed. *Orphan to Apprentice: Child Indentures as Social Welfare*. Madison, NJ: Museum of Early Trades & Crafts, 2012.

Forman-Brunell, Miriam, and Leslie Paris. *The Girls' History and Culture Reader: The Nineteenth Century*. Urbana: University of Illinois Press, 2011.

Formanek-Brunell, Miriam. *Made to Play House: Dolls and the Commercialization of American Girlhood, 1830–1930*. Baltimore: Johns Hopkins University Press, 1993.

French, Stanley. "The Cemetery as Cultural Institution: The Establishment of Mount Auburn and the 'Rural Cemetery' Movement." *American Quarterly* 26, no. 1 (March 1974): 37–59.

Frick, John W. *Theatre, Culture and Temperance Reform in Nineteenth-Century America*. New York: Cambridge University Press, 2003.

———. "Uncle Tom's Cabin on the Antebellum Stage," *Uncle Tom's Cabin* and American Culture. University of Virginia: http://utc.iath.virginia.edu/.

Gac, Scott, *Singing for Freedom: The Hutchinson Family Singers and the Nineteenth-Century Culture of Reform*. New Haven, CT: Yale University Press, 2007.

Gänzl, Kurt. *Lydia Thompson: Queen of Burlesque*. New York: Routledge, 2002.

Graham, Franklin. *Histrionic Montreal: Annals of the Montreal Stage*. Montreal: John Lovell, 1902.

Grant, Ulysses S. *Personal Memoirs*. New York: C. L. Webster, 1885–86. *Bartleby.com*. Last modified 2000. www.bartleby.com/1011/. Accessed July 2, 2013.

Association for Gravestone Studies. "Some Common Symbols/Emblems Found in Nineteenth-Century Cemeteries." Accessed for download, April 6, 2012.

Griffith, Barbara J. "All the Lovely Sisterhood: The Ladies of the Theatre in the California Gold Rush." *Journal of the West* 37, no. 1 (January 1998): 7–10.

Grimsted, David. *Melodrama Unveiled: American Theatre and Culture, 1800–1850*. Chicago: University of Chicago Press, 1968.

Grossman, Barbara Wallace. *A Spectacle of Suffering: Clara Morris on the American Stage*. Carbondale: Southern Illinois University Press, 2009.

Gubar, Marah. *Artful Dodgers: Reconceiving the Golden Age of Children's Literature*. New York: Oxford University Press, 2009.

———. "Who Watched *The Children's Pinafore*? Age Transvestism on the Nineteenth-Century Stage." *Victorian Studies* 54, no. 3 (2012): 410–26.

———. "Entertaining Children of All Ages: Nineteenth-Century Popular Theatre as Children's Theatre." *American Quarterly* 66, no. 1 (March 2014): 1–34.

Gurr, Andrew. *The Shakespearean Stage 1574–1642*. 4th ed. New York: Cambridge University Press, 2009.

Harbin, Billy J., Kim Marra, and Robert A. Schanke, eds. *The Gay and Lesbian Theatrical Legacy: A Biographical Dictionary of Major Figures in American Stage History in the Pre-Stonewall Era*. Ann Arbor: University of Michigan Press, 2007.

Hawes, Joseph M., and N. Ray Hiner. *American Childhood: A Research Guide and Historical Handbook*. Westport, CT: Greenwood Press, 1985.

Higonnet, Anne. *Pictures of Innocence: The History and Crisis of Ideal Childhood*. London: Thames and Hudson, 1998.

Hough, David. "The Playmakers." In *Farewell Cinderella: Creating Arts and Identity in Western Australia*. Edited by Geoffrey Bolton, Richard Rossiter, and Jan Ryan. Crawley, Australia: University of Western Australian Press, 2003. Google e-book, accessed April 16, 2012.

Huff, Helen. "The Haunting of Celebrity and the Construction of Nationalism." In *Masculinities, Femininities, and the Power of the Hybrid in U.S. Narratives*. Edited by Pascual Nieves, Laura Alonso-Gallo, Francisco Collado-Rodriguez. Heidelberg, Germany: Universitätsverlag, 2007.

Hughes, Amy. *Spectacles of Reform: Theatre and Activism in Nineteenth-Century America*. Ann Arbor: University of Michigan Press, 2012.

Hutton, Laurence. *Curiosities of the American Stage*. New York: Harper & Brothers, 1891.

———. "Infant Phenomena." *Frank Leslie's Popular Monthly* 21, no. 4 (April 1886): 439–48.

Hunter, Jane H. *How Young Ladies Became Girls: The Victorian Origins of American Girlhood*. New Haven, CT: Yale University Press, 2002.

James, Allison. "Agency." In *The Palgrave Handbook of Childhood Studies*. Edited by Jen Qvortrup, William A. Corsaro, and Michael-Sebastian Honig. London: Palgrave, 2009.

James, Allison, and Alan Prout. *Constructing and De-Constructing Childhood*. London: Falmer Press, 1997.

Jefferson, Joseph. *The Autobiography of Joseph Jefferson*. New York: Century Company, 1891. Repr. Edited by Alan S. Downer. Cambridge, MA: Harvard University Press, 1964.

Johnson, Claudia. *American Actress: Perspectives on the Nineteenth Century*. Chicago: Nelson-Hall, 1984.

Keister, Douglas. *Stories in Stone: A Field Guide to Cemetery Symbolism and Iconography*. New York: MJF Books, 2004.

Kendall, John S. *The Golden Age of the New Orleans Theatre.* Baton Rouge: Louisiana State University Press, 1952.

Kincaid, James. *Child-Loving: The Erotic Child and Victorian Culture.* New York: Routledge, 1994.

King, Grace. *New Orleans: The Place and the People.* New York: Macmillan & Co., 1895. Repr., New York: Negro University Press, 1968.

Knoper, Randall. *Acting Naturally: Mark Twain in the Culture of Performance.* Berkeley: University of California Press, 1995). California Digital Library, accessed February 6, 2012.

Kolbert, Elizabeth. "Spoiled Rotten: Why Do Kids Rule the Roost?" *New Yorker Magazine*, July 2, 2012.

Lamb, Edel. *Performing Childhood in the Early Modern Theatre: The Children's Playing Companies (1599–1613).* New York: Palgrave Macmillan, 2009.

Leavitt, M. B. *Fifty Years in Theatrical Management.* New York: Broadway Publishing Company, 1912. *Internet Archive*, 2007, accessed April 18, 2012.

Lepore, Jill. "Historians Who Love Too Much: Reflections on Microhistory and Biography." *Journal of American History* 88, no. 1 (June 2001): 129–44.

Lerman, Nina E. "Preparing for the Duties and Practical Business of Life: Technological Knowledge and Social Structure in Mid-19th-Century Philadelphia." *Technology and Culture* 38, no. 1 (January 1997): 31–59.

Lessing, Lauren. "Roses in Bloom: American Images of Adolescent Girlhood." In Holly Pyne Connor et al., *Angels and Tomboys: Girlhood in Nineteenth-Century American Art.* San Francisco: Pomegranate Communications, Inc. and Newark Museum, 2012.

Levine, Lawrence. *Highbrow/Lowbrow: The Emergence of Cultural Hierarchy in America.* Cambridge, MA: Harvard University Press, 1988.

Linden-Ward, Blanche. "Strange but Genteel Pleasure Grounds: Tourist and Leisure Uses of Nineteenth-Century Rural Cemeteries." In *Cemeteries and Gravemarkers: Voices of American Culture.* Edited by Richard Meyer. Ann Arbor, MI: UMI Research Press, 1989.

Lott, Eric. *Love and Theft: Blackface Minstrelsy and the American Working Class.* New York: Oxford University Press, 1993.

Louden, J. C. *On the Laying Out, Planting and Managing of Cemeteries, and on the Improvement of Church Yards.* London: Longman, Brown, Green, and Longman, 1843.

Luskey, Brian P. "'What Is My Prospects?': The Contours of Mercantile Apprenticeship, Ambition, and Advancement in the Early American Economy." *The Business History Review* 78, no. 4 (Winter 2004): 665–702. Accessed July 23, 2010. http://www.jstor.org/stable/25096953.

Macdonald, Cordelia Howard, and George P. Howard. "Memoirs of the Original Little Eva." *Educational Theatre Journal* 8, no. 4 (December 1956): 267–82. Accessed July 20, 2010. http://links.jstor.org/sici?sici=0013–1989%28195612%298%3A4%3C267%3AMOTOLE%3E2.0.CO%3B2-Y.

Macintyre, Stuart. *A Concise History of Australia*. Cambridge, UK: Cambridge University Press, 1999.

MacLeod, Anne Scott. "The Caddie Woodlawn Syndrome: American Girlhood in the Nineteenth-Century." In *The Girls' History and Culture Reader: The Nineteenth Century*. Edited by Miriam Forman-Brunell and Leslie Paris. Urbana: University of Illinois Press, 2011.

Mallios, Seth, and David M. Caterino. "Mortality, Money and Commemoration: Social and Economic Factors in Southern California Grave-Marker Change during the Nineteenth and Twentieth Centuries." *International Journal of Historical Archeology* 15 (2011): 429–60.

Marino, Daniela. "Prayer for a Sleeping Child: Iconography of the Funeral Ritual of Little Angels in Mexico." *Journal of American Culture* 20, no. 2 (Summer 1997): 37–44.

McArthur, Benjamin. "'Forbid Them Not': Child Actor Labor Laws and Political Activism in the Theatre." *Theatre Survey* 36, no. 2 (November 1995): 63–80.

———. *The Man Who Was Rip Van Winkle: Joseph Jefferson and Nineteenth-Century American Theatre*. New Haven, CT: Yale University Press, 2007.

———. *Actors and American Culture, 1880–1920*. Philadelphia: Temple University Press, 1984.

McConachie, Bruce A. *Melodramatic Formations: American Theatre and Society, 1820–1870*. Iowa City: University of Iowa Press, 1992.

———. "H. J. Conway's Dramatization of *Uncle Tom's Cabin:* A Previously Unpublished Letter." *Theatre Journal* 34, no. 2 (May 1982): 149–54.

McKillop, Heather. "Recognizing Children's Graves in Nineteenth-Century Cemeteries: Excavations in St. Thomas Anglican Churchyard, Belleville, Ontario, Canada." *Historical Archeology* 29, no. 2 (1995): 77–100.

McMahon, Heather M. "Profit, Purity, and Perversity: Nineteenth-Century Child Prodigies Kate and Ellen Bateman." PhD dissertation, Indiana University, 2003.

MacMinn, George. *The Theatre of the Golden Era in California*. Caldwell, ID: Caxton Printers, 1941.

McTeague, James H. *Before Stanislavski: American Professional Acting Schools and Acting Theory 1875–1925*. Metuchen, NJ: Scarecrow Press, 1993.

Meer, Sarah. *Uncle Tom Mania: Slavery, Minstrelsy and Transatlantic Culture in the 1850s*. Athens: University of Georgia Press, 2005.

Merrill, Lisa. *When Romeo Was a Woman: Charlotte Cushman and Her Circle of Female Spectators*. Ann Arbor: University of Michigan Press, 1999.

Mintz, Steven. *Huck's Raft: A History of American Childhood*. Cambridge, MA: Harvard University Press, 2004.

Mullenix, Elizabeth Reitz. *Wearing the Breeches: Gender on the Antebellum Stage*. New York: St. Martin's Press, 2000.

Mullenneaux, Nan. "Our Genius, Goodness, and Gumption: Child Actresses and National Identity in Mid-Nineteenth-Century America." *Journal of the History of Childhood and Youth* 5, no. 2 (Spring 2012): 283–308.

Murray, James V., and John Swantek, eds. and comps. *1813–1993: The Watervliet Arsenal: A Chronology of the Nation's Oldest Arsenal*. Watervliet, NY: Watervliet Arsenal Public Affairs Office, 1993.

Myers, Robert J., and Joyce Brodowski. "Rewriting the Hallams: Research in 18th Century British and American Theatre." *Theatre Survey* 41, no. 1 (May 2000): 1–23.

O'Connor, Jane. *The Cultural Significance of the Child Star*. New York: Rutledge, 2008.

Odell, George. *Annals of the New York Stage*. New York: Columbia University Press, 1927.

Officer, Lawrence H., and Samuel H. Williamson, "Purchasing Power of Money in the United States from 1774 to the Present." *MeasuringWorth.com*. Accessed December 10, 2011.

Pike, Martha V., and Janice Gray Armstrong. *A Time to Mourn: Expressions of Grief in Nineteenth-Century America*. Stony Brook, NY: The Museums Stony at Stony Brook, 1980.

Phelps, H. P. *Players of a Century: A Record of the Albany Stage*. 2nd ed. Albany, NY: Joseph McDonald, 1880.

Postman, Neil. *The Disappearance of Childhood*. New York: Vintage, 1982. Repr., 1994.

Quimby, Ian. *Apprenticeship in Colonial Philadelphia*. Master's thesis, University of Delaware, 1963. Repr. New York: Garland, 1985.

Qvortrup, Jens, William A. Corsaro, and Michael-Sebastian Honig, eds. *The Palgrave Handbook of Childhood Studies*. London: Palgrave, 2009.

Rainville, Lynn. "Hanover Deathscapes: Mortuary Variability in New Hampshire, 1770–1920." *Ethnohistory* 46, no. 3 (Summer 1999).

Rapport, Lisa J., and M. Meleen. "Childhood Celebrity, Parental Attachment, and Adult Adjustment: The Young Performers Study." *Journal of Personality Assessment* 70, no. 3 (1998): 483–505.

Reinier, Jacqueline S. *From Virtue to Character: American Childhood, 1775–1850*. New York: Twayne, 1996.

Rinear, David L. *Stage, Page, Scandals, and Vandals: William E. Burton and Nineteenth-Century American Theatre.* Carbondale: Southern Illinois University Press, 2004.

Roach, Joseph. *It.* Ann Arbor: University of Michigan Press, 2007.

Rorabaugh, W. J. *The Craft Apprentice: From Franklin to the Machine Age.* New York: Oxford University Press, 1986.

Roost, Alisa C. "Melodrama or Tragedy? The United States Worldview since 9–11." Paper presented at the annual conference of the Popular Culture Association, San Francisco, March 22, 2008.

Rourke, Constance. *Troupers of the Gold Coast.* New York: Harcourt and Brace, 1928.

Russett, Cynthia Eagle. *Sexual Science: The Victorian Construction of Womanhood.* Cambridge, MA: Harvard University Press, 1989.

Rutherford, Sara. *The Victorian Cemetery.* Botley, UK: Shire Publications, 2008.

Sánchez-Eppler, Karen. *Dependent States: The Child's Part in Nineteenth-Century American Culture.* Chicago: University of Chicago Press, 2005.

Schulz, Constance B. "Children and Childhood in the Eighteenth Century." In *American Childhood: A Research Guide and Historical Handbook.* Edited by Joseph M. Hawes and N. Ray Hiner. Westport, CT: Greenwood Press, 1985.

Senelick, Laurence. *The Age and Stage of George L. Fox.* Boston: Tufts University Press, 1988.

———. "Boys and Girls Together: Subcultural Origins of Glamour Drag and Male Impersonation on the Nineteenth-Century Stage." In *Crossing the Stage: Controversies on Cross-Dressing.* Edited by Leslie Ferris. London: Routledge, 1993.

Sentilles, Renée M. *Performing Menken: Adah Isaacs Menken and the Birth of American Celebrity.* New York: Cambridge University Press, 2003.

Sherman, Robert L. *Chicago Stage: Its Record and Achievements.* Volume 1. Chicago: Robert L. Sherman, 1947.

Simon, Louis M. *A History of the Actors' Fund of America.* New York: Theatre Arts Books, 1972.

Singley, Carol J. "Neither Indentured nor Adopted: Harriet Wilson's *Our Nig.*" In *Orphan to Apprentice: Child Indentures as Social Welfare.* Edited by Siobhan Fitzpatrick. Madison, NJ: Museum of Early Trades and Crafts, 2012.

Skinner, Maud Otis. *One Man in His Time: The Adventures of H. Watkins, Strolling Player 1845–1863.* Philadelphia: University of Pennsylvania Press, 1938.

Slout, William L., ed. *Olympians of the Sawdust Circle.* Copyright © 2005 by William L. Slout. http://www.circushistory.org/Olympians/OlympiansB1.htm.

Smith, Ophia D. "The Early Theatre of Cincinnati." *Historical and Philosophical Society of Ohio Bulletin* 13, no. 4 (October 1955). Smithsonian Institution Libraries.

———. "The Cincinnati Theatre, 1817–1830." *Historical and Philosophical Society of Ohio Bulletin* 14, no. 4 (October 1956). Smithsonian Institution Libraries.

Snyder, Ellen Marie. "Innocents in a Worldly World: Victorian Children's Gravemarkers." In *Cemeteries and Gravemarkers: Voices of American Culture.* Edited by Richard E. Meyer. Ann Arbor: UMI Research Press, 1989.

Staenberg, Marc R., and Daniel K. Stuart. *Children as Chattels: The Disturbing Plight of Child Performers.* 32 Beverly Hills Bar Assn. Journal 21 (1997). Retrieved from A Minor Consideration, http://www.minorcon.org, January 20, 2000.

Stott, Richard D. *Workers in the Metropolis: Class, Ethnicity, and Youth in Antebellum New York City.* Ithaca, NY: Cornell University Press, 1990.

Stowe, Harriett Beecher. *Uncle Tom's Cabin.* 1851. Repr. Bedford, MA: Applewood Books, 2008.

Swift, Mary Grace. "Dancers in Flames." *Dance Chronicle* 5, no. 1 (1982): 1–10.

Titone, Nora. *My Thoughts Be Bloody: The Bitter Rivalry That Led to the Assassination of Abraham Lincoln.* New York: Free Press, 2010.

Toll, Robert C. *Blacking Up: The Minstrel Show in Nineteenth-Century America.* New York: Oxford University Press, 1974.

Trainor, Kevin. "*Pars pro toto:* On Comparing Relic Practices." *Numen* 57 (2010) 267–83.

Turbin, Carole. *Working Women of Collar City: Gender, Class, and Community in Troy, New York, 1864–86.* Urbana: University of Illinois Press, 1992.

University of Virginia. "*Uncle Tom's Cabin* and American Culture." Website © 2009. http://utc.iath.virginia.edu/index2f.html. Accessed September 26, 2012.

Van Ravenswaay, Charles. *Saint Louis: An Informal History of the City and Its People, 1764–1865.* St. Louis: Missouri Historical Society Press, 1991.

Varty, Anne. *Children and Theatre in Victorian Britain.* New York: Palgrave Macmillan, 2008.

Vey, Shauna. "Good Intentions and Fearsome Prejudice: New York's 1876 Act to Prevent and Punish Wrongs to Children." *Theatre Survey* 42, no. 1 (May 2001): 53–68.

———. "An American Antebellum Child-Actor Contract: Alfred Stewart and the Shift from Craft Apprentice to Wage Laborer." In *Entertaining Children: The Participation of Youth in the Entertainment Industry.* Edited by Gillian Arrighi and Victor Emeljanow. Palgrave Macmillan, 2014.

Welter, Barbara. "The Cult of True Womanhood: 1820–1860." *American Quarterly* 18, no. 2 (1966): 151–74.

Waite, John G., Douglas C. Bucher, Stacy Pomeroy Draper, and Walter Richard Wheeler. "History of Second Street and its Surroundings." In *The Marble House in Second Street: Biography of a Town House and Its Occupants 1825–2000*. Edited by John Waite Associates. Troy, New York: Rensselaer County Historical Society, 2000.

Welter, Barbara. "The Cult of True Womanhood: 1820–1860," *American Quarterly* 18, no. 2 (1966): 151–74.

Weston, Effie Ellsler, ed. *The Stage Memories of John A. Ellsler*. Cleveland: The Rowfant Club, 1950.

Wilmeth, Don B., ed. *Staging the Nation: Plays from the American Theatre 1787–1909*. Boston: Bedford Books, 1998.

Wilson, Arthur Herman. *A History of the Philadelphia Theatre 1835–1855*. New York: Greenwood, 1968.

Zelizer, Viviana A. *Pricing the Priceless Child: The Changing Social Value of Children*. Princeton, NJ: Princeton University Press, 1994.

INDEX

Italicized page numbers indicate figures.

Act to Prevent and Punish Wrongs to Children (1876), 118
advertisements and publicity devices: cast members featured in, 28, 32, 68–69, *134*; for Cincinnati engagement, 56–57; connections to local events, 91; eroticization of child actresses in, 72; focus on middle class and fashionable audiences, 58; for Louise Arnot Troupe, 118–19; *Marsh's Juvenile Dramatic Era*, 33, 63, 132; scale and novelty emphasized in, 16; for *Uncle Tom's Cabin*, 21
agency: children and, 7–8, 147–49; concept of, 7; exercise of, by Georgie Marsh, 133, 145; exercise of, by Louise Arnot, 12, 42, 107–12, 121–22, 145
Age of Innocence, The (Reynolds), *5*
Aiken, George, 20–21
Airey, Walter T., 110
Albany Rural Cemetery, *139*
Aldrich, Louis, 57; Actors Fund Home and, 139–40; on child performers, 118; on 1857 Panic, 37; marriage to Clara Shropshire, 97; with Marsh Troupe, 17, 55–56, 84–86, 93; star status, 117; in Tom Maguire's stock company, 113
Amazon marches (Zouave performances), 31, 144, 164n108
American Ladies Seen through the English EyeGlass (play), 112
Anae, Nicole, 89
apprenticeships, 47–52, 122, 167n33
Argus (Melbourne, Australia, newspaper), 89–90, 100, 106, 109, 110
Ariès, Philippe, 4–5, 99
Arngrim, Alison, 102
Arnot, Jenny: appearances with Louise Arnot, 116; benefit performances for, 90; leave taking from Marsh Troupe, 94; in *Lurline*, 115; marriage of, 98; with Marsh Troupe in California, 86–87; with R. G. Marsh at the New Idea, 98; during Sydney engagement, 89–90; in *Toodles*, 133; on tour in New Zealand, 95; in *Uncle Tom's Cabin*, 1–2, 93

Arnot, Louise, *105*, *111*, *122*; agency and autonomy of, 12, 42, 107–12, 121–22, 145; in Australia, 89–90, 99, 108–9; benefit performances for, 31, 61, 90, 109–10; in *Black-Eyed Susan*, 24, 108; childhood training in Marsh Troupe, 123; conflict between Nagle and Marsh over, 39–42; cross-dressing roles, 102–9, 114; in *The Drunkard*, 92; in *Lady of Lyons*, 108–9; Louise Arnot Troupe, 116, 119; in *Lurline*, 115; marriage to Bartine, 94, 107, 110; at Mary Marsh's gravesite, 14–15; as model of child actor/apprentice, 99–101; mother's attempts to remove from troupe, 38, 41; with Mr. Mason's Dramatic Company, 110; in *The Naiad Queen*, 30–31; New York engagements, 24; in New Zealand, 107–8, 115; public persona, 10; with R. G. and Georgie Marsh in California, 112; roles in Marsh Troupe, 15, 17; Sacramento engagement, 113–14; stage persona and style adaptations, 12–13; talent of, 22; touring as star attraction, 118–19; touring in 1890s, 120–21; in *Uncle Tom's Cabin*, 2, 93; voice of, 104–6
Arnot-Gunn vaudeville team, 123
Australia: Louise Arnot in, 108–10; Marsh Troupe in, 87–94, 108

"Baby Peggy," 8–9, 77, 127
Barnum, P. T., 28, 92
Bartholomew, Freddie, 167n20
Bartine (trapezian), 93–94, 107–8, 110
Bartine, Jennie, 108
Bartine, Mary, 117
Bateman, Ellen, 9, 48, 70, 101–3
Bateman, Hezikiah L., 25, 48
Bateman, Kate, 9, 48, 70, 101
Bateman, Sydney Cowell, 48
Beckley, Fanny, 116
benefit performances, 19, 28, 91, 96–97. *See also names of individual performers*
Bernstein, Robin, 64, 77, 93
Bertolucci, Bernardo, 127
Bieber, Justin, 146
Billings, Hammatt, 66, 68, 71
Black-Eyed Susan (play), 24, 108, 162n71
blackface performances, 19, 101–2
Blondin, Charles, 107
Boone children, 36
Booth, Edwin, 31
Boston engagements, 26–27, 33–35
boy performers, during English Renaissance, 23, 47–48
Brian O'Linn (play), 35
Brigand, The (play), 89
Brisbane Courier (Australian newspaper), 110
British Blondes, Lydia Thompson and, 114–15
Brown, Richard D., 2–3, 142–43
Brown, T. Allston: on Alfred Stewart, 61; on George Marsh, 133, 138; on Louise Arnot, 24, 41, 116; on R. G. Marsh, 18, 138
burial practices during nineteenth century, 79–80, 176n93
burlesque, and convention of cross-dressing, 114
Burton, William E.: Georgie Marsh and repertory of, 125–26, 132; R. G. Marsh and, 18; script for *The Naiad Queen*, 30; self-reinvention, 136; and *Toodles*, 25
Burton, William Shakespeare, 125

Carroll, Lewis (Charles Dodgson), 71
cartes de visite, 144
cash-wage jobs, shift toward, 49
cast lists, Boston engagement, 26
celebrity photos, as publicity devices, 28
Chanfrau, S. F., 33–35
child actor/apprentice model, Louise Arnot and, 99–101
childhood: artificial stages of, 146; changing definitions and conceptions of, 3–4, 9, 22–23, 146–49, 172n9; classism and racism in concept of, 64; creation of, and development of melodrama, 68; emergence of, with rise of middle class, 63–64; extinction of, 77; idealization and protection of, 4–6, 65, 83; infantilized, exemplars of, 38, 145
childhood studies scholars, 10
child performers: acting craft and talent of, 128–29; antebellum prodigies, 9; audiences' beliefs about, 132; in California, 86; Charles Dickens and, 128; child-star phenomenon in twentieth century, 66–68; competence and dependence of, 9; conceptions of, in nineteenth century, 3, 70; critics on, 36; eroticization of, 62, 70–72; financial agency of, 147–48; inability to bridge gulf between childhood and adulthood, 146; in liminal zone between child and adult, 64; literacy of, 10–11; Marsh children as exemplars of professional, in nineteenth-century theatre, 2–3; poor outlook for, following 1857 Panic, 37; prejudice against, 126–27; protective legislation for, 117–18; public personae of, 9–10; public's interest in, 88–89; salaries for, 46–47; in seventeenth-century England and in vaudeville, 15–16; use of androgyny of, 101–2
children: Act to Prevent and Punish Wrongs to Children, 118; African American and immigrant, 6; competence and agency of, 7–8, 147–49; of deceased fathers, 44; idealized, 64, 144; identity of, 55; practice of living away from home, 39; sentimental versus economic value of, 6–7, 22, 42, 64–65; shift in images of, beginning in seventeenth century, 5; stage roles versus reality of work roles, 76; theatre attendance by, 57–58; training of, by acting families of nineteenth century, 48; on Victorian stage, 70; view of, in modern times, 147
chorister companies, all-boy, 47–48
Cincinnati engagements, 20–21, 32, 56–57
Cincinnati Enquirer (newspaper), 60–61, 76
Cinderella (play), 35, 113–14, 124
Clipper (New York newspaper): on aging of Marsh children, 84, 88; on Arnot's marriage to John Wilson, 116; on child performers, 36; coverage of Mary Marsh's fatal accident, 60; on 1857–58 theatrical season, 37; on Georgie Marsh, 135; on Louis Aldrich, 55–56; on Marsh-Stewart controversy, 53–54, 58–59; on return of Marsh Troupe to California, 97

Conjugal Lesson, The (play), 19
consolation literature, 81–82
contact relics, 83
Conway, H. J., 19, 21
Coogan, Jackie, 9, 135, 147
Crabtree, Lotta, 2, 86, 97, 119, 137
Crisp, William H., 58
critics' reviews: in Australia, 89–90; of *Cinderella*, 113–14; of Georgie Marsh, 26, 93, 124, 129, 131; of Jenny Arnot, 87; on Louise Arnot's adult performances, 104–6, 107–8, 112, 118–20; on Louise Arnot's childhood performances, 10, 100–101, 121; of Marsh Troupe, 2, 10, 15; of *The Naiad Queen*, 30–31; of R. G. Marsh, 19
cross-dressed actors and performances, 101–2, 103–9, 114–15
Culkin, Macaulay, 8–9
"Cult of True Womanhood, The: 1830–1860" (Welter), 65
Cushman, Charlotte, 70, 103
Cyrus, Miley, 146

Davis, Jim, 103
Diamond, Jared, 7
Dickens, Charles, 30, 128
Dime Museum, Washington, D.C., 118
Disney, Walt, 11
Dodgson, Charles (Lewis Carroll), 71
domestic abuse in nineteenth century, 113
Don Caesar de Bazan (play), 33
Douglas, Ann, 65, 77, 81–82
Dred Scott case, 40
Drunkard, The (play), 92
Dunedin, New Zealand, 94–96, 108
Du Souchet, H. A., 120
Dutcher, Jane C., 18, 20, 136–37

economy, mid-nineteenth-century, 49
Edwards, Harry, 113
Ellsler, John, 19–20, 22, 55
eroticization of child performers, 62, 70–72

familial relationships, parent-managers and damage to, 147–48
family-based troupes in nineteenth century, 15, 36, 48, 158n3
family values, commodification of, 144
fatalities from theatre fires, 72, 76–77
Federal Fair Labor Standards Act (1938), 118
financial agency, child actors and, 147–48
Fisher, Clara, 103
Florence, Mr. (actor), 131
Forty Thieves, The (play), 19
Frank Leslie's Popular Monthly (periodical), 127
freedom dues, 50
French, Stanley, 79

Georgia Circuit, 58, 61
Germon, Greene C., 20–21, 136
Gerry, Elbridge, 118
Glessing, Carolina, 125
Golden Axe, The (play), 33
Grace, Rowena, 126
graves and gravestones: of Georgie F. Guerineau, *139*; of Mary Marsh, 79–81, *81*, 81–82, *82*, 83, 85
Gubar, Marah, 72
Guerineau, George Washington. *See* Marsh, George Washington ("Georgie")
Guerineau, Georgie Frederick, 137–38, *139*
Guerineau, Jane C. Dutcher (Mrs. Robert Marsh), 18, 20, 136–37

Guerineau, Mary Eliza. *See* Marsh, Mary
Guerineau, Robert. *See* Marsh, R. G. (Robert Guerineau)
Gunn, Tom, 121

Hallam company, and apprenticeship system, 48
Hanlon, William, 107
Happy Man, The (play), 35
Hawk's Bay Herald (New Zealand newspaper), 96
Higonnet, Anne, 5, 63–64
Honeymoon, The (play), 33, 107
Howard, Caddie Fox, 20, 48
Howard, Cordelia, 9, 20–21, 46, 48
Howard, George C., 20
Howard Athenaeum newspaper, 33, 63, 132
Howard Athenaeum playbills, *29*, *45*
Hutton, Lawrence, 10, 63, 71–72, 126–28, 132

Ince, Annette, 113
Invincibles, The (play), 31
Ixion (play), 114

James, Allison, 7, 148
Jefferson, Joseph, 89, 92, 125
Johnson, Hattie, 95

Keene, Laura, 92, 180n72
Kendall, John S., 132, 134
Kincaid, James, 63, 71–72, 77
Kingsley, Omar, 101

Lady of Lyons (play), 108–9, 115
LaFont, Tom, 98
Last Emperor, The (movie), 127
Leah, the Forsaken (play), 119
Lease, Mary E., 119–20
Leffingwell, M. W., 113–14
leg shows, 114
Lepore, Jill, 3
Liddell, Alice, 71
Little Detective, The (play), 119
Louise Arnot Troupe, 116
Ludlow, Noah, 28–30
Lurline (play), 115
Lyon, Salma. *See* Aldrich, Louis

Macintyre, Stuart, 110
MacLeod, Anne Scott, 106
Macon, Georgia, 14, 72, 78–79, 120–21
Maguire, Tom, 96–97, 113–14
Marsh, George Washington ("Georgie"): abilities of, compared to adult professionals, 129–32; benefit performances for, 90; birth of, 18; in *Black-Eyed Susan*, 24; during Boston engagement, 26; in *Cinderella*, 124; as comedic performer, 125; comfort with audiences, 133; death of sister Mary, 141; following disbanding of Marsh Troupe, 97–98; exercise of agency by, 133, 145; in *Marsh's Juvenile Dramatic Era*, 33; in *The Naiad Queen*, 30–31; at the New Idea (Victoria, British Columbia), 98; in *Our American Cousin*, 92; playing opposite Mary, 70; precociousness of, 26; publicity photographs, 28, *34*, *134*; public persona, 10; relationship with father, 13, 148; role in Marsh Troupe, 15, 17; self-reinvention and obituaries of, 135–37; during Sydney engagement, 89–90; talent of, 22; in *Toodles*, 25, 86, 125, *130*, 130–31, 133; in *Uncle Tom's Cabin*, 20, 93, 132; William E. Burton repertoire and, 125

Marsh, Jane C. (Dutcher), 18, 20, 136–37
Marsh, Louisa. *See* Arnot, Louise
Marsh, Mary, *69*; benefit performances for, 20–21; birth of, 18; in *Black-Eyed Susan*, 24; during Boston engagement, 26; dual identity of, 62–63, 65–66, 70; as embodiment of ideal child, 12; as exemplar of infantilized childhood, 145; fatal accident at Ralston Hall, 38, 60, 72–73; grave and gravestone, 79–81, *81*, 81–82, *82*, 83, 85; Louise Arnot's visit to gravesite of, 120–21; as "martyred child," 74–75; media reaction to death of, 76; in *The Naiad Queen*, 30–31; persona after death, 73–78; portrayal in advertisements and publicity devices, 28, 68–69; public persona, 10; public response to death of, 73; roles in Marsh Troupe, 15–17; talent of, 22; in *Toodles*, 25, 133; in *Uncle Tom's Cabin*, 20, 66, *67*, 68
Marsh, R. G. (Robert Guerineau): acting career, 18–19, 126; birthplace of, 17; challenges to image of, in case of Alfred Stewart, 44–46; coaching by, 128; company alignment with local politics, 95–96; final years, 138–39, 140, 148; and Georgie's professional development, 124; legal battles, 91; as manager of Marsh Troupe, 7, 15, 38–39; on Mary as foundation of troupe, 62; Mary's death and, 61, 73–75; in *The Naiad Queen*, 18–19, 30–31; theatrical innovations of, 91, 143–44; in *Uncle Tom's Cabin*, 18–19; in Victoria, British Columbia, 97–98
"Marsh Children, The" (drawing), *27*
Marsh's Juvenile Dramatic Era (newspaper), Howard Athenaeum, 33, 63, 132
Marsh's Royal Lyceum, Melbourne, 91
Marsh-Stewart contract and controversy, 11–12, 43–47, 49–52, 54, 58–59
Marsh Troupe of Juvenile Comedians (Marsh Troupe): actors reported to have performed with, 153–55; aging of juvenile performers, 87–88; as case study, 3; disbanding of, 97; during 1857–58 season, 37; during 1859–60 season, 84–85; as exemplars of child professionals in nineteenth-century theatre, 2–3; founding of, by Robert Marsh, 15, 22; life span of, 1–2; as model for theatrical managers, 143; new direction after losing Mary and Alfred, 84; and realities of antebellum theatre, 144; repertory of, 16–17, 23, 25, 33–34, 91–92, 126; respect from professional peers, 144; scale and novelty of, 15–16; and Shakespeare, 84; success of, 23
matinees, 57
McArthur, Benjamin, 1–2
McGill, W. M., 56
McLaughlin, Louisa. *See* Arnot, Louise
McLaughlin, Mrs., 41
Melbourne, Australia, 89–90, 100
Melbourne Herald (Australian newspaper), 89
Meleen, Matthew, 140

melodrama, 24–25, 42, 68
Menken, Adah Isaacs, 25, 103, 115
microhistory, value of, 2–3, 142–43
mimicry, in nineteenth century, 126
Mintz, Steven, 5, 8
Morris, Clara, 55, 171n75
mother-managers, 148
Mousely, Georgiana, 72, 85
Mullenix, Elizabeth Reitz, 103, 114, 115
Mullenneaux, Nan, 10
My Friend from India (play), 120
My Husband's Mirror (play), 26
My Neighbor's Wife (play), 26

Nagle, J., 39–40
Nagle's American Juvenile Comedians, 36
Naiad Queen, The (play): Alfred Stewart and, 44–45; basis for success of, 72; complimentary benefit for All England Eleven cricket team, 91; death of Mary Marsh and, 60, 86, 141; Howard Athenaeum playbill, *45*; as mainstay of Marsh Troupe, 25, 26, 126; Marsh Troupe productions of, 30–32, 35, 56, 95; R. G. Marsh's performance in, 18–19, 126
nautical melodramas, 24–25
New Idea theatre (Victoria, British Columbia), 98
New Orleans engagements, 35–36, 58, 61
New York Central Railroad, 19
New York engagements, 19–20, 23–24, 32–33
New York Times (newspaper), 23
New Zealand: Louise Arnot in, 107–8; Marsh Troupe in, 94–96
Nichols, Mrs. H. F., 25
nostalgia in nineteenth-century culture, 77

O'Connor, Jane, 66–68, 134
Ole Olsen (play), 119–20
Otago Daily Times (New Zealand newspaper), 94, 96, 100, 108
Our American Cousin (play), 91–94

Panic of 1857, 36–37
parents as agents or business managers, 140–41, 145, 147–48
Perth Inquirer (Australian newspaper), 110
photography, in marketing Marsh Troupe, 16, 28, *34*, 133, *134*, 144
Plain Dealer (Cleveland, Ohio, newspaper), 73, 79–80
playbills and programs, 26–28, *29*, *45*
Pomare IV (queen of Tahiti), 96
Postman, Neil, 3, 63
public, defined, 68
publicity devices, 28, 33, 63; celebrity photos, *134*
Putnam's Magazine (periodical), 70, 127

Quebec Colonist (Canadian newspaper), 131
Queen, Frank, 59
Quinn, Anna Marie, 36, 88–89, 103, 165n146, 178n46

rail travel, 31–32
Ralston Hall (Macon, Georgia), 14, 72
Ramous, Sam, 98
Rapport, Lisa J., 140
Raymond, J. T., 131

Regan's Luck (play), 121
relics, in Victorian-era burial practices, 83, 176n93
repertory of Marsh Troupe, 16–17, 23, 25, 33–34, 91–92, 126
Reynolds, Joshua, 5
Rice, T. D. "Daddy," 20–21
Rinear, David, 25
Roach, Hal, 11
Roach, Joseph, 83
Robinson, Sue, 86, 113–15
Romance of Coon Hollow (play), 120
Rorabaugh, W. J., 49, 169n48
Rose Hill Cemetery (Macon, Georgia), 14, 78–79, *81*, *82*
Roselle, Amy, 102
rural cemetery movement, 78–79
Russell, Jeannie, 102

Sarony Photography studio, 144
segregation, racial, 21, 27
Sentilles, Renée, 164n108
Shropshire, Clara, 97
Smith, Sol, 30, 58
Smith, William H., 92
Spaulding, "Doc" Gilbert, 35, 58, 165n135
steamboat travel, 28–31
Stewart, Alfred: with Marsh Troupe, 32–33, 35, 71; R. G. Marsh's contract with, and surrounding controversy, 11–12, 43–47, 49–52, 54, 58–59; work as solo performer, 53–54, 61
Stewart, Hannah, 32, 44, *52–53*, 58–60, 145
St. Louis engagements, 28–30
St. Louis Leader (newspaper), 30, 41–42
St. Louis Missouri Republican (newspaper), 30, 42
stock company style of education and training, 122
Sydney engagements, 89–90, 108
Symons, D., 91

Taylor, C. W., 19
Taylor, Tom, 91–92
temperance movement in Australia, 92
Temple, Shirley, 8–9, 71
theatre companies: adult, compared to Marsh Troupe, 16; all-boy, in seventeenth-century England, 23, 47–48; juvenile, spread of, 36, 143. *See also names of specific companies*
theatre fires, 72
theatre historians, and nineteenth-century American theatre, 2
theatre industry, Marsh Troupe's impact on, 143
Thompson, Lydia, 114–15
ticket auctions, 27–28
ticket prices, 26–27, 37, 61
tomboys, in Victorian era, 106
Toodles (play), 25, 33–35, 86, 125, 130–33
touring by Marsh Troupe: in Australia, 12, 87–94; Boston engagements, 26–27, 33–35; Cincinnati engagements, 20–21, 32, 56–57; discomforts of travel, 17, 28–31; Georgia Circuit, 58, 61; journeys to California, 85–86, 96; New Orleans engagements, 35–36, 58; New York engagements, 19–20, 23–24, 32–33; in New Zealand, 12, 94–96; southern states, 85; in spring of 1857, 39–40; St. Louis engagement, 28–30
Triangle Shirtwaist factory fire, 12
Twain, Mark, 130

"Uncle Sam," 159n19
Uncle Tom's Cabin (play): dropped from Marsh Troupe repertory, 22–23; Georgie Marsh in, 132; Louise Arnot in, 2, 93; Marsh Troupe's performances of, 1–2, 19–20, 125; R. G. Marsh's roles in, 18–19; R. G. Marsh's version, 92–93
Uncle Tom's Cabin (Stowe): adaptations for the stage, 19–21, 92–93; Billings arbor scene illustration, 66, 68, 71
Under Southern Skies (play), 121

vaudeville, rise of, 119
Victorian era: burial practices, 79–80, 176n93; consolation literature, 81–82; tomboys in, 106

Warden, Edward, 54
Washington Critic (newspaper), 118–19
Watkins, Harry, 17, 31–32, 144
Weathersby, Eliza, 115
Welter, Barbara, 65
Wemyss, Francis, 72
Wheatley, William, 33
Wheatley's Gift (magazine), 33
Whittle, Charles, 20
Wilson, John, 116, 117
Wilson, Kate, 113–14
Wilson, Sam, 159n19
Wilton, Marie, 102
Wiseman, Alice, 109
women, idealization and dependence of, 65
Wood, Henry, 24, 26, 39
Wood, Sarah, 137
Woodlawn, Caddie (fictional character), 106

Zampillaerostation, 107
Zavistowski Sisters, 124
Zelizer, Viviana, 42, 64, 76
Zinn, Howard, 1
Zouave performances (Amazon marches), 31, 144, 164n108

Theater in the Americas

The goal of the series is to publish a wide range of scholarship on theater and performance, defining theater in its broadest terms and including subjects that encompass all of the Americas.

The series focuses on the performance and production of theater and theater artists and practitioners but welcomes studies of dramatic literature as well. Meant to be inclusive, the series invites studies of traditional, experimental, and ethnic forms of theater; celebrations, festivals, and rituals that perform culture; and acts of civil disobedience that are performative in nature. We publish studies of theater and performance activities of all cultural groups within the Americas, including biographies of individuals, histories of theater companies, studies of cultural traditions, and collections of plays.

Queries and Submissions
Scott Magelssen, Editor
magelss@uw.edu

Founder and Editor, Robert A. Schanke, 2000–2014

Other Books in the Theater in the Americas Series

Shadowed Cocktails: The Plays of Philip Barry from "Paris Bound" to "The Philadelphia Story"
Donald R. Anderson

A Gambler's Instinct: The Story of Broadway Producer Cheryl Crawford
Milly S. Barranger

Unfriendly Witnesses: Gender, Theater, and Film in the McCarthy Era
Milly S. Barranger

The Theatre of Sabina Berman: "The Agony of Ecstasy" and Other Plays
Translated by Adam Versényi
With an Essay by
Jacqueline E. Bixler

Staging Social Justice: Collaborating to Create Activist Theatre
Edited by Norma Bowles and Daniel-Raymond Nadon

Messiah of the New Technique: John Howard Lawson, Communism, and American Theatre, 1923–1937
Jonathan L. Chambers

Composing Ourselves: The Little Theatre Movement and the American Audience
Dorothy Chansky

Ghost Light: An Introductory Handbook for Dramaturgy
Michael Mark Chemers

The Hanlon Brothers: From Daredevil Acrobatics to Spectacle Pantomime, 1833–1931
Mark Cosdon

Richard Barr: The Playwright's Producer
David A. Crespy

Women in Turmoil: Six Plays by Mercedes de Acosta
Edited and with an Introduction by
Robert A. Schanke

Rediscovering Mordecai Gorelik: Scene Design and the American Theatre
Anne Fletcher

A Spectacle of Suffering: Clara Morris on the American Stage
Barbara Wallace Grossman

American Political Plays after 9/11
Edited by Allan Havis

Performing Loss: Rebuilding Community through Theater and Writing
Jodi Kanter

Unfinished Show Business: Broadway Musicals as Works-in-Process
Bruce Kirle

Staging America: Cornerstone and Community-Based Theater
Sonja Kuftinec

Words at Play: Creative Writing and Dramaturgy
Felicia Hardison Londré

Entertaining the Nation: American Drama in the Eighteenth and Nineteenth Centuries
Tice L. Miller

Documentary Trial Plays in Contemporary American Theater
Jacqueline O'Connor

Working in the Wings: New Perspectives on Theatre History and Labor
Edited by Elizabeth A. Osborne and Christine Woodworth

Cuba Inside Out: Revolution and Contemporary Theatre
Yael Prizant

Stage, Page, Scandals, and Vandals: William E. Burton and Nineteenth-Century American Theatre
David L. Rinear

Contemporary Latina/o Theater: Wrighting Ethnicity
Jon D. Rossini

Angels in the American Theater: Patrons, Patronage, and Philanthropy
Edited and with an Introduction by Robert A. Schanke

"That Furious Lesbian": The Story of Mercedes de Acosta
Robert A. Schanke

Caffe Cino: The Birthplace of Off-Off-Broadway
Wendell C. Stone

Teaching Performance Studies
Edited by Nathan Stucky and Cynthia Wimmer
With a Foreword by Richard Schechner

Broadway's Bravest Woman: Selected Writings of Sophie Treadwell
Edited and with Introductions by Jerry Dickey and Miriam López-Rodríguez

The Humana Festival: The History of New Plays at Actors Theatre of Louisville
Jeffrey Ullom

Our Land Is Made of Courage and Glory: Nationalist Performance of Nicaragua and Guatemala
E. J. Westlake

SHAUNA VEY is an associate professor at New York City College of Technology, City University of New York, where she teaches theatre and communication courses. Her work has been published in *Theatre Survey* and *Theatre History Studies*.